NOT WAVING BUT DROWNING

Not Waving But Drowning

The Troubled Life and Times of a Frontline RUC Officer

Edmund Gregory

MAINSTREAM
PUBLISHING
EDINBURGH AND LONDON

First published in Great Britain in 2004 by
MAINSTREAM PUBLISHING COMPANY (EDINBURGH) LTD
7 Albany Street
Edinburgh EH1 3UG

ISBN 1 84018 917 7

Extract from *Great Expectations*, OWC by Charles Dickens (1993)
is reproduced by permission of Oxford University Press

'Not Waving But Drowning' by Stevie Smith is reproduced
by permission of the Estate of James MacGibbon

A catalogue record for this book is available from the British Library

Typeset in Stone
Printed and bound in Great Britain by
Antony Rowe, Chippenham, Wiltshire

This book is dedicated to the memory of my brother, John, and our mother, Trilby Elizabeth Gregory. I pray my story may shed some light upon their troubled lives and may God grant them peace at last.

NOT WAVING BUT DROWNING

Nobody heard him, the dead man,
But still he lay moaning:
I was much further out than you thought
And not waving but drowning.

Poor chap, he always loved larking
And now he's dead
It must have been too cold for him his heart gave way,
They said.

Oh, no no no, it was too cold always
(Still the dead one lay moaning)
I was much too far out all my life
And not waving but drowning.

ACKNOWLEDGEMENTS

First and foremost, I would have to thank my wife Agnes. No other woman could have been such a pillar of strength and provided the support I needed through my darkest days and horror-filled nights. I will always love her; without complaint, she held my fabric together, watched over me and, more importantly, gave life to our children, Robert and Cassandra.

I will never be able to repay the debt of gratitude I owe to Miss Ruth Colvin, who provided me with the confidence to make my own way in life. She took me under her wing as a traumatised young boy, taught me right from wrong and waved goodbye to a young man as I set off into the big bad world to seek my misfortune.

It would be remiss of me to proceed much further without paying a particular thank you to Mrs Allison Murphy, MSSc Dip PD. At every turn, she encouraged me and set in motion the train of events which have led to you reading this book. After reading the first rough draft, she would not rest until it was finished and she spent many weeks proofreading: thank you, Allison.

I also owe a debt of gratitude to Professor Liam Kennedy of Queen's University in Belfast for his wisdom and encouragement. He read my work, advised me to remove much angry and heavily judgemental material, and pointed me in the right direction.

I would like to thank all the *decent* men and women who served with me in the Royal Ulster Constabulary. When all is said and done, the RUC has been good to me, and my career provided me with the means to give my wife and children the comfortable life I felt they deserved.

Thanks must also go to all the members of my family who have given so freely of their time. This book is as much for them as it is for me. My brothers and sisters have also harboured the hurt of their childhood and I have been assured that, by sharing their story, they too will derive some comfort.

Last but not least, I also have to thank Bill Campbell, Ailsa Bathgate and all the highly professional team at Mainstream Publishing. By having the foresight to publish this book, Bill has unwittingly pointed me towards the path of recovery and for that I thank him very much.

CONTENTS

PREFACE

What you are about to read may be considered by some to be very good material for a novel, and indeed in some respects it probably is. However, these are, in fact, my memoirs, written primarily to record my life for the benefit of my family. I felt it was vitally important that when my grandchildren, Andrew and Nicole, grew up, they would know what it was like to live through Northern Ireland's darkest days and that they would glean some insight into my own poverty-stricken life as a child growing up in a very troubled family during the 1960s.

This book is also a record of my career as an officer in the Royal Ulster Constabulary and is an attempt to come to terms with the horrors that I experienced on the frontline of the war against terrorism that raged for over 30 years in this divided Province. According to Interpol, we were fighting the worst terrorist onslaught that ordinary policemen have ever had to face anywhere in the civilised world.

I served in the RUC for 21 years and my career was cut short not by my own choosing but as the result of events stretching back over those years. The pent-up emotions and underlying stress had subconsciously eaten away at me until my body told me in no uncertain terms that it could take no more. I was diagnosed in 1990 and again in 2000 by the RUC Occupational

Health Unit as suffering from Post-Traumatic Stress Disorder (PTSD), which ultimately led to my medical retirement from the force in 2001. I was one of literally hundreds of officers who have had their careers cut short by this illness, which is described by the World Health Organisation in the following terms:

> Post-Traumatic Stress Disorder [PTSD] arises as a delayed and/or protracted response to a stressful event of an exceptionally threatening or catastrophic nature. The event is likely to cause pervasive distress in almost anyone (e.g. natural or man-made disaster, combat, serious accident, witnessing the violent death of others, or being the victim of torture, terrorism, rape or other crime). Typical symptoms include episodes of repeated reliving of the trauma in intrusive memories (flashbacks) or dreams. There is usually a state of hyper-vigilance, an enhanced startle reaction and insomnia. Anxiety and depression are commonly associated with the above symptoms, and a suicidal tendency is not infrequent. In a small proportion of patients, the condition may show a chronic course over many years and a transition to an enduring personality change. People who have suffered abuse as children or who have had other previous traumatic experiences are more likely to develop the disorder.

Bearing in mind my very troubled upbringing, I now believe that I should never have been found suitable for service in the police at all. I feel I carried over the trauma of my childhood into my police career and it undoubtedly weakened my resistance. I subconsciously manufactured an imaginary 'chest of memories' deep inside my head to which I would consign the more unsavoury aspects of my police service. Once they were hidden away, I felt confident enough to carry on, but I soon realised that my chest was already full of the horrors of my childhood and there wasn't much room left for what was to come during my police career!

To exacerbate the situation further, I was never made aware of any trauma counselling available after witnessing these horrific incidents; I just washed off the blood and guts and opened a few bottles. I feel this situation led to the high level of suicides amongst officers in the RUC – more than in any other force in the world.

I am not making the case here that I have had more than my share of bad experiences. God knows, there are men out there who have suffered more than I. Three hundred and three RUC men and women have lost their lives, many have lost limbs and thousands have received other very serious injuries which are not always apparent. Every officer has a story to tell and it is a tragedy that so many members of the Royal Ulster Constabulary died before they could put their own lives into words.

Most of what I am about to impart has never been divulged to anyone. I make no apology for not glamourising this book with fancy quotes and exaggerated claims of my involvement in certain incidents; poetic licence will not influence my version of these events. I have not set out to try to impress anyone but to attempt to convey to you in layman's terms what it was like to be on the receiving end of the terrorist onslaught in Northern Ireland. You do not need to lose your life or limbs to be a victim of terrorism.

CHAPTER 1

OUR MOTHER WAS DRIVEN
TO DISTRACTION

In the little world in which children have their existence whosoever brings them up, there is nothing so finely perceived and so finely felt, as injustice. It may be only small injustice that the child can be exposed to; but the child is small, and its world is small, and its rocking-horse stands as many hands high, according to scale, as a big-boned Irish hunter. Within myself, I had sustained, from my babyhood, a perpetual conflict with injustice.

Charles Dickens, *Great Expectations*

I was born on 24 June 1956, the third child of a family living in a small, run-down, semi-detached cottage two miles outside the town of Newtownards in the county of Down in Northern Ireland. With no car at our disposal and a very poor local transport system, my mother had to rely on our neighbour, Mrs McBurney, to telephone for an ambulance when she went into labour. This kind lady, who lived in a big detached house in the corner of a field across the main road, was by now accustomed to the annual arrival of another member of the Gregory clan.

With a tug and a good smack, I was dragged kicking and screaming from my warm sanctuary and out into this cold cruel world. If I had known what horrors lay ahead for me in later life, the screaming might never have stopped.

My earliest recollection is of that old farm dwelling in a little townland called Ballyrickard, which is roughly halfway between Comber and Newtownards in the midst of the fertile County Down countryside. It is an area that could easily be described as the back garden of Ulster, as most of the top-quality vegetables found in the markets of Belfast are grown in its rich dark earth. Our claim to fame in Ballyrickard was the fact that there were the remains of a Norman hill fort behind our tiny house, way down at the bottom of the neglected garden. It was a mound of earth about 40 feet high, upon which, a thousand years ago, stood a wooden fortress, protection for the English landowners against marauding Irish raiders of that time. We called it a 'fairy glen'. The local farmer once cut down one of the old trees that grew upon its summit and his best cow died that same night. That seemed like too much of a coincidence for us and so we assumed he was being punished. There was a rickety old gate at the bottom of the garden leading into this magical place but I never ever went near it, just in case.

The cottage itself was very old. It was badly constructed in a basic oblong form, with a dividing wall between two separate dwellings, one being slightly smaller than the other. I don't remember anyone living in the other half of the building, though there may have been at some point. Inside, there was a very thin, wooden dividing wall painted in the most depressing shade of chocolate brown. This partition created two rooms and a little kitchen area. The ceiling was made from hardboard tacked onto the rafters in the most haphazard fashion, while the floor was made of old slate flagstones, which were always damp and very cold to walk on. The only sanitation was a cesspit at the bottom of the garden. The poor conditions of the house meant that my siblings and I suffered a constant succession of colds, chills and bad chests.

I do have happy memories of playing outside in the fields that surrounded that small cottage and of sitting on the cracked concrete platform nearby upon which the neighbouring farmer would place his full churns of fresh milk ready for collection, but on the whole my childhood was a time of great hardship. I was born into a poverty-stricken and troubled family, and eventually had two brothers and three sisters. The eldest was my sister Sadie, then my brother John, myself, my sister Cherie, my brother Tom and lastly our baby sister Irene. To this day I still question the sanity of my parents for bringing so many children into the world when there was no money to feed them. We always seemed much worse off than other families around us at that time. Our cousins had new clothes, shoes and plenty of food, while we always had to make do with very little. But worse than the financial hardships we suffered was the emotional deprivation. No matter how hard I try, I cannot remember any occasion in my early years when I received any love or affection. If there were any instances, they have obviously been overshadowed by the other miserable memories.

My father worked as a bus driver for the Ulster Transport Authority during the summer season and spent a lot of his time away from home. The crack and bang of his trusty motorbike was the only signal I ever had of his departure in the early hours of the morning as he made his way to collect his bus at the depot. I have very few memories of my father from this earliest period of my life, as he was always gone at first light and didn't return from work until well after our bedtime. On a few precious occasions, I was allowed to sit in the driver's cab with him for a short trip in the shiny green bus. It seemed that he was king of the road. Approaching cars always gave way as we slowly chugged and clanked our way down the narrow pot-holed roads of rural Ulster. Through the smoky haze of cigarettes I would clean the misted windows with my jumper sleeve while perching on my knees on the plush seats, bursting with excitement and afraid of missing something outside. These episodes were very few and far between, however, and even at that young age I had the feeling that he would rather be anywhere other than with his wife and children. On the rare occasions I do remember him being at home, he and my mother would always be arguing about his prolonged absences and the lack of money coming into the house.

Mother did the best she could just to keep our heads above water, but she was fighting a losing battle and we ran about in old, tattered clothes. One dark Christmas Eve when I was about three and a half years old, she fell into a fit of deep depression when it became common knowledge among the wider family circle that there was nothing under the tree for her children. My father was nowhere to be found, so his brother Bobby cycled all the way from Newtownards with very small and inexpensive gifts he had bought in a corner shop. Mother was crying her eyes out as he peered in through our bedroom door. He was shocked to see all us children huddled up in one bed covered by old blankets and coats, our dirty little faces lit up by reflected light from the open doorway. I have only a vague memory of this but it is still clear in my uncle's mind today.

A few months later, just as I was reaching school age, we moved from the cottage into a reasonably new council house in Donard Avenue in the town of Newtownards. There was a massive re-housing plan being put into action by local councils at that time across the Province. Far too many families like us were living in substandard housing, suffering all the medical conditions associated with such an environment. I was thrilled by our new house as it was warm and dry with doors and windows that actually worked. We had a front and rear garden but, as my father did precious little with them, they soon became overgrown.

It was to this house that I can clearly remember my baby sister Irene arriving after she was born in Newtownards Hospital in 1961. I was only five years old at the time and, full of curiosity, I tried to reach up to see into her pram. Unfortunately, when I gripped the handle, I tipped her out and onto the floor. No real harm was done but my mother was furious and I was badly beaten for this silly mistake. I can vividly remember cowering under the table in a frantic bid to escape the onslaught from my mother, hardly able to see for the tears welling up in my eyes. I eventually managed to run outside and I hid in the overgrown garden for most of the day, too afraid to go back into the house. In the end, the cold forced me indoors, whereupon I went straight to hide in my bed. For years after that I was terrified to go anywhere near my baby sister in case I received another beating. It always seemed that Mother had plenty of time and affection for her daughters, while we boys were nothing but a nuisance.

It was also in this house that I was introduced to my elder sister Sadie. To say I was confused would be an understatement; I was totally baffled. I had never seen Sadie before in my life, as she had spent all her seven years living with her aunt and namesake in the tiny village of Carrowdore, six miles away. It was a fairly common practice in large families for relatives to help out by looking after one or more of the children. Sadie had been returned to us as my aunt was now pregnant with her own child and could no longer look after her. I don't even remember hearing her name mentioned before she appeared. John was even more confused than I was and refused to accept that she was one of the family, stating that his only sisters were Cherie and Irene. It took some time for us all to get used to having Sadie around.

The chasm between my mother and father was growing ever wider. They were now fighting and arguing on an almost daily basis, and my brothers and sisters and I would invariably be caught in the middle. I would hide but at the same time watch as they verbally and physically assaulted each other, with my mother usually coming off worse. My father was a control freak and imposed his will on everyone in the household. He seemed to believe that it was his duty in life to keep his wife in subjugation and he was unable to control his jealousy. Mother was beautiful and he knew it, so he denied her money for good clothes, make-up and indeed anything else that would make her look and feel more attractive.

When I was about six years old, in a cry for help my mother bought several packets of Phensic painkiller tablets and sent us out to the corner shop for even more. When she had collected enough, she took a couple, emptied the rest down the drain, left the empty packets in the kitchen and feigned an overdose. She was taken to hospital to have her stomach pumped and when news of this reached the wider family circle it meant that my parents' marital problems were out in the open and my aunts and uncles were now aware of the deepening conflict between them. While our other relatives were concerned about my mother's state of mind, apparently my father put her actions down to attention seeking, but he must have felt some kind of pressure upon him as he agreed to Mother taking a job as a machinist in Walker's Linen Mill in Newtownards.

A period of relative calm followed as she was now bringing her own money into the home and we were able to buy more of the things that we needed. But this tranquillity could never last and just when I began to hope that things were on the up, the fighting started again. It was a vicious circle: my mother was now buying the things she needed to make herself look good and my father hated it. She was going out with her colleagues after work and it drove him crazy trying to keep a constant watch on who she was with. Their relationship was a continual psychological battle that often descended into physical abuse.

At this point in my life, the only stability I had was during my time away from home at the Model Primary School on the Scrabo Road. I settled in quickly and soon became teacher's pet. It was as if my teacher could sense that I was starved of affection at home, as she often let me sit upon her knee. Such kindness was a revelation to me. Religion also played a very important role in my life then, as our weekly attendance at Sunday school meant another chance to escape from home. In reality, I think it was also a chance for our parents to get rid of us on a Sunday afternoon but I didn't mind; I enjoyed it. Our house was always festooned with the many pictures presented to each of us in turn for consistently good attendance, our colourful little certificates pasted on their reverse.

After about three years in this rather elegant part of town, we were on the move again to another council house in Newtownards, this time in Queen's Square. The relationship between my parents continued to deteriorate. My father didn't seem to realise, or perhaps he just didn't care, that his constant arguments with our mother had us children living in total fear. He couldn't bear to hear any noise from us even when we were just playing normally. More times than I care to remember we would be playing in our beds instead of sleeping – as all children do – when suddenly the bedroom door would be flung open, slamming hard against the wall, and a slipper would be thrown at us from the open doorway. We would then be left to cry ourselves to sleep, while making damn sure we didn't make any more noise. My father was from a very large family and, from what I have learned, he was also bullied by his father, so maybe for him, it was his payback time in relation to his own children. Our neighbours disliked him as he was forever shouting and banging on shared walls, complaining that they were also making too much noise. Kids outside were shouted at on a daily basis, which in turn only fuelled the aggravation of their parents. 'There is something wrong with that man,' was the general consensus on our street.

Things gradually went from bad to worse and Mother was the first to crack under the strain. When I was about eight years old, she spent a few weeks in the Newtownards Hospital Psychological and Neurological Unit suffering from severe depression. My father was unable to cope with six children on his own and the situation got so bad that, instead of facing up to his responsibilities, he voluntarily put us into welfare care. It seemed to me that he had just had enough of us and took the easy way out; what else was I to think when we were so cruelly abandoned?

Strange cars with police escorts arrived in Queen's Square to take us away. The appearance of more than one reasonably new car entering this working-class cul-de-sac always caused a sensation and on this occasion the neighbours came out in force. As well-dressed welfare officers escorted us into the back seats of their gleaming vehicles, for a moment I almost imagined that I was the envy of the friends I was leaving behind. But in reality, concerned neighbours stood at their open doorways with arms folded, shaking their heads and 'tut-tutting' as they chatted amongst themselves, no doubt glad to see that some attention was at last being paid to our plight.

We were all taken to Childhaven Children's Home just outside the little coastal town of Donaghadee, seven miles away. I can vividly remember arriving there very late in the evening. Once inside, it was the heat that struck me first: I was used to being constantly cold and I couldn't believe just how warm and inviting this building was. I gazed in wonder at the high ornate ceilings and spiral staircase; I had never been in such a posh house before and I was initially excited that I was to stay there for a while. After a bath administered by the staff and having our hair thoroughly checked for lice, we all sat up on our beds at midnight eating large bowls of Corn Flakes covered with fresh ice-cold milk and sugar. I was really hungry and had never tasted anything so good. This was the first time in my life I had experienced the luxury of my own bed and it felt strange and lonely without the other little bodies beside me. I was also afraid of wrinkling the immaculately clean sheets and the heavy blankets that ensured my warmth throughout that first night.

The next morning, it felt just like Christmas Day. I was awoken by the sound of my brothers' and sisters' laughter and saw that a member of staff was laying out new clean clothes on our beds. We each got a new toothbrush and a tin of tooth powder. Somewhat puzzled, I looked up at the lady. She must have realised I didn't know what to do with them as she took us all into the bathroom to instruct us how to clean our teeth, something we had never done before.

I knew kids who had been traumatised by their incarceration in children's homes but at first it was different for us. I initially looked upon this stay in Childhaven as a holiday and was mostly just excited by it all; we had never been away from home before. During quieter moments, though, I couldn't help but worry about what was going to become of us all. A few days later, when the first excitement had begun to wear off, I spent hours maliciously picking off small pieces of old brown paint from the banisters of the massive oak staircase as I wondered what I had done wrong to end up in a home. Things got worse when I had to go through the humiliation of attending a different school in Donaghadee and sit amongst the well-heeled pupils as they quizzed me about why I had been sent to live at the poor kids' home up the road.

We stayed in Childhaven for some weeks but were then sent back to a situation much worse than it had been before we left. Mother had just arrived home from the hospital and would spend all day making up little plastic bags for knitting wool as part of her therapy. She looked tired and drawn, and any interaction with us children irritated her. The fights between her and my father soon picked up where they had left off and we were caught in the middle yet again. After my time in the sanctuary of Childhaven, I had very nearly forgotten the hurt of seeing my parents tearing themselves apart. But it soon came flooding back and I recall huddling on the stairs with Sadie, trying to work out with which parent our loyalties lay, both of us crying our eyes out as we watched them throwing each other around the room.

At this stage, I developed my own special way of dealing with all the hurt around me: I would sing and hum my way through my favourite tunes as I tried to blank out the sights and sounds of my parents destroying each other. As they grew louder, so did I, to the extent that I think I only added to their rage. Then again, however, my behaviour managed to get them to stop fighting for a while as they concentrated on trying to keep me quiet.

A short time later, my father also took his turn in Newtownards Hospital suffering from the effects of his turbulent marriage to my mother. It became obvious to all that Mother just couldn't cope with the six of us on her own, so the welfare department again took us into care and sent us this time to Marmaine, another children's home, this time in the sleepy little town of Holywood in County Down. The sight of the welfare cars arriving in Queen's Square didn't cause quite so much of a stir on this occasion.

Marmaine was a palatial house set in its own grounds on Church Road and had the most fantastic tiered gardens I had ever seen. The front lawn was vast and for the first time in my life I rolled and played on clean cut grass. Magnificent spruce trees and rhododendrons formed a small fragrant wood at the bottom and I revelled in my new-found ability to climb really high into their branches to observe my latest domain. Beside the house, we had our very own railway carriage, a gift from the Belfast and County Down Railway. Its wheels had been removed and it sat on a low brick wall. The seats had also been removed and replaced with tables and chairs. It felt so good sitting in there as it rained heavily outside. We would pretend we were on our way across the world as I handed out old tickets from a big wooden box.

In stark contrast, however, my time inside the main house was a living hell due to the wicked cruelty inflicted upon me by one particular member of the staff. I can remember once sliding down the banister and into the front hall, as any young boy was likely to do. I was caught red-handed and beaten so badly that I was bruised for days. My injuries were put down to a fall from the banister that did not take place. I was knocked breathless as this 'carer' repeatedly thumped my back with her fist while dragging me up the stairs to bed. I cried myself to sleep with the covers pulled over my head, desperate to know what awful crime I had committed to be sent away to this prison. I was always told it was only bad boys and girls who were sent to homes. I had done nothing wrong so why was I here?

The six of us were generally well looked after in this home, as there was plenty of good food and activities, but there was also a total lack of affection or understanding for already traumatised children. I believe that the psychological effect of the upheavals we had been through led me to develop a severe stammer at this time. I knew what I wanted to say but I was suffering from a total lack of self-confidence. I was sure that anything I had to say would be scoffed at, so I stammered rather than spoke. I just could not get the words out and had to endure the cruel taunts of the other kids in the home and at Holywood Primary School. One of the young teachers tried as hard as she could to save my speech from deteriorating further by instructing me in skills aimed at controlling my emotions. To a certain degree, it seemed to be working: I still stammered but with control and timing I could now communicate at my own pace.

From the wide family circle of aunts and uncles, only a few ever helped us out. In those days, it would have been the norm amongst close families for relatives to step in and look after the children until the situation settled down. My aunt Sadie in Carrowdore did indeed take three of us on numerous occasions while our parents tried to settle their differences. But our relations all had children of their own and it would have been totally unfair to burden them further. They knew we were being shipped from welfare home to welfare home, so Uncle Bill offered to take Cherie under his wing. Our father refused this kind gesture by stating, 'If you're taking any of them, then take them all, they're not being split up.' To this day, it is still a thorny issue within our ageing family circle. The issue is never raised by any of us children but some of our relatives obviously still feel guilty that they were unable to do more to help us.

After a long period in Marmaine, we were sent home again to a situation that had not improved. This intolerable state of affairs lasted until I was about ten years old, when things got so bad that our parents eventually separated and our mother left home, taking all six of us with her. After finding ourselves living in a little house in John Street in Newtownards for a week or so, we were told we were heading to the city of Belfast.

OUR MOTHER WAS DRIVEN TO DISTRACTION

While we prepared for yet another move, I was playing in the vacant room upstairs when I stood on a piece of wood with a big rusty nail protruding from it. The nail went straight through my right foot adjacent to my big toe. I screamed out more in horror than pain as I looked down to see the bloody nail poking out through the top of my plastic sandal. By the time Mother made her way upstairs, I had stood on the piece of wood with my other foot and pulled my injured foot off the nail; blood was now all over the floor. There was no way that this was going to delay our move, however, and just as I thought I was heading to the hospital to have it looked at, I was bundled into the welfare minibus as we set off for Belfast. I had my foot bandaged up with a scarf and believed it would get better soon because my mother had told me so!

CHAPTER 2

WHAT HAVE WE DONE
TO DESERVE THIS?

I was excited about the minibus trip, as I didn't get to travel much in those days, except for the odd run to the little village of Carrowdore to see Aunt Sadie. I had so many clothes on, though, I could hardly sit down, and in a way my discomfort detracted from the thrill of the journey. Mother had told us to put on as many layers of clothing as we could to save carrying them and I was wearing three pairs of trousers and underpants, about four shirts and as many jumpers. I was not alone, as even the girls were dressed in all they could wear. Tom reminded me of the Michelin man as we sat and sweated buckets the whole way from Newtownards, hardly able to turn around to see out of the windows.

We eventually arrived in Belfast in the dying light of evening. The strange lights and tall buildings of the city centre initially enthralled us as we repeatedly asked, 'How far to go now?' My excitement about the city began to wear off, however, as we drew closer to the area in which we would be living. Inner-city Belfast was different from anything I had experienced before. I was used to the countryside of Newtownards, where we had constant supplies of fresh air, colour and green grass, and I now found myself in a grey urban sprawl. The smell became overpowering as the cars, buses and trucks added to the pungent atmosphere of coal fires and industrial smoke, creating a choking blanket that hung menacingly over the city. The contrast was unbearable and the only thing that kept me from crying was my naive belief that it wouldn't be too long before our parents got back together again and we would be heading back home to Newtownards.

We were dropped off at an old condemned house at 100 Dover Street, just off Divis Street at the lower end of the Falls Road. The Victorian house was mid-terrace, red brick and typical of the larger houses built to replace the slums that had previously occupied this site. When we got inside, I stood there speechless in the only clothes I had to my name, trying to balance in the doorway on my uninjured foot. We set down our few boxes in the grubby hall and surveyed our surroundings, which were much worse than I could have imagined: it was filthy.

Mother, of course, looked upon this move as some kind of exciting adventure and tried to convince us to see the positive benefits of Dover Street. Obviously she was either blind or she was seeing this awful place through Valium-tinted glasses. If the truth were told, she had not brought us to Belfast because she couldn't bear to be separated from her children or because she hoped that she could give us a better life there; instead, the six of us represented an easy income in the form of child benefits.

We had three floors and attic rooms at our disposal, and in the room upstairs we children were to share, the only piece of furniture was a stinking, piss-stained double bed. There were no blankets or curtains, just our own pile of coats and the clothes we stood up in.

Sadie screamed out in horror at the top of the stairs as she came face to face with an enormous growth of fungus protruding menacingly from one of the walls of the landing. It looked like a giant pig's ear and, with some trepidation, I set about scraping it off with an old piece of wood I had found lying on the floor. It hit the floor with a damp 'plop', causing a cloud of dust and spores to drift up as the girls recoiled and ran back down to the bottom of the stairs.

Mother had the pick of the bedrooms and hers was resplendent with carpet, bed, blankets and even the luxury of curtains. Downstairs, the rooms were damp and smelly with missing and rotten floorboards. The kitchen was a mess. It had an old Belfast sink complete with rotten draining boards. The stench was unbearable as they fell away in our hands. Only the cold water tap worked; a rusty discharge was all we could ever get out of the hot tap. The only room of any use was the rear scullery, which was attached to the kitchen. It was the only place in which we could get the fire to work and we would huddle in there on an old broken settee as we burnt anything we could lay our hands on. The coal bunker in the yard had already been scraped clean by the previous tenant but there was plenty of old wood lying around, so John and I set about breaking it up the best we could with an old axe we had found and by jumping off the step onto the larger pieces as the girls gathered up the sticks. This was the first time I became aware of a fire's ability to generate a welcoming glow in even the most dingy of hovels.

On our first night there, we were sent to that stinking damp bed on the first floor without a bite to eat. We laid down some coats to give us a dry surface to sleep upon, then covered ourselves with the rest and anything else we could lay our hands on. There was a strong smell of warm urine emanating from an old rusting paint pot in the corner, as no one dared venture out into the backyard in the dark. Bad as things might have been at home, they were never this bad.

'What have we done to deserve this?' I asked God as I said a little prayer. Panic bombarded my mind and I could not lift my head from under the coats for fear of what I might see, such was the noise of scurrying mice and the icy wind whistling through the broken glass as it rattled the old sash window. In my whispered little prayer, I begged for swift deliverance from this horrible place. I also said the Lord's Prayer, and it had never seemed so poignant as I clung on to my sisters and we cried ourselves to sleep.

The next day we were woken by the cold. No matter which way we lay, we were freezing as the rain lashed in through the broken glass. We had slept in all the clothes we had to our name and had nothing warmer to put on. As we stood shivering and starving in the scullery, John realised things were really bad, so he suggested we head out around the doorsteps to collect a few bottles of milk to heat. I looked at John and without much deliberation we set off into the icy cold morning.

John was always a bit more worldly wise than me and pointed out that it wouldn't be such a good idea to pinch from the neighbours' houses, so we headed into Boundary Street. The area was totally deserted at this early hour, so we lifted one bottle each and headed back to the house. No sooner had we made off than we heard a car horn. We looked around to see a car chasing after us at speed. My bandaged foot, stuffed into my untied shoe, was now killing me and running was near impossible.

'Oi! Come back here, ye thievin' wee bastards,' I heard the driver shout out at the top of his voice, so loud it scared the daylights out of me.

'Christ! What do we do now?' I called to John.

John was at this stage some distance ahead and already hiding behind a car in a side street. He shouted, 'Split up!', so I hobbled over some waste ground and made my escape home. John arrived a few minutes later, totally out of breath and laughing his head off. Half expecting to get my head in my hands for stealing, I was somewhat disturbed to find I was being pardoned by Mum. This was unnerving after years of having it drummed in to me that stealing was totally wrong. Now it seemed I was allowed to carry it out with impunity.

As my foot was throbbing unbearably, I sat down and removed the bandage only to see a seeping mess of pus. Apparently there was a hospital just a short distance up the road, so Mum gave me a shilling and told me to go to the casualty department. 'On my own?' I asked her.

'Go on, you big baby, you're supposed to be a big boy now,' she said.

I stood at the bus stop on Divis Street for what felt like ages before the red trolley bus arrived. The sight of that big machine really scared me. Trolley buses were much larger than the ordinary buses I had previously known and they had two big arms reaching up from the roof to touch cables that seemed to be part of a massive spider's web covering the city.

'Come on, son,' the conductor said as he saw my bandaged foot. 'I take it you want off at the Royal?'

'No, mister. I have to go to the hospital,' I replied.

'That's the Royal you want, son, the Royal Victoria Hospital. I'll give you a shout when we reach it,' he said as I tried to hand him my shilling. 'That's OK, son, you keep that for sweets, looks like you need them,' he added with a big Belfast smile on his face.

A few minutes later, the conductor pulled the cord and the distinct 'ding, ding' signalled the driver to stop. When we reached the front entrance of the hospital, I hobbled my way to the rear door of the bus and the conductor lifted me up and set me down on the pavement. I was touched by his kindness and even though no words were exchanged I knew from his broad smile that he wished me well.

It was somewhat exciting to be the focus of all this attention as another Samaritan now came my way. No sooner had I arrived at the front door than a young porter rushed over with a wheelchair to take me to the casualty department. I screeched out in agony and horror as the nurse cleaned my wound and put a fresh bandage on it; then, with a jab on the bum, I was sent on my way. I felt much better and stopped to buy Kola Kubes in a corner shop with my shilling as I limped back to Dover Street.

The rest of that day was spent exploring our house, such as it was. Mother had by now spent all her money on a bottle of QC wine and some cigarettes, and there was nothing left for food until she could claim more benefit. Then she spied the gas meter sitting on a shelf in the corner of the scullery. With a nod and a wink, John and I set about breaking off the lock with the axe we had found in the yard. I had never seen so many shillings in my life as I emptied the contents of the cash box onto the floor. With a pocketful, I was told to run down to the shop at the end of the street to buy bread and a few other things. We were going to make toast on the fire that John was lighting. I'm sure the shopkeeper knew fine well I had robbed the gas meter, seeing as I had no money except shillings. People in the city invariably kept them for the gas and rarely spent them in the corner shop but I would imagine that every meter in the street had been robbed at some stage. To our great surprise and excitement, later that day a coalman arrived in the yard and tipped two bags into the small roofless coal shed. As kids, we were totally oblivious as to who had bought it or indeed how we came to receive it but our faces lit up as we realised we would be warm that night. Seems the gas money was being put to good use after all!

WHAT HAVE WE DONE TO DESERVE THIS?

The backyard of the house was an absolute mess. It was filled with all kinds of junk and rotting foodstuff, and it stank to the high heavens. It was great entertainment for me to watch the rats scurrying about all over the mound outside the scullery window. 'Rats like cats,' I would shout out to frighten the girls, but a few days later, some men from the Belfast Corporation arrived and set about clearing the disgusting rubbish. At least now we could get to the only toilet this property had – a foul, supposedly white toilet in an old outhouse beside the coal shed. The bowl was the most revolting shade of brown one could imagine. Copious amounts of bleach only appeared to make it worse and the stench was overwhelming, ensuring you only ever stayed in there as long as it took. There was no toilet roll for us; instead, we cleaned ourselves up with strips of the *Belfast Telegraph* hanging on a string. Mother was the only one to have soft toilet roll and she kept it hidden in her room.

What a culture shock living in the city was to us country kids. We hadn't really got a clue what was expected of us or, indeed, even just what to say to the kids playing on the street outside. We must have appeared so strange to them. For a start we were, by their standards, very quiet. Belfast kids have a loud and angry way of speaking to each other, and our accents seemed to make them think we were a bit snobbish. The cap certainly didn't fit. How could we be snobs when they saw the abject poverty in which we were living? By and large, though, they viewed us as outsiders and left us to our own devices.

Kids from provincial towns invariably have their own little idiosyncrasies and we were no different. At home in Newtownards, we would try to dress as smartly as possible for Sunday school and we felt we had to follow on with this tradition when we first attended Sunday school at the Shankill Road Mission. We arrived, each with a little flower in our buttonholes, only to be laughed at by the other children there, as this practice was not in vogue in Belfast.

Mother didn't escape scrutiny either. She was warned a number of times by concerned neighbours for leaving the front door key in the lock – normal practice at that time back home. In any case, we never had anything to steal. Any self-respecting burglar would probably have taken pity on our dire situation and left us stuff instead.

I was in my final years of primary school by this stage and so attended Brown's Square Primary School at the lower end of the Shankill Road. This was a great little school, though the Victorian building was now seriously dilapidated. The floors were full of holes that had been repaired with patches of board tacked down with shiny copper nails, and the many broken windows allowed all the noise and smog of the city to enter. Our well-worn flip-top desks were scarred with the names of hundreds of former pupils who had sat upon these perches.

Each morning, I looked forward to being issued with my big shiny brass disc that entitled me to my free lunch in the school canteen across the street. To some kids, it would have been a degrading experience to be called out in front of the class to collect it, walking a line of cat-calls of 'gypsy, gyppo'. As far as I was concerned, however, it was survival: this was our ticket to the only hot meal we would get that day. I would cry my heart out if school were closed for more than a few days. I seemed to suffer more than the rest of my brothers and sisters from hunger, and sometimes the pains would be so excruciating that John or Sadie would have to find something to quell them.

From Brown's Square, I progressed to Ballygomartin Secondary School in 1967 and found myself in the company of some of the hardest kids I had ever come across in my short life. This was a predominantly Protestant school and among my fellow pupils was Samuel McAllister, later to become one of the infamous Shankill Butchers. His comrade and fellow Butcher Robert 'Basher' Bates had left school the previous year but would meet McAllister most days at the school gates. Within ten years, they, along with their leader Lenny Murphy, had joined the Ulster Volunteer Force and would be responsible for over 19 of the most brutal and bloodcurdling murders Northern Ireland has ever witnessed. Their full story is graphically told in Martin Dillon's book *The Shankill Butchers*.

At school, Bates and McAllister often held the other kids to ransom with knives. In the toilets, they would beat the shit out of boys who wouldn't pay them protection money. When they found out I was from the slums of Dover Street, I escaped this demand, as they knew they were wasting their time on me: I had no money. But to say that life at Ballygomartin was difficult for me would be an understatement. I had arrived on their turf with what they termed a 'Fenian' name and despite my attempts to convince them that I was one of them – a Prod – the fact that I lived in Dover Street just off the Catholic Falls Road didn't help my case at all. I was subjected to the most brutal of beatings at school, literally having to hide for my life on some occasions. On more days than I care to remember, I had to fight my way home as I ran the gauntlet of Protestant thugs queuing up at the gates to beat the shit out of this supposed 'Fenian newcomer' on their turf. Lenny Murphy had suffered similar problems, as he too was raised a Protestant with the burden of a Catholic name. The abuse and vilification he received as a boy was thought by some to be the very reason he turned into a Catholic-hating psychopath. It's ironic and quite frightening to think just how much we had in common.

My elder brother John was not very good at confrontations and he played truant on an almost daily basis rather than deal with the hate in Ballygomartin. When he did attend, he too was forced to run the gauntlet and between us we would devise all sorts of escape plans. He would make them believe he was heading out of one gate as I escaped out the other. As he was always a faster runner than me, they never caught him and we would eventually meet up again at the top of the Shankill Road.

Academically, John lagged way behind the rest of us and he was always very conscious of this. He had resigned himself early on to the fact that schooling was not for him. He was ridiculed and punished by teachers for failing to complete the work assigned to him and it was only later in life that it was discovered that he was chronically dyslexic. It almost breaks my heart when I think back to the times he would ask me for help with his homework. He would plead with me to help him, with tears running down his face, as he was terrified about the reaction he would get at school the next day if he didn't get it done. This in turn scared me, as John was my big brother and he was not supposed to cry.

As an attempt to escape from the daily bullying, I became absorbed in my schoolwork. While never at the top end of the academic scale, I managed to hold my head above water, which was not bad considering I had been to six schools in as many years. I also found what I thought would be an interest I could sustain and became involved in the school orchestra.

As a direct result of the enthusiasm I was showing, my music teacher asked if I would like to try an instrument and after trying most of them I decided that it was to be the concert flute for me. I progressed really well and started to show some promise, probably due to the fact that I would stay to practise long after school was over to escape the beatings.

I really got to grips with this music scene and was eventually sent to the Belfast School of Music in Donegall Pass on Saturday mornings for further instruction. I could hardly believe this turn of events, as here I was, this grubby kid from the slums of the Lower Falls, amongst all the snobs from Campbell College and Belfast Royal Academy. An advanced student/instructor by the name of James Galway from Carnalea Street sometimes showed up. His father, known to his mates as 'Jumbo' Galway, worked in the Harland and Wolff shipyard. He would go without his cigarettes and drink to ensure James had a new flute to play. When James played at the school, I would be completely awestruck and the whole class would halt their work just to listen to the harmony from down the hall. He made a great name for himself playing this instrument and it was a tremendous honour to have been at the School of Music with him.

One day, when I was 11, my instructor came over and asked me to stay after class. 'Christ, what have I done now?' I thought. There was no need for me to worry, though, as he told me that he thought I had potential and wanted to offer me the chance to have my very own flute on loan. I was somewhat taken aback and didn't really know how to reply. He assured me that it was OK and I walked out half an hour later with a brand-new silver concert flute in its black box under my arm. The whole way home, I was walking on a cloud. Here I was at last with the first possession I could call my own.

At home, by and large us kids were left to our own devices at that time, as our mother took very little interest in what we were doing or how we were getting on. She was more interested in whichever new man she had in her life. Somehow, however, we managed to keep ourselves busy and out of serious trouble. When it was open, we had the run of a council playground behind us in Boundary Street. At that time in Belfast, and throughout Northern Ireland, playgrounds were habitually locked on Sundays. The swings were systematically chained and padlocked on Saturday night, as were the see-saws, roundabouts and slides. This course of action was the result of an edict from the ruling Unionist authorities. As a child, I didn't understand the politics behind this order but could not miss the outcry from the other residents when the 'lock man' would appear. Amid taunts from the local Catholics, he would set about his sorry task with glee. Taking obvious pride in his work, he would chase the children out and finish off by locking the high gates that surrounded the playground. The Protestant government wanted us all to keep Sunday holy and they were going to browbeat us into it; it seems pathetic when I think of it now.

For something to do on the long summer days we would all tramp the streets – a tribe of kids, the eldest no more than 13 or 14 years old, walking unaccompanied throughout the troubled city. We once even managed to walk the whole way to the little town of Holywood and back, some 13 miles, without money, food or anything to drink. I missed the green fields and clean fresh air of Newtownards and I think I was checking my bearings and contemplating a possible escape route in case we should ever need one. We were a family of children trying to come to terms with our plight and surviving the best we could. We all looked out for one another and had no choice but to grow up fast; at this stage I was 11 going on 16.

We survived only because of the regular handouts of food hampers, second-hand clothes and plastic sandals donated by the Shankill Road Mission, which was a Presbyterian Church housed in the most elaborate premises I had ever seen. It was a grand old building that really did seem to contain some kind of holy presence. It dominated the front of the lower Shankill Road close to the junction of Agnes Street. After you passed through the huge, brown-painted double doors, you were led to the main hall, which was circular with the most ornate balcony held up by a series of heavy, black, cast-iron pillars.

The Shankill Road Mission was a godsend for me. The members of the congregation were totally genuine and really did care for us, and I soon established myself within its Boys' Brigade. The 36th Belfast Boys' Brigade instilled in me the core values of discipline and respect which would otherwise have slipped away as a result of the way we were living day to day.

I now had a goal and something I could look forward to on a weekly basis. I took great pride in keeping my uniform clean and the belt and buckle polished, and I took part in parades and organised displays. Even though I had fairly limited responsibilities within its ranks, I still felt that at last I could make a valuable contribution and this helped to build my confidence and self-esteem.

I am sure, looking back, that many secret meetings must have been held between the elders concerning the best way to take my brothers and sisters and me under their wing, such was the effect our condition had upon them. I was really the only one of the family who got actively involved, though. For the first time in my life I was taken away on field trips and camping in Scotland, all paid for by the Mission. My musical skills again came to the fore as I was given a bugle to play. Due to a severe shortage of instruments, I was given one that had certainly seen better days. Damaged, dented and covered with filthy green dirt and mould, it took hours of scrubbing to get it shining, but I managed it and it sounded sweet.

As well as all the time I spent within the welcoming walls of the Mission, I would also spend hours hanging around the junction of the Shankill Road and Agnes Street, as this place held an eerie fascination for me. On the wall of the bank there was an old cast-iron street sign emblazoned with the words 'Agnes Street'. I etched my initials into its flaking paint with a rusty old nail, never realising for one moment just how significant that name would become to me in later life.

CHAPTER 3

I THINK IT WAS OUR ABJECT POVERTY THAT SAVED US

From what I can remember, my father was pretty elusive at this stage in our lives. He now had a car, which enabled him to make the trip from Newtownards to see us, but he had other interests now that he no longer had a wife and six kids to look after. On many occasions, we sat for hours on the dusty bare-board stairs in Dover Street awaiting his arrival, only to be told late in the evening that our vigil had been in vain. You can't tell a child to go and play as they wait for something exciting; they always want to be there to see it happen. We would not be content playing upstairs or out on the street as we waited for him to appear; I felt so insecure that I wanted to be at the door just in case I missed him.

I now believe there never was a set schedule for visits. Mother can't have known if he was planning to come, as we had no telephone to allow them to make such an arrangement. In retrospect, I think it was her cruel way of building up false hope within us, possibly in an attempt to keep us quiet and out of her hair for a while.

He did arrive once and make a vain effort to take us away in his old black Morris Minor. A heated argument developed on the street, resulting in blows being exchanged between him and Mother's present lover. It cheered me beyond belief to know that my father cared enough not only to make the ten-mile journey but also to actually fight for us. In a way, I felt a bit proud of him that day, but it was sad to see him square up to this hard man only to come off worse. As the row continued, our dad tried to plant a real haymaker on his opponent's chin. He misjudged badly and fell to the ground, banging his head on a cast-iron drainpipe. I was terrified about what was going to happen and couldn't bear to watch any more, so I fixed my gaze on something to try to blank out the noise. I ended up staring at the little flip-up orange direction indicators synonymous with Morris Minor cars of that time. It may seem weird but somehow this did help me to switch off. I remember that one of the indicators was out of its socket as if indicating a turn. Its pulsating flash of warm orange light somehow seemed to mask the sound of human struggle going on around me.

Bloodied from the cut to his head, my father eventually clambered defeated into his car and drove off empty-handed; I didn't see him again for what felt like years. I cried until I could cry no more. I wanted to go back to Newtownards and would have gladly accepted the troubled life we had had there. It was never as bad as the living hell in Belfast in the care of a mother who devoted all her attention to her latest lover and QC wine.

I was always starving and one day I spied a box of Weetabix breakfast cereal amongst other items of food sitting in the cupboard in my mother's bedroom. I shouted out with delight as I made my way over to get it, thinking they were for us. But almost immediately the truth dawned as I received an almighty thump on the back of the head and was thrown out of the room. 'They're not for you,' Mum told me. She and her lover would have them for breakfast and in fact they would eat and drink very well while we managed on scraps.

We didn't know it at the time, but our situation was so bad that someone reported my mother to the National Society for the Prevention of Cruelty to Children. I remember someone from the society talking to each of us on an individual basis and then together as they tried to assess what was going on. They must have been concerned, as we were given some financial help to get some clothes and food, but, like all other money that came into the house, it went on more important things than children.

To quell our hunger pains, we would make what we considered to be a great delicacy out of whatever was left in the bare cupboards. It would be made from broken-up bread mixed with warm tea and sugar in a jam jar, as we didn't even have enough mugs to drink from. Sadie was the best at making up this concoction. It seemed to all of us that she possessed the secret recipe so we would make sure it was always her turn. This delicacy had been very popular among the poorer families of the city for a long time before our arrival in Belfast and was in fact called 'panade'. This was so strange as it rhymed with her name and for ages we honestly believed it was a testimony to her culinary skills.

We really were living in squalid surroundings. We had to endure the constant coming and going of some of the most unsavoury characters Belfast had to offer. In the other bedsits in our building, we could hear the drunks, prostitutes and perverts laughing and carrying on their sordid deeds well into the night. Conditions were so filthy that I contracted a severe case of ringworm on the back of my neck and, much to my delight, I had to spend Christmas and New Year in the Royal Victoria Hospital for sick children. I had been bitten by an infected cat or even a rat while I was sleeping, as at that time both animals had the run of the house. I suffered a disgusting, reddish-brown, scaly ring on my neck that had to be painfully scraped, cleaned and painted with iodine each day.

My time in hospital was truly an oasis of calm during this turbulent time in my life. I seemed to make a good impression on the young nurses and they constantly asked for locks of my curly ginger hair. I suppose I was a mannerly and well-spoken child compared to the rough and ready Belfast street kids who would normally have crossed their path. There was open criticism among the staff about the fact that no one came to see me regularly. I had only one visit from my mother and that was on Christmas Eve when she brought me a little Airfix plastic model of the *Golden Hind* in a plastic bag. I wasn't expecting anything at all but I could see the disapproving look on the face of my nurse when she realised that Christmas meant so little to me and indeed my mother. The caretaker took pity on me and spent the night making me a big wooden fort from leftover scraps of wood in his workshop. I couldn't believe my good fortune: at last I had something to play with and I didn't stand out from the rest of the kids on the ward so much. I got to take it home when I left hospital but I never did get any soldiers to man its battlements.

I was due to be discharged from hospital earlier but the nurses, on seeing my dismay at this prospect, decided with Matron's approval to keep me in over the New Year. I enjoyed my first happy festive season and was spoilt rotten. For those two weeks, I closed my mind to everything out in the real world, even my brothers and sisters. I was living in a haven of clean sheets, warm food and the love and attention of caring staff. I would perch on top of the radiators, grinning like a Cheshire cat as I wallowed in the warmth and security of this safe environment.

Bad as it was, however, that house in Dover Street was not the worst of our hovels. After two months, the landlord had been forced to fix the windows, so it was now basically dry, if filthy. One good thing about the house was a fantastic council gas lamp outside the front door. We were very lucky, as IRA fighters, in a bid to cover their movements in the dead of night, had smashed all the others. Ours was painted green and, when lit, it shone through the smog of a thousand coal fires and gave a warm iridescent yellow glow around the front door of our house, as if laying out our boundary to the exclusion of all others. We assumed ownership of that lamp by tying our ropes to the ladder-rests, thereby making a swing, which amused us for hours. It was also our guiding light in bed as it shone into our bedroom on the first floor, generating that warm, flickering magnetism only produced by gaslight.

Play in Dover Street was now interspersed with bouts of the very serious rioting that was flaring up in Belfast. Coming as we did from the quiet backwater of Newtownards, we had no experience of this engrained hatred and didn't really even understand the reasons for it. At that time, Newtownards had no religiously entrenched ghettos and people lived side by side in relative harmony, so it was distanced to a certain degree from the sectarian conflict that was mounting within Northern Ireland. In true boyhood fashion, I was somewhat excited watching the barricades being built at the end of our street and observing the running gun battles between the police and the rioters. I could hear the gunshots ringing out in the dead of night as we lay safely tucked up together in our own little huddle away from the windows, hiding from the hate-filled adult world outside.

On more than one occasion I found 'B' Specials (reserve RUC officers noted for their brutality) hiding in our backyard or camped out in the other derelict houses beside us. They would huddle into small rooms and corners behind piles of bricks and wood, heating soup and tea on small stoves boiling away on a few old bricks. I described our local delicacy of panade to them but they winced at the thought of it. I could see their guns poking out through broken windows and holes in the walls they had made by removing a brick or two. It was very exciting to think there were policemen camped beside my house, spying on all that was happening on the Falls Road, though I wasn't entirely sure *why* they were there. If things were reasonably quiet, they would normally talk to me but during the really bad times, they would chase me away and move to another street. They asked me to keep the fact that they were there a secret and, after promising with my right hand up to God, I kept my word. I'm not sure that they believed me, though. They were a good bunch of lads and many had kids of their own.

Tensions continued to rise between the two factions and one morning, following a night of protracted violence, the cold light of day exposed the damage that had been wrought. Whole families were being burnt out of their homes in some sort of ethnic cleansing process, while the police seemed to stand by and watch. Young as I was, I was still very concerned as I realised the implications for us as a Protestant family living in the Catholic end of Dover Street – we were prime targets for retaliation. To be quite honest, I think it must have been our abject poverty that saved us – there would have been nothing to gain from burning us out, as the house was so run down it was obviously condemned anyway.

After Protestants had witnessed a night's rioting between gangs from the Shankill and Falls roads, they agreed that they should build their own defences. Catholic youths had started to stone and petrol bomb any passing vehicles and also began attacking the police station in Hastings Street. Protestants in Dover Street began fighting with the B Specials in an attempt to get at the Catholic rioters, who in turn invaded Dover Street, carrying corrugated iron sheets as they tried to push the Protestants back. Several more houses were burnt out. The police commenced a baton charge on the Catholic end of the street, while IRA gunmen began firing in their direction. A few streets away, other IRA gunmen fired at the police, who were trying to push the Catholic crowd back into the Falls Road. Later on that evening, the IRA again opened fire on Protestant crowds in Dover Street.

This was a very frightening time for us, as it must have been for most kids living in the area. But then out of the blue we were blessed with the arrival of a new man in Mum's life. Pat appeared on the scene and provided the strong male presence that had been lacking for so long in our lives. Pat filled the void that had been left by our father and he instilled in me the required Belfast etiquette that would ensure my survival on the street. He also had a great effect upon Mother, who now seemed to be on a more level keel. Her mood changed from one of constant despair to one of hope, and for the first time in many years she was visibly happy. Pat even took some of us up to his sister's home in Andersonstown, where we had a great weekend with her family and kids. The spectre of the Troubles was never far away, though, and the fact that we were Protestants staying in this Catholic area caused me a lot of anxiety. I need not have worried, however, as we hid it well and had a great time.

Despite this new semblance of stability, I was still showing signs of being a disturbed child. The unconscious habit of singing and humming that I had developed some years previously was just as prevalent now. It was greatly annoying to everyone around me but it was my way of coping. After much discussion, Pat decided that it might be a good idea to channel this singing in a constructive direction, so he suggested I join the local Catholic choir in the chapel just around the corner in Divis Street. For the first time in my life I came face to face with the fundamental differences between being a Protestant and the demands of the Catholic Church. In order to join this choir, I would be expected to attend Mass and partake in their traditions, which were alien to me. I felt really uncomfortable about this, especially as I had already established myself in the Shankill Road Mission. I think Pat got the message and the subject was never raised again. My subconscious singing never did stop and to this day continues to annoy my long-suffering wife.

In many other ways, though, I was an ordinary, inquisitive and mischievous boy. There were certain rooms in the Dover Street house that were worse than others due to infestation, filth and missing floorboards. In total ignorance of the dangers and as a form of excitement, I discovered the fun that could be had with electricity. I would tentatively stick my fingers in the light sockets in a vacant room while standing on a chair. The buzz was not at all painful, more like a great tingle down my arm, possibly because I had isolated myself to some degree with the chair I was standing on. I even managed to encourage my sister Cherie to do the same thing. While she stood on the chair, I told her to put her finger into the light bulb holder as I turned on the switch. She jumped off the chair and ran away screaming. In reality, it wasn't that bad and I put her reaction down to a case of girls being girls. Now, of course, I realise how stupid I was being and Cherie has also never let me forget it.

One day, in a dark and stinking attic room, Cherie and I found a large steel water tank covered with a heavy wooden lid. It was built into the far corner of the wall and looked to me as if it had been there for a hundred years. It was rusting very badly along its bottom edge and there were water stains all over the floor underneath, where leaks had obviously caused some of the floorboards to rot. There were holes in the floor through which I could peer into the unoccupied room below. The pipes leading out of the tank were bashed and bent out of shape as if someone had taken a hammer to them in an effort to close off the flow. I somehow managed to lift the lid and peek in, as any curious child would have done. It was so dark in the room, which had only one very small hinged window in the roof, that I had great difficulty seeing what was in the tank. In an attempt to investigate, I put my hand into what I thought would be water.

'Holy shit!' I shouted out in disbelief.

I could feel something really slimy and disgusting between my fingers, not water as I had expected. I pulled my fingers out only to see that they were covered in the most disgusting mess. It stank to high heaven and the shock of not really knowing what it was set me back on my feet somewhat.

'Cherie, I can't see in. Away down and get the candle in our room, and the matches,' I shouted towards her as she stood in the open doorway.

She went down to get a candle but I knew from her hesitancy she didn't really want anything do with this adventure at all. I heard her heavy footsteps come back upstairs and enter the room, then she stopped dead in her tracks at the door.

'I'm not coming over there, you can come over here and get it, I'll leave it here,' she said as she placed the candle and matches on the floor at her feet.

I dropped the heavy lid back onto the tank with a dull thud and made my way over to the doorway where she stood. Cherie recoiled into the landing area away from the stench that I had brought with me in a waft of air.

I lifted the candle and matches, and gazed back towards the darkened corner. Twilight was fast approaching and the room was growing darker by the minute. I detected a warm mist swirling around the room; whatever was in that tank was certainly warmer than room temperature. The meagre daylight emanating from the small skylight caused a pin-sharp ray of light through the dusty atmosphere of the room as I looked back over, wondering if it was such a good idea to return to that corner.

Cherie was by now intrigued enough not to leave and my brother Tom had joined her, wondering what was going on. I felt they also wanted to know what was in there but were too afraid to look for themselves.

'Come on over with me, Tom. I need you to hold up the lid.'

Tom's face drained and I could tell that he was not at all enamoured with the prospect of this task. But at that time Tom would have been more daring than me. Whereas I would stop and think a situation through, he would invariably jump straight in with both feet and think about it later. So, despite his obvious reservations, no sooner had I suggested it than he was over lifting the lid.

I lit the candle and shone it in only to see a mucky mess of every shade of brown goo, which filled the tank right up to the top. The harder I looked, the more my eyes were becoming accustomed to the weak candlelight. I could now see over towards the darkened edges under the lid.

'Tom, it looks like slurry, you know, the stuff the farmers put on the fields.'

He looked in and his nose must have caught a whiff of the stench.

'Jesus, it looks like shite,' he shouted out, nearly dropping the lid on my fingers as I held onto the edge of the tank.

'Twat,' I shouted at him. 'You nearly scared the shit out of me there, now hold the bloody thing.'

I peered in again, this time over to the far corner to something which seemed to be breaking the film which covered the otherwise level surface. I studied it really hard as I poked it with an old broken coat hanger I had picked up from the floor.

'Christ,' I shouted out. 'I think there's a bit of hair floating over there.'

Tom peered in and almost immediately we both slammed the lid shut with an almighty bang. We gazed at each other in total disbelief; we hadn't a bloody clue what it was but we were now both very scared indeed. My heart was pounding in trepidation as Tom ran off.

The overwhelming stench caused by the lid being closed so forcibly seemed to soak us in its wash; it seemed to stick to our very clothes and skin.

'Mum!' I shouted out at the top of my voice.

The girls at the doorway, now holding their noses, also shouted down and the echo filled the stairwell: 'Mum, come up till ya see what Edmund has found.'

It seemed like ages but Mum eventually appeared at the top of the stairs. I really did think I was about to get the biggest hiding for disturbing her and I cowered behind the girls thinking maybe they would get thumped first – the first hit was always the hardest with our mum; she seemed to settle down a bit as her anger subsided.

'What's happening up here?' she asked in a stern voice.

'Look in that tank,' I told her. 'There's something yuck in there and it stinks,' I added excitedly.

'Is that what that smell is?' she said, looking at me as if I had farted. 'Light that candle. You shouldn't be playing with matches up here, anyway,' she continued and I got a clip round the ear.

I lifted the lid up and she peered into the tank, holding the candle at the end of her nose. Being taller than Tom, I managed to lift the lid up higher, in fact I nearly lifted it off altogether. Mother screamed out in disbelief. She slammed the lid shut, creating another disgusting waft of stench which filled the room and my head – the kind of stink that takes your breath away momentarily, leaving you unable to breathe again until you're well away from it.

'Get you downstairs right now and get all those filthy clothes off you.'

She had now instilled a degree of panic in us all as I raced down the stairs, not really understanding what she meant. I went into the scullery and stripped down to my underpants as she brought the 'Baby Burco' boiler in from the yard. This was our only bath in those days and the six of us, eldest first, would be washed on Saturday night in front of the fire. Poor Irene! By the time it was her turn the water was always cold and filthy. Mother plugged the Burco into the electricity socket and started filling it from the tap as Sadie filled the kettle and placed it on the stove. As I stood shivering, I realised the predicament I was in: I had now stunk the scullery out as well.

Within half an hour I was standing in the boiler with warm water lapping at my feet and being scrubbed down with 'Lifeboy' carbolic soap. It stung my eyes and got up my nose but I didn't care; I now felt clean. Sadie lifted my stinking clothes up with a stick and threw them into the yard.

Someone from the Belfast Corporation came out to inspect the tank later that day and called the police. I remember the house was full of people as a visibly nauseated female officer told Mother that she thought it was human excrement dumped in there by one of the previous residents. The only explanation suggested was that the room was four floors up at the top of the house and the only toilet available was outside in the yard. The authorities then blocked up the water taps somehow – we had noticed a filthy brown liquid coming out of one of them for weeks before but had thought it was rust. They then slapped some sort of an order on the house and, with a policeman slamming the door behind us, we were moved out to Allworthy Avenue post-haste.

CHAPTER 4

MOTHER HAD FLED

'God! Does it not get any better?' I remember saying to myself when I first set eyes on our next hovel in Allworthy Avenue. It looked even worse than the one we had just left.

We had pushed all our worldly belongings there in a baby's pram, along Agnes Street and Clifton Park Avenue. All the well-to-do-residents could be seen peering out from behind their lace curtains, no doubt wanting to know where these gypsies had come from and, more importantly, where they were going.

The landlord had allocated us some rooms in a condemned, derelict corner shop. We entered by the side door, which led into the only room with a coal fire, and just off this was what would become our mother's warm and cosy bedroom. The other bedroom was on the top floor of the building, and in there all six of us children would again share one bed – three up and three down. The stench of damp rotting wood and plaster filled my nostrils as I gazed up at the fusty peeling wallpaper, trying in vain to detect any of the original patterns. The windows of our bedroom were broken and boarded up but I managed to remove one piece of wood to reveal an intact pane of glass. This small opening provided me with a peephole to the outside world and at night I would stare out for hours at my only distraction – the cars going by on the street below. I would jot down their registration numbers and listen intently to their distinctive sounds. I could tell by the engine and exhaust noise which make of car was passing down my street as I lay in bed. This was my only respite during the long and cold winter we spent there. But I would soon realise what a dangerous hobby it could be.

One evening there was a fatal shooting in Cliftonville Avenue. I heard the shot and jumped to the window in time to log the number of the getaway car. I was, however, smart enough to realise that if I gave this information to the police, it would get me into serious trouble, so I burned all my numbers the next morning, just in case, and kept my mouth shut about what I had seen.

Again, it was so cold in the room that at night all six of us huddled together in a big ball to try to keep warm in the middle of another filthy double bed which had no doubt witnessed all kinds of seedy life before us. I had to wear my only jumper as pyjama bottoms and we covered ourselves up with any available coats and mouldy old curtains as blankets. On some freezing nights, it was so cold that we would play with the ice that formed on the inside of our window. The fleas that also inhabited the bed were intolerable. Each morning, one or more of us would find new bloodstained bites somewhere on our bodies. I would hunt the folds of the mattress and knew that their favourite hiding place was down in the button recesses. It was instant death for any I captured, as I crushed them between my fingernails. Mother eventually managed to get some dog flea powder and it was relative bliss for a while. The powder, whether good or bad for humans, even made the mattress smell almost inviting.

Although the house itself was a nightmare, there were some good points about where we were now living. The Waterworks Park could be reached through a hole in the hedge; this was a vast area between our house and the Cavehill Road. Through some trees I found two lakes, one of which had been drained, leaving a wonderful playground for any imaginative kid. I knew every nook and cranny of that lakebed and spent my days digging for treasure and harassing the snobby kids as they sailed their expensive model boats on the upper pond. Constant supplies of sticklebacks and frogs ensured I kept out of serious trouble.

In the bedsit on the first floor between our bedroom and my mother's room on the ground floor of the building lived a very gentle and quiet middle-aged man with his two young daughters aged about eight to ten. They appeared to me to be twins, as they were so alike in every way. Their front-facing room was always warm and well decorated, and was packed to the roof with books; they even had a television, for God's sake – something I hadn't seen since leaving Newtownards. Having said that, they were just as poor as we were. The lovely clothes the girls wore had been mended and patched often but they were always clean and well pressed.

I believed the man was a teacher, as he could often be found coaching his daughters in reading and writing, with soft music playing in the background. They were certainly far better educated than we were and I marvelled at the big words they used. I had never seen such a close bond between a parent and his children before and found it hard to comprehend that any man could be so caring. It only served to emphasise how starved of affection I felt. I would ache with envy when hearing laughter and the clatter of dishes and cutlery from within their room. This, combined with the sound from the television in the corner and the warmth of the paraffin stove, made their lives seem blissful compared to my grey existence.

At Christmas, however, it became apparent that their father had no gifts for the twins. To our shock and dismay, Mother told Cherie to hand over a doll she had just received from Santa that morning. Cherie was gracious enough on the outside but inside, as you can imagine, she was heartbroken; we had so few toys ourselves. Pat had provided enough funds for one gift for each of us and now Cherie had been forced to give hers up. The only reason I can come up with for Mother's sudden display of charity was that she must have taken a shine to this man and maybe this was her way of currying favour with him. In the end, however, I think he was too astute and saw right through her game.

As we moved into the New Year, 1968, it seemed as though we were getting settled for once, as Pat was building a pigeon loft out in the backyard. This was a good time for me, as I got close to Pat and he took an interest in us, more than our mother did, certainly. I helped him to build the loft and I would look after and feed his birds on a daily basis until he appeared to lose interest in them. Many were flying off never to return and I remember thinking how lucky they were.

One day I got my eyes opened wide when he sent me off to the local shop to buy an eraser. I was baffled as I sat and watched him cut and carve for hours at this little piece of rubber, not knowing exactly what he was doing or hoping to achieve. Then it all became clear. He had carved a certain number on it and used it with black ink to alter the payment amount on our family allowance book from the welfare services. After all the pages had been altered, he burned the rubber and ink to remove all traces of his actions. I can't really remember if he got away with it or not but if he had been caught I think I would have been aware.

Pat was a sign writer by trade but was also a talented landscape artist. I remember that at one point he was painting a large information sign for a building company by the name of Gilbert Ash. It took up nearly the whole of the living room and got in everyone's way as he tried to complete it on time. However, the smell of the special sign-writing paint he used was a pleasant contrast to the usual stench that permeated our hovel.

His skill was awe inspiring to me as a child. One time when he was short of money, he painted a fantastic large oil painting of the Antrim Coast on a piece of hardboard he had first prepared by priming it with white emulsion. I watched every brush stroke, completely enthralled as this masterpiece came to life. It was getting late, though, and no amount of yawning could keep me awake, so I went to my crowded bed now warmed by all the little bodies already in there. I found my spot and snuggled in, and after I pulled the overcoats on top of me I fell asleep dreaming of that exciting new world being created in the room below.

The next morning, I could hardly get out of bed early enough to see the finished painting but I had to wait, as Mum and Pat were still sleeping and woe betide anyone who woke them up. As usual, we crept around like mice getting our breakfast – thanks to Pat, food was now more readily available – and after a few hours, Mum and Pat were out of bed and I could at last see the finished painting. It looked amazing to me and I was so disappointed when he told me that we had no choice but to sell it. He sent me off to the shop to buy some sheets of brown paper and sticky tape, and when I got back we started to wrap up the still-wet painting, taking great care not to smudge it in any way.

I felt so proud when he then asked me to take it down to Smithfield second-hand market in downtown Belfast and get the best price for it. I knew why he had asked me: he didn't want the embarrassment of selling it himself, knowing that he would look desperate to the stallholders. I didn't mind though, I could live with that. I set off with my younger brother Tom to the market, where I haggled like an Egyptian carpet-seller with all the stallholders and somehow managed to get £50 for it. I then returned home with my precious wad of money safely tucked away in the deepest recess of my trouser pocket, keeping a sharp eye out all the time for any potential robbers.

Pat was over the moon with the £50 I gave him and we ate well that night. In fact, I can vaguely remember that it was the first time I tasted Chinese food. I went to bed a happy and very proud man of 11 years old. I had been given a man's job to do and completed it to the satisfaction of all.

Life carried on with this semblance of stability for the next few months or so and then, suddenly, Pat was gone. Just like his pigeons, he disappeared into the night. I thought I would never see him again and it tore my heart out to lose him. Things at home started to go downhill rapidly again as the money dried up. I was by now shouting out 'Tele, Sixth, Tele' as I sold the *Belfast Telegraph* newspaper from the corner of Castle Junction in the afternoons, bringing home a few pennies. I would collect two dozen at a time from their building in Little Donegall Street and sell them all. It felt good to be entrusted with 24 papers. I was given a job to do and I carried it out to the best of my ability. Having said that, theft was pretty rife among the boys and I wondered how the hell the *Telegraph* ever made any money at all. It almost seemed to me as if the *Telegraph* was more concerned with the boys' welfare on the streets and, as in my case, the contribution it made to the household.

On one occasion I was sent by my mum, cap in hand, to St Malachy's College on the Antrim Road, where Pat was now working painting rooms. I was so pleased to see him but so ashamed when I had to beg him for money for food. After that, I never saw him again.

Not long after this, we were evicted due to the massive rent arrears that had built up. It seemed that there were always more important things to spend money on than rent. We found ourselves back on the street with the loaded pram as the landlord slammed the door behind us. This time we made our way to another bedsit, in Clifton Park Avenue, which we were to share with May, a prostitute friend of our mother.

Again, we kids were given the shitty end of the stick and had a disgusting upstairs room in yet another flea-infested hovel – things always seemed to go from bad to worse. The house was stinking with damp and the putrid wallpaper that fell off the walls forming rotting heaps on the floor. I began to think that every house in Belfast was like this. We resorted to burning the oil-cloth floor covering and breaking up the floorboards of a vacant front room to burn in the fire we needed to heat food and keep warm. Our education about the seedy side of Belfast life continued as all manner of lowlifes crossed our broken threshold at night. Between our mum and her friend, countless men were brought into the house and up to the only decorated room upstairs, emerging late into the night and long after we had retired to the only warm place we could call our own – our bed.

I've learned from speaking to members of her family in recent years that Mother's behaviour at this time was apparently completely out of character. She was from a stable family from Newtownards and had gone completely off the rails. I often wondered why it was I rarely visited my maternal grandparents until I learned they had opposed her marriage to my father as they felt she was marrying 'beneath herself'. This resentment also led them to ostracise the children that resulted from the marriage. On one occasion when we were desperate, Mother travelled from Belfast looking for some money and assistance only to be turned away from their doorstep.

Her behaviour continued to deteriorate and she became completely dependent on alcohol, cigarettes, Valium and the goodwill of various men. I was too young to make any judgements but I realised that things were going badly wrong. John must also have sensed the disaster that was looming, as he used bus money borrowed from May to make his way to our father's house back in Newtownards. John had always been my father's favourite and hoped that he could somehow get him to help us. A few days later, Father bundled him into his car and drove him to Glenravel Street

RUC station, where it was decided that some action should be taken about our situation. In the meantime, Mother had fled.

We had all been cruelly abandoned as she took off for the bright lights of London. She had told Sadie where she was going and that she would be back. Presumably she also told May where she was off to, but to the rest of us she didn't say a word. In order to raise funds for her escape, she sold the concert flute that had been given to me on loan from the Belfast School of Music. It bought her a single airfare into oblivion. I still find it unbelievable that any mother could totally abandon her six children in such dangerous surroundings. If she had left us at the doors of some children's home for safe keeping, then that would have shown a certain degree of concern and love for us. As far as I am concerned, nothing can excuse her actions.

We were left there in that freezing bedsit to fend for ourselves for three whole days with only the clothes on our backs and no food. May was still carrying on her business, with seedy men frequenting the house in the dead of night and I would sit and worry over the possibility of my sisters being drawn into her web. Sadie would often spend time in May's room and on many occasions I would stand on an old chair and peek in the small stained-glass window above her door making sure nothing untoward was going on. I wasn't stupid and I knew full well what was happening in that house!

Hunger was getting the better of us, so I was forced to steal bread from the local shop in Manor Street, getting caught many times into the bargain. The owner, on seeing who it was he had caught by the scruff of the neck, always let me go. I think he was only too aware of our predicament, as I would plague him on a daily basis for any broken biscuits, out-of-date bread and damaged tins. Thank God Sadie now had a part-time job working in a chip shop around the corner on the Antrim Road. In lieu of her wages, she would bring home our only hot meal of the day: fish and chips at midnight. We were lonely and frightened children aged from six to fifteen, left alone for days before the authorities were eventually made aware of our condition.

I shall remember until the day I die the scene in Clifton Park Avenue when welfare services and the police came to round us up. Net curtains were twitching the whole length of the street as if it was all some form of entertainment. Cherie was literally holding onto the front door of the house, screaming in anguish at the loss of her mother and the thought of never seeing her again. I had never heard her curse so profanely. All her fear and despair came flooding out and it took two officials to get her into the car. Cherie still hoped that Mum would come back to get us, as she had promised Sadie, and she believed that if we left the house, Mum would never be able to find us again. In contrast to her hysteria, I was totally submissive and it was almost a relief to be placed into the rear seat of a police car, safe in the arms of a burly policeman who no doubt had children of his own, as he was so caring towards me. He was evidently moved by our plight and tried to reassure me that everything was going to be OK. This was the first time in my short life I had been so close to my new heroes – the police – and I had never felt so safe and secure.

We were then driven to the High Court in Belfast, where Judge Babington made us all wards of court and placed us into welfare care. After court, we were sent to Macedon Children's Home, a Dr Barnardo's home in Newtonabbey, just outside Belfast, where a case conference was called as they tried to decide what to do with us.

CHAPTER 5

A HAND ON A SHOULDER
IS A LOADED GESTURE

The result of the case conference was to lead to further misery, as, for reasons that were never made clear to us, we were split up and sent to different children's homes. John and I were sent to Bawnmore Boys' Home just outside Belfast, while my sisters and Tom were sent first to Glendhu Children's Home, then on to Williamson House on the Antrim Road in Belfast a few weeks later.

We had depended on each other throughout the traumas of our young lives and this separation following the disappearance of our mother was almost too much to bear. I was enraged and constantly demanded to know where my brother and sisters had been sent, but for weeks I was kept in the dark. We didn't know if we were ever going to see one another again. This was particularly cruel and I formed the distinct impression they were trying to break up our family group. John and I were determined to find the others and when we discovered where they were being held, we repeatedly ran away from Bawnmore and tried to make our way to Williamson House. Before we could get to see them, however, a car would always arrive from Bawnmore to cart us away.

NOT WAVING BUT DROWNING

Bawnmore was a large, red-brick house just off the Mill Road in Belfast. It had formerly been the estate house and gave its name to the surrounding area but most of the vast acreage had been sold off for redevelopment. This fine old residence was typical of a turn-of-the-century house. Its bay windows and ornate plasterwork suggested a former grandeur but the interior had been butchered to a certain degree by the installation of modern electrical appliances and central heating.

Bawnmore was a living hell for John and me, as it was for most of the other boys incarcerated there. We had been tossed into Belfast's seething pool of juvenile criminals and hard cases. Although we had also committed various petty crimes, we had been forced into that position in order to survive; we were not juvenile delinquents or vandals and couldn't understand why we had been sent there.

The choice facing us was fight or suffer the consequences. This was no place for wimps, as any sign of weakness was met by the most severe of beatings from the older lads. The staff failed to investigate any complaints and some even seemed to condone some of the things that went on. Indeed, they too inflicted harsh punishments and physically abused many of those in their care.

Carrying on from my note-taking exploits in Allworthy Avenue, I started to write down details of boys there with me: their names, their ages and what they did. In no way was this a conscious attempt at compiling a record of what went on there; it was just my way of keeping busy while this hell was going on around me. The lad in the next bed reported me to a member of staff. He came up to the room, took my book and glanced through it. I was dragged downstairs and forced to watch as he burnt it in an old bin out in the yard. The severe beating that I then received was warning enough for me never to take such a risk again.

I worried a lot about John during this time. He was still experiencing learning difficulties and had to attend a special-needs school at Mount Vernon, not too far away on the Shore Road. John was by nature a very quiet lad, always on the lookout for some escape from his world. He was also easily led, and I soon began to feel uncomfortable about how close he seemed to be to certain male members of the Bawnmore staff. I couldn't have explained why, but something made me very uneasy about the whole situation.

John would spend a lot of time in the company of one particular carer. He would take John away on weekend trips and fill his head with tales of foreign lands and adventures he had experienced on his travels. It turned out later that John had fallen into dangerous hands – even though this man was in a position of trust, employed to protect children in need.

Years later, Bawnmore was linked to a sex-abuse scandal when allegations were made in the local press that certain high-ranking members of society were involved in abusing young boys at Kincora Home on the Newtownards Road in Belfast and other institutions across the city. A full police inquiry commenced and numerous senior civil servants, members of the clergy and even politicians were hauled over the coals as the police attempted to gather enough evidence to take the matter to court.

My own experience of sexual abuse in Bawnmore was of the occasional member of staff putting his hand down my pyjamas and playing with my genitals while I lay in bed, helping me shower or a spanking by way of correction. This was happening to a number of the other boys there, so we thought this was normal behaviour. As an 11-year-old boy, you don't question a male carer in a white coat as he helps bath you; you accept his way or face the consequences. Having said that, I never heard any of the boys complain about this treatment while they were there, possibly because in some cases the staff would buy their silence. Some of the boys from very deprived backgrounds enjoyed the attention, free radios and pocket money. Others, of course, were just too intimidated to speak out.

Some of the boys were singled out for more serious abuse and I can recall that, on different occasions, a few of us would be called in from playing outside and in the presence of a number of well-dressed men, who were total strangers to us, we would be asked all sorts of personal questions about everyday things as they eyed us up and down. It occurred to me later in life that this must have been some kind of sordid selection procedure for potential conquests.

The following is an extract from the then RUC Chief Constable Sir John Hermon's account of this appalling affair taken from his autobiography,

Holding the Line. I take this opportunity to thank Sir John for his kind permission to reproduce this extract, as I feel his account is authoritative and cannot be improved upon.

On the 24th of January 1980, an article written by Peter McKenna appeared in the *Irish Independent* under the headline 'Sex Racket at Children's Home'. McKenna was the paper's chief news reporter, and the article related to allegations circulating about an official cover-up of the recruitment of boys for homosexual prostitution at a boys' home, known as Kincora. A member of its staff was also alleged to have been involved with a loyalist paramilitary group called 'Tara'.

The home had been opened at 236 Upper Newtownards Road in East Belfast in January 1958 by the Belfast Welfare Authority Department. It was a hostel for boys in the fifteen to eighteen years age group, and could accommodate up to a dozen of them. The building itself was a detached house with living and dining areas on the ground floor, and also an office with a door from it into a one-bedroomed flat.

The warden of the home, Mr Joseph Mains, occupied that flat from 1964 until the home was closed in 1980. Another staff member occupied a different bedroom on the first floor, beside the bedrooms of the boys.

Peter McKenna's newspaper article alleged that individuals employed within the social services were well aware that serious sexual abuses were taking place at the home, but that 'reports on certain cases were destroyed under orders from a senior member of the Social Services Department'. Yet, throughout its twenty-two years, no victim of abuse at Kincora had ever made a complaint to the RUC.

With such serious allegations raised in this article, it was clearly a matter requiring immediate police investigation, and the day after the article's publication, a small team of officers, led by Detective Chief Inspector George Caskey, began an urgent investigation into the allegations. Initial inquiries by the Caskey team did find sufficient evidence to justify the suspension of three members of the Kincora staff, namely Joseph Mains and the Assistant Warden, Raymond Semple, and also William McGrath, who was described as the 'Housefather'.

On the 16 of December 1981, all three, having pleaded guilty to various offences including indecent assault, gross indecency and buggery, were sentenced to several years' imprisonment, Mains for six years, Semple for five years and McGrath for four. The meticulously thorough RUC investigation also resulted in the detection of four other men, whose behaviour in two other boys' homes in Belfast and one in Newtownabbey led to their convictions for similar crimes.

Far from assuaging the public and media concern, these convictions opened a veritable Pandora's Box of allegations, based on the suggestion that Kincora had been a focal point of a vice ring involving senior government officials over a period of years. It was suggested that facts had been suppressed by the RUC, and that there had been cover-ups to protect public figures and high-ranking officials. The revelation that William McGrath had been involved in the small loyalist paramilitary group 'Tara' gave rise to further speculation that he was blackmailed into reporting to the British security service, MI5. It was alleged that MI5 knew about the criminal abuse at Kincora, but had used that knowledge for intelligence purposes to intimidate prominent politicians and others believed to have been implicated. The suggestion that dirty tricks were being played by MI5 to disseminate black propaganda against politicians and others meant that stories about an RUC cover-up of Kincora frequently appeared in local newspapers.

Realising the damage that unsubstantiated rumours could do to the community's confidence in the investigative integrity of the RUC, the Chief Constable, Sir John Hermon, decided that these allegations should be thoroughly examined by the same team of detectives, led again by George Caskey. Simultaneously, he announced in a press release on the 18th of February 1982 that he had asked Her Majesty's Inspector of Constabulary to appoint an independent chief constable to investigate allegations about a police cover-up. He made plain that 'The appointed Chief Constable, Sir George Terry, will have full access to all the papers past and present and in addition will have general oversight of the continuing investigations'.

My own personal view is that Terry, being an Englishman, was somewhat confused in relation to the complicated subculture prevalent in Northern Ireland, therefore, I feel, he made somewhat hasty and inaccurate judgements. Sir John Hermon concluded, after the convictions and the subsequent Terry investigation, that the whole sickening episode had begun and ended with a small number of perverted Kincora staff degrading some unfortunate disadvantaged boys placed in their care. None of those convicted, even when in jail and with nothing further to lose, ever alleged that they had been blackmailed or coerced by MI5 or military personnel. In 1983, Hermon was able to state publicly that the reports from the further RUC investigation and that of Sir George Terry had been forwarded to the Director of Public Prosecutions for Northern Ireland, and he had decided there was nothing in them to warrant the institution of criminal prosecutions.

My brother John had already admitted to me that he was a member of 'Tara' at that time and that he had been taken by a member of staff from Bawnmore to Kincora on visits. I don't know his exact involvement as he clammed up when I asked him in Australia in 1997. I can only speculate but, considering the psychological damage that had obviously been inflicted on him and all the circumstantial evidence available to me, I cannot help but come to the conclusion that he was abused to some degree. This all clicked into place as I conducted my own research when I joined the RUC. John departed very quickly for Australia in 1973 and it appeared to me that he was running away from something – or, even more sinister, someone. He always believed that someone was out to get him.

After the horrors of Bawnmore, we were all eventually reunited in 1968 and moved into what was termed a 'Family Group Home' at 10 Benview Avenue, Belfast. This home was part of a new initiative reflecting a growing belief that more progress could be made with children in care if family groups were kept united in one location: a complete reversal of the previous policy that had seen us cruelly separated.

It was an ordinary house in all respects in a very ordinary street. As it was an end-of-terrace house, it had four bedrooms. All six of us, along with two other small children, could now live under one roof and were cared for by someone who, to all intents and purposes, was our surrogate mother. Miss Ruth Colvin took on this unenviable task and has been a great influence in my life ever since. She looked after us very well and the neighbours were full of praise for Ruth's work and her competence in bringing up eight children – especially when they discovered that she was only 23 years old. We grew very fond of Ruth and I felt much closer to her than I had ever done to my own mother. The love and gratitude I have for her is still as strong today, over 30 years later, as it was in those early years.

While we were obviously delighted to be reunited, we had all by now been psychologically scarred by our experiences over the previous years and this exhibited itself in different behavioural problems. But unbelievably, in a classic example of how the welfare system can completely fail vulnerable children in its care, the staff in this new home were not made aware of our recent history and no help or evaluation was therefore forthcoming.

Sadie and John found it damn near impossible to settle into the ordered routine of family life over the next year or so. They constantly bickered and fought with Ruth, to the extent that they started to alienate themselves from the rest of us, as we were pretty happy with our lot in life at that time. At 14 years old, John was both smoking and drinking in an attempt to escape his demons and I would do all in my power to cover up his actions from Ruth. Sadie, meanwhile, at 15 was a somewhat rebellious girl and thought of as easily led. She refused to conform to Ruth's strict 'mainstream' dress code of skirts and dresses, and defied her by secretly buying a pair of black trousers. Ruth confiscated them and in doing so set in motion a train of events that ultimately led to the breakdown of trust between them.

Sadie was also finding her own way in life in relation to boys and came home one evening with a few of them in tow. There were at least four of them outside the house fighting amongst each other because her boyfriend was a Catholic. I observed most of this from an upstairs window and will never forget the savagery of that fight. They were literally kicking and punching each other into oblivion. As the bloodbath raged on the street outside, Sadie was safely imprisoned in the house, having been dragged inside by Ruth. Not happy with this enforced custody, however, Sadie tried her hardest to get past Ruth and out to the thugs fighting on the pavement. I have never seen such an exhibition of hate shown towards a person who, at the end of the day, was there to protect her. Sadie both physically and verbally abused Ruth, who had probably never experienced such venom before in her life. Ruth cried out for help as I sat in a cold sweat glued to the stairs. I was afraid and at the same time torn as to where my loyalty should lie. For all intents and purposes, Sadie had been our mum for the past few years and here I was being forced into conflict with her.

I now know this incident hurt Ruth deeply and the damage was done there and then between them. After all, Ruth was employed to care for us and did not have to stand for this kind of treatment. Shortly afterwards, Sadie was voluntarily removed from the home after refusing to apologise to Ruth. She was moved to another home called Ettaville very close to the Newtownards Road. John also departed as soon as he was 15 and headed back to Newtownards to stay with our father, eventually getting himself a job working at the local coffin-makers.

CHAPTER 6

THESE WERE THE MOST STABLE YEARS OF MY LIFE

The rest of us thankfully adjusted more successfully to this new environment and enjoyed some settled years there after all the moving around we had previously experienced. I attended the Boys' Model School on the Ballysillan Road and can vividly remember my first day there. At that time, the Boys' Model had the reputation of being one of the better schools in Belfast and entrance and class placement were usually secured through success in your Eleven Plus. Due to my chaotic upbringing and disrupted schooling, I had never taken any exams but the headmaster was prepared to accept me into the school as a favour to the welfare department. He was unsure, however, as to which class to place me in, so he devised a 'simple' test for me as I stood quaking in his office. Ruth was sitting in the corner of the room as he bombarded me with questions on subjects I had never even heard of before. I mean, he even asked me a question on algebra. I was near to tears as I panicked about the possible repercussions of my failure. What if I could not answer his questions correctly, would I be removed from the very place in which I had at last found peace? I was so scared that I couldn't think straight at all but somehow I managed to get through the ordeal and was placed in a middle class, where I stayed throughout my final years of school.

These were, without a doubt, to be the most stable years of my life and I could finally get down to my studies. I never was very good academically but excelled at the more practical subjects. I could often be found in the woodwork or metalwork rooms, even after class. My standard of technical drawing, woodwork and metalwork was very high and my projects were always gaining top marks for imagination and skill.

Sport was another area in which I struggled. The Boys' Model was a great rugby school in those days and I can proudly state that I played absolutely no part at all in maintaining that great tradition. I was pathetic in shorts and remember trying rugby on one occasion only. On a freezing cold morning, I decided that maybe it was about time I started playing with the big boys and so I headed out onto the field. I received an enthusiastic welcome from the rest of the team but that was soon to evaporate when they saw me play. I was an abject failure at this teamwork business and after that first disastrous outing I decided to steer well clear.

One of my mates at the time had a fascination with anything explosive. Christ! He would bring small grains of home-made gunpowder and other substances into school hidden in his pencil case. Picking his moment when the teacher left the room, impromptu experiments would take place as he mixed a few grains and proceeded to blow the lid off some poor sod's desk; this guy was crazy and he was barred from the chemistry room at all times. After leaving school, I heard that he had turned into a freelance bomb-maker, working for anyone who could pay for his products on the understanding he would have no part in the planting of the bombs. He was seen some years later minus his right arm and half his face, sucking soup through a straw. It would seem that one of his works of art had blown up in his face as he built it.

Life in Belfast in those days was always fraught with danger due to the escalating sectarian conflict and street disorder. Hardly a night went by without a corpse being found lying in a pool of blood in some back alley of the city or in Carr's Glen behind my school. We had somehow become accustomed to walking through the barricades and the constant drone from army helicopters hovering overhead day and night. Their powerful 'night sun' searchlights would illuminate troublesome hotspots in the republican enclaves of the Oldpark Road and Ardoyne, making it damn near impossible for terrorists to move about undetected.

Even in the relative safety of our surroundings in Benview Avenue, it was impossible to escape the Troubles. One night after midnight, we were all awoken by an almighty explosion. The glass from our windows came raining down as we lay in our beds. A bomb had been planted in the Spar shop 50 yards away and the blast was so intense that somehow it managed to suck out the kitchen window. Its frame was moved in its socket by about an inch and a mighty crack developed in the adjacent wall. It later transpired that the owners of the Spar had refused to pay protection money to the local paramilitaries on numerous occasions, something that wasn't recommended in those days.

This was only one of the many incidents that occurred in that area, which was, and still is, a hotbed of loyalism. There is hardly a household that has not been touched by the horrors of the Troubles in some way. Most of the lads I went to school with have ended up in prison at some stage of their lives and many are dead.

Because of the elevated position that Benview Avenue enjoyed, nestling as it did on the slope of Squires Hill, I would lie in my bed with the window open on those dark nights and listen to the gun battles in the city below. To be quite honest, I had no real interest in the political struggle and found it very hard indeed to tell the factions apart. I was no angel, though, and remember once getting caught up in a riot between loyalist thugs and the army while I was visiting my friend John's home just off the Bilston Road. We were going about our own business when all of a sudden a crowd about 50-strong appeared from nowhere and began pelting the soldiers with stones and bottles. Kids being kids, we joined in the fun and before I knew it I was breaking up bricks that were being removed from some poor neighbour's garden wall to be used as missiles. Our riot was quickly over when I felt the collar of my shirt being lifted by John's father, who frogmarched us the whole way to the safety of his home around the corner. I managed to get my own trophy of the event, though, in the shape of a long black rubber bullet fired at us by the soldiers. I found out later that these were much sought-after souvenirs of the Troubles. About nine inches long, two inches thick, made of quite flexible black rubber with a very smooth rounded tip, they were nicknamed 'the widow's delight'. I wish I had kept it, as it would be worth a fortune now.

Our summer holidays were spent in Portrush, where we stayed in a large privately rented house in Princess Street for the whole month of July. Ruth and her assistants, June and Margaret, would also move up with us but take it in turns to stay. I loved Margaret and June: not in a physical sense as I was too young for that but I loved them as surrogate parents. Having said that, it didn't stop me peeking into their bedrooms as I inquisitively tried to see what a naked woman looked like! In their early 20s, they were very young to hold such a position of responsibility but to me they seemed very grown up. I loved being in their company and in some ways I believe they understood what was going on inside my confused head as I commanded lots of attention by holding hands and sitting beside them.

Portrush was the premier seaside resort in Northern Ireland and a great place for family holidays. While there, I would indulge in all the activities available to a young lad. Totally unknown to Ruth, I would walk the rocks and swim all day at a little beach beside the Arcadia ballroom. With my pocket money, I would buy all manner of things like fishing rods and even a Polaroid camera. I proceeded to take pictures galore and still have many of them today.

Back in Belfast, with John and Sadie now away from Benview, there was some room in the house for other vulnerable children to seek sanctuary. One day, out of the blue, a young girl arrived to stay for a while. Carol was always smiling and laughing, and her bubbly personality infected us all. I was somewhat smitten and found myself looking forward to her company more and more. We were the best of friends and revelled in each other's company; Cherie and Irene were somewhat out of favour during the year she was there and they knew it.

Those years I spent at Benview Avenue were halcyon days indeed. We were living in what seemed like luxury to us. There were new clothes and food whenever we needed them and we were looked after by someone who actually cared for us. Our father was always given the option to visit us but his visits were very rare and it got to the stage where I didn't really want to see him anyway.

I left school in the summer of 1971, aged 15, and was offered a job working for a friend of Ruth's by the name of Jack McMurray. He was the owner of a DIY shop on the other side of the city. The prospect of diving into the big bad world initially filled me with excitement until Jack told me I was only to be paid £5 per week, an incredibly low sum even in those days. Still, I took up the job and worked like a navvy, doing all the mucky jobs no one else wanted. I clearly remember my very first morning, as he made me clean up all the rubbish and rotting wood lying out the back of his shop on the Castlereagh Road. It was the biggest mound of rotting wood scraps I had seen since Dover Street and made me think long and hard about the men I had watched so intently clearing that rat-infested yard. Just like them, I knuckled down and just got on with it, doing what I thought was a good job even though it took me all day.

I learnt a lot in that year. I was often left to my own devices in some grotty house tracking walls for rewiring or ripping out old window frames, and I also had the pleasure of meeting 'Big John' the carpenter. Big John was a fantastic character and loved by everyone who met him: a true gentle giant with hands like shovels. He worked as a baggage handler at Aldergrove Airport outside Belfast but in order to make more money he would resort to his trade as a carpenter and complete any work that Jack needed done. He was a true craftsman and his skill was legendary. I would be fascinated just watching him construct a window frame or a door. We worked together quite a lot, as more often than not he would be fitting new windows after I had ripped out the old ones. We spent many days talking and I could feel he was starting to take me under his wing and instruct me in the ways of the world.

Not long after we had started working together, I think he must have noticed I was beginning to grow fluff on my chin and starting to take more than a casual interest in girls. Big John would tease me when a pretty girl walked past and my face would turn a deep shade of red. He knew I was getting to the stage in life when my hormones were starting to race and, God bless him, he did all he could to try to get me fixed up with a date. By way of kick-starting my desires, he even introduced me to my first mucky magazine while we were repairing someone's roof, a real hard-core foreign one that left nothing to the imagination. He was wasting his time, though: I was far too shy and lacked the confidence to ask girls out. These endeavours of John's went on for some time and I think he was starting to get fed up with my lack of progress when I made a fatal mistake that would embarrass me beyond belief.

The two of us were working in the shop one day when a very pretty girl dressed in her green school uniform walked in through the side door. My blood was racing and John knew it. He must have thought this was it, as he made a beeline straight over to her and started talking, throwing backward glances in my direction.

I was transfixed but, unbeknown to me at that time, this gorgeous girl was in fact Ruth, the boss's daughter.

John could see me looking over as he headed back towards me. 'What do you think, Ed?' he asked.

'She's beautiful, mate. The prettiest-looking girl I've seen today,' I told him.

No sooner had I uttered those words than the tramp headed straight back over to her to pass on my compliments. Christ! I could have killed him there and then. I have never been so embarrassed in my life. I wished a great big hole would open up in the floor of the shop and I could fall into it, never to be seen again.

I looked over and made eye contact with her; she chuckled and looked away from my gaze.

'God! What have I done?' I said to myself as she walked over towards me. I was having real trouble standing due to the weakness now starting to develop in my knees.

When she came over, she introduced herself and thanked me for the compliment, but she then told me she already had a boyfriend, Basil. I was mortified, though, to be honest, I wouldn't have had a clue what to do if she had agreed to go out with me.

She headed out of the shop with her friend and I gave a huge sigh of relief and got on with my work. I thumped Big John as he passed but seeing that his arms were so bloody big it probably felt like a tickle to him. I did wonder afterwards, though, if she'd just been making an excuse. After all, what girl would go out with a boy called Basil?

CHAPTER 7

MY NEW-FOUND FRIEND

I continued living in the children's home in Benview Avenue until 1972. I was now travelling across Belfast every day to the shop on the Castlereagh Road, catching two buses and not getting home until late at night. One evening as I stood waiting for my bus in Royal Avenue, thousands of starlings flew overhead in the dying light of day, searching for their favourite roosts in the high buildings and under the Lagan bridges. Their twilight chorus made it very hard to hear anything else in that bustling city. Believe it or not, a few years later the bombing in Belfast was so bad that even the starlings departed for places of safety. They are only now starting to return in their vast numbers.

Suddenly, like the starlings when it is their time to leave the nest, I just knew it was my time to go. Something inside just let me know that I was ready to make my own way in the world. But I had to literally beg to leave Benview, as Ruth didn't think I was prepared to face the big bad world. I now realise she was right in some respects. I should have listened to her but, kids and human nature being what they are, I didn't. There was never any pressure for me to leave and I could have stayed there for a few more years. Ruth had already made a tentative enquiry trying to get me a place in Rupert Stanley College to study art and design but, rightly or wrongly, my mind was made up.

NOT WAVING BUT DROWNING

It is with deep shame that I recall the way I treated Ruth prior to my departure. I invented totally false stories of unhappiness to strengthen my case for leaving, as the overwhelming desire to flit to a new life in Newtownards had clouded my judgement. I recall informing someone from the welfare department that I was generally unhappy in Benview and wanted to return to my father, someone I didn't even know very well. I think I really hurt Ruth and can only hope that she has forgiven me. I'm still not sure what got into me but I had been making a few trips home to see my brother John, who was living with my father. The situation there seemed much better and I felt like I needed to take the next step in my life.

The house at Benview Avenue has now gone. It was not well constructed and once the children's home was relocated to a new property off the Lisburn Road in 1974, Benview became so run down that no one wanted to live there any more. The terraces of what were once beautifully modern, grey-brick houses were demolished, as they were becoming a danger to children playing in the area. It's ironic to think that this house was built to help children in danger only to be torn down to prevent them coming to any harm. I was nearly moved to tears upon seeing the vacant plot upon which had stood a house where I had spent the happiest days of my childhood. It was as if someone was trying to remove all physical evidence of my stay there, but I still have my memories.

I eventually got my way and headed back to Newtownards to live with my father. I soon realised that I had made a big mistake and that my short visits had given me a false idea of what life would be like living with him once again. He was a short, stocky, argumentative man with receding hair, who was never happy with his lot in life. He was constantly complaining that everyone in the world was out to shaft him. If he had stood still long enough to glance in a mirror, he would have realised that his own personality was his biggest enemy. He had few friends, which was hardly surprising as most people just couldn't be bothered striking up a friendship with a man who had such a negative outlook on life.

His small, red-brick house in Newtownards was typical of the council houses of the '60s. Inside, it was obvious that he took no pride in the appearance of his home. It was generally run down with the decoration having deteriorated so much that it was hard to tell what the original colours had been. The hall leading up to the kitchen was carpeted with old remnants, while in the kitchen itself the first thing that met your eye was a stainless steel sink that clearly wasn't living up to its name, discoloured as it was from years of tea stains. Any white-painted surfaces in the whole house were tainted by years of nicotine and neglect, and there was a heady atmosphere of stale cigarettes and damp. The combination of small windows and heavy blinds only emphasised the dingy state of the small cramped rooms. It wasn't a lack of money that had led to this deterioration in the state of the house – soap and paint are cheap; it just boiled down to my father's lack of interest in his surroundings.

Once I moved in, it wasn't long before the old troubles of the past resurfaced. My father still had a short temper and also, as far as I was concerned, tried to take control of my life. He had set up a job for me in the same warehouse in which he and Uncle Bobby were working, up at the old disused quarry in Newtownards, but he demanded a large portion of my pay packet each week for board and lodgings. It seemed to me right from the start that, just like my mother and the child benefit, all he was interested in was my earning potential, not the chance to get to know his long-lost son.

Life with him was intolerable. I was not allowed to watch the programmes on the television I wished to see, mealtimes were always dictated by him and usually meant running through to the adjacent chip shop for a fish supper. I was never allowed to come into the house after 11 p.m., even at weekends. If I was any more than two minutes late, the door would be locked and I would have to get my brother John out of bed by throwing stones at his window. I eventually had enough of this treatment and started to stand up for myself, as any teenager would do in those circumstances. The verbal arguments started to turn nasty and a shoving match would result. There were many times when John had to get between us to prevent blood being drawn. In my father's eyes, John was the 'golden child' and his namesake, so he could do no wrong.

John sympathised with me about my father and, as we were sharing a room, we would talk long into the night as he puffed away at his Woodbine cigarette, his last charge of nicotine until morning. Never far from a drink,

John would habitually have his last slug of brandy then turn to the wall and sleep. His drinking worried me but I soon realised that John's demons tortured him most in the darkness of night and he needed all the help he could muster. Many nights he would scare the life out of me when he would wake screaming and soaking with sweat.

By that stage, he was awaiting his passage to Australia. I was very envious and wished I had the courage to make such a bold break. But then I didn't have the driving force that was pushing him, as I'm sure he hoped that he might find some peace on those antipodean shores. John's memories of Bawnmore must have been so painful that all he wanted to do was get out of this country as soon as he could.

I felt trapped in the house with my father, but I soon found a welcome distraction and excuse to get out. I had been home in Newtownards for some weeks when I met up with a cousin called Roberta, the eldest of Uncle Bobby and Aunt Margaret's four girls, whom I hadn't seen for years. She and a few of her friends had planned going for a long walk the next day down to a local beauty spot along the coast called Barr's Bay and wanted to know if I would like to join them. I would have done anything to get out of the house, so I shyly agreed. Unbeknown to me, I was being 'set up' for a potential date with a friend of hers by the name of Elizabeth.

The next day we were greeted with glorious sunshine and at the appointed time we all met up to start our long trek. The happy band included Roberta and her boyfriend Jim, my brother John and his girl Margaret Pyper, the aforementioned Elizabeth and her friend Mary Spence, and Mary's younger sister Agnes, who had just left school at 16 and was working as a packer in the Berkshire factory in the town.

We had a great time as we walked and laughed along the shore of Strangford Lough, and while I wasn't particularly taken by Roberta's friend Elizabeth, I did take a shine to Agnes. I didn't have the confidence to speak to her, however, or attempt to cross that threshold between unknown acquaintance and possible friend. It seemed that the trauma of Belfast had followed me down here to Newtownards. After years of having to look after myself in strange surroundings, I was continually on the defensive and found it very hard to let my barriers down enough to get to know new people.

After we went home, I couldn't get Agnes out of my head and I was impatient to see her again. The next opportunity presented itself at a gathering at my uncle Bobby's home. Uncle Bobby lived just across the way from my father's. In contrast to our home, however, his house was clean, cosy and warm, and had that lived-in feeling that can only come from caring occupants. I could feel the love in the air as I gazed around at the pictures of his four daughters fighting for pride of place on every wall and surface.

Bobby and my father were brothers but like chalk and cheese. Bobby was the younger brother and yet he was by far the more mature. He had a great outlook on life and lived it to the full, making the most of the good times and taking hardship on the chin. I really admired Bobby and wished in so many ways that he could have been my dad; I know I would have been the son he always longed for.

When I first saw her that evening, I thought that Agnes was looking radiant. It was obvious to me she had gone to a lot of trouble as her shiny fair hair was sitting perfectly on her shoulders. But again, I was too shy to speak to her. I was scared that maybe she was going out with someone else and the last thing I wanted to do as a newcomer was to start a confrontation. At the end of the night, we all walked Agnes to her home in the nearby Scrabo Estate. On the way there, the other members of our group dwindled away and I eventually decided to muster all my courage and break the ice. Once we started chatting, I couldn't believe how easily we seemed to get along. It almost felt as if we were old friends who had met again after a long time apart. There was a real chemistry between us and I was delighted to find out that she didn't already have a boyfriend. After seeing her home and securing a date for the next night, I said goodnight and headed back to my father's house in order to make my curfew of 11 p.m.

For most of that night I lay and thought about my new-found friend. Although we had only spoken briefly, I had felt a real connection between us. I know people are going to say that because I had been starved of affection for so long I was going to latch onto the first girl to flutter her eyelashes at me but they would be so wrong. She really seemed to like me and, with my battered self-esteem, that was something that would take me a very long time to comprehend.

I called after work the next day to see her as arranged and I was introduced to her mother, Sarah. Sarah was a great woman who showed all the signs of having had a hard life. Not only did she look after a husband who was fond of a drink but she also single-handedly managed to raise a large family of seven girls and one boy. After chatting to her for a while, Agnes and I then headed out for a walk that was to become a milestone in our relationship. The country road we walked along was narrow and winding, and was very quiet in those days. On this warm and beautiful evening, we stopped beside the ivy-covered bridge of the old disused railway and this was to be the scene of our first kiss.

I wanted to kiss Agnes so much but to tell the truth I didn't really know what to expect. Our first effort was clumsy and felt a bit awkward. I was shaking in my boots but it was beautiful as she responded by placing her arms around my shoulders, standing on her tiptoes to do so. My emotions were now in overdrive as I tried to regain control of myself. We headed on, walking up the road and growing closer with every step. I was so proud to be with her and surrendered totally to her charms.

From that day forward, our relationship became serious. We complemented each other's characters and started to look forward to a future together as a loving couple. No girl had ever asked or wanted to be in my company before and Agnes's interest enchanted me. For the first time in my life I had someone who wanted me for who I was. Her adoration melted my heart, nothing else mattered any more – I felt complete.

The group next met at her aunt's house on the following Thursday night. This was a relatively new council house in the Glen Estate and, due to its elevated position, had a fantastic view of the town to the front. Her aunt made us all welcome and this became a regular haunt where we could all watch *Top of the Pops* in peace. It was there that we made the announcement that Agnes and I were now an item, much to the approval of all present. My father, in contrast, was totally against me seeing Agnes. I couldn't understand his reasons at all and it led to serious arguments between us. The only reason I could think of was that Agnes also came from a large working-class family and perhaps he had wanted to see his son going out with a girl from a wealthier part of town, whose parents were higher up the social ladder. His attitude infuriated me and all I could think about was a way of getting Agnes and myself out of this bloody place and as far away as possible on our own.

Agnes's brother Jackie was in the army and was based in Warminster in England. I saw this option as the way out for Agnes and me, so in 1973 I applied to join the Royal Navy as a junior seaman. After what I perceived to be a very simple selection procedure in Belfast, I was posted to HMS Raleigh in Plymouth for my basic training. While Agnes wasn't over the moon at the prospect of our extended separation during basic training, and cried on a daily basis about the prospect of my departure to England, I think she eventually resigned herself to the fact that this could be our way out in years to come when I got married quarters.

For the first time in my life I had to travel alone and somehow I managed to get myself to Plymouth without incident. I met up with a few fellow recruits on the train and we all shared our trepidation and anticipation about this latest adventure in our lives. Without doubt, I was the worst dressed among the party. I was sitting in my only good trousers and jacket, surrounded by all these fashionably kitted-out young lads. I felt somewhat out of place, like an Irish navvy just off the boat. We eventually arrived in Plymouth and were whisked across on the Torpoint Ferry by navy staff to our new home for the next few months.

HMS Raleigh was an imposing shore base, similar to any other military camp in the country. Before arriving there, I'd had some idea that it might have been an old ship, or something along those lines, with a nautical feel about it, but of course it was nothing of the sort. The base was set on a rolling hillside overlooking the harbour, where there were various large navy ships at anchor, including the aircraft carrier HMS *Eagle*. This scene only heightened the excitement we all felt on that first day and in some way bestowed the required nautical ambience on the shore-based camp.

The old black army Nissen huts that were to be our home were laid out in rows along the sides of the large imposing parade ground and, after collecting our kit, we settled into what would be our routine for the foreseeable future. There was a lot of banter about me being an Irish 'Paddy', which was perhaps only to be expected in the midst of so many English recruits and training staff. The jokes came thick and fast but I was new on their turf and just hoped that the novelty would eventually wear off for them.

The training started almost immediately and at times was intense. On one occasion we performed a scenario where we had to don gas masks and enter a sealed room that was slowly being filled with tear gas. This was to test not only our mask's ability to keep out gas but also our reactions to a gas attack. Before you were allowed to leave the room, you had to remove your mask and experience the effect of the gas on your face. I found no problem at all with this exercise but one of the lads was having real difficulty finding his way out. With the instructor's permission, I went back in and, after groping around in the dark, I found him slumped on the floor. I managed to drag him out to the praise of everyone present but we both coughed and cried for the rest of the day. Tear gas affects people in different ways. Our instructor appeared to have built up some form of immunity, having been exposed to it so often, and could be seen entering the room without a mask, after we were finished, to retrieve the spent cartridge.

The navy put me through class work to bring my educational skills up to scratch and prepared me for further exams required for progress through the ranks. Ship husbandry and sailing skills were my forte, and I even managed to pass their strict swimming test. I was trained to a high standard of fitness and had no problem at all completing the required assault course. We were then split into teams and put into a large room designed to look like the inside of a ship. The scenario was that we were inside a damaged ship and, after the door was closed, water would be pumped in through holes in the hull and split pipes, filling the room. Our duty was to use all the available tools and timber shoring to stop the leaks. We worked very hard that day and completed the exercise to the satisfaction of all. The instructors were observing our every move while looking for the 'leaders and followers' within our group. I drew upon the many practical skills I had acquired in previous years and adopted a leadership role, encouraging the more inept recruits who obviously had never wielded a hammer before. My experience of working with Big John the carpenter stood me in good stead. This test of teamwork and practical skills went a long way in building my self-confidence and proving to me that I could have some useful purpose in life after all.

After a few hard weeks drilling on the parade ground followed by intense class work, all we wanted to do was to get out of the camp for a few hours, and we were eventually granted some shore leave. I headed out to Torpoint with a few of the lads, after being warned to watch each other's backs with regard to the resident skinheads and – even more dangerous – the Torpoint women. At this stage in my life I had no experience at all of alcohol and it didn't take long before I was feeling the effects. Bearing in mind I was drinking scrumpy, it is no wonder I was starting to suffer. No one warned me how strong it was and at the time I thought it was only apple juice I was drinking as I could still see bits of fruit floating in the glass. I got very drunk but thankfully evaded detection at the front gate when returning to camp.

Despite the satisfaction I was gaining from the course, dark clouds were again gathering on the horizon. In those days, things were very tough indeed in the junior ranks if you were a 'Paddy' and there was only so much a boy of 17 could take. I had thought that the initial ribbing would calm down after a while, but even after several weeks in, I was still being ridiculed and vilified not only by other recruits but also by the training staff. At every turn there would be damaged kit, comments made, group bullying and I would be ostracised even in our bunkroom, which I had to share with 20 other recruits. I just couldn't understand what I had done to deserve this treatment.

All I wanted was to be given a chance in life and I was being denied at every turn. I had completed part one of my basic training and was about to be transferred to HMS Ganges for my next phase but, after suffering a severe bout of homesickness, I no longer felt able to cope with the escalating discrimination I was encountering and applied to leave after only four months. Because I was only a junior seaman and hadn't yet signed up for my minimum 12 years, I could leave under what was called PVR or Premature

Voluntary Release. I was forced out and, with a heavy heart, I realised that my navy career was over.

After talking to a retired petty officer later in life, I discovered that it was not until the late '80s that ritual bullying and degrading initiation ceremonies were banned from navy training altogether.

CHAPTER 8

I DEPARTED JUST AS SHE DID
ALL THOSE YEARS AGO

When I arrived back home, my relationship with Agnes went from strength to strength as we made plans for our marriage and a place of our own. To tell the truth, all Agnes really wanted at that time was to have me home with her and the whole experience away from each other only strengthened the bond between us. After the fatted chicken had been eaten in celebration of the return of his prodigal son, my father again had the gall to ask me why I was still with Agnes, saying, 'I thought you might have found someone else while you were away.' This pathetic comment filled me with hate and rang continually in my head.

Then I received news from Sadie that upset me beyond belief. Just when I thought I had laid the ghosts of the past to rest, one of them had come back to haunt me.

Sadie had married the previous year and was living in a small house on the Circular Road in Newtownards with her husband Sammy. Out of the blue, Mother had appeared at Sadie's home. It had been seven years since she had set eyes on her and, to be honest, we had all thought she was dead. Mother was, in fact, quite ill as she had had a breast removed due to cancer.

I was very disturbed on hearing this news and turned to Agnes for support and guidance about what I should do. She felt that I should at least pay Mother the courtesy of going and seeing her; my inner voice had been saying the same thing and, though I couldn't think of any reason why, I somehow just knew I should go.

'Do you want me to come with you?' Agnes asked.

'Yes, pet, I don't think I could do it alone,' I replied. In fact, I was afraid to see Mother alone, I don't know why but I was just plain scared of her. So we made our way up there together and knocked on Sadie's front door.

Mother's presence and the thick, mask-like make-up she was wearing shook me to the core, and I could find no feelings of love or affection for her at all; I looked upon her as a total stranger. She was only 40 years old and yet she looked more like an old woman of 70. Obviously the drink and drugs had taken their toll on her once-memorable beauty and figure. I winced in shock at the sight of her and Agnes must have felt my hurt as she squeezed my hand even tighter.

'Hello, wee son,' Mother said to me as she emerged from the kitchen in her tightly wrapped dressing gown, the absence of her breast all too apparent. Holding onto the doorframe with one hand and a king-size cigarette in the other, she looked over towards me, but didn't have the courage to look me straight in the eye. She didn't even use my name; in all honesty, I don't think she knew which son I was.

'Hello,' is all I could manage in return. What else could I say in a situation like this? This woman was my mother and yet she had never displayed any maternal instinct towards me whatsoever. The conversation continued amongst the other people in the room as I tried to come to terms with this unfolding scene.

'Is this your friend?' Mother asked, as her eyes momentarily glanced towards Agnes.

'Yes, this is my girlfriend Agnes, we are getting married in a few months,' I replied but I could have spoken to the wall such was the response I received. My comments appeared to go in one ear and out the next as she looked away from Agnes in a flash.

That was it for me. I felt I didn't have to sit there and take part in that charade any longer. Though I was glad I had listened to Agnes and had had the courage to see Mother, this would be the last time. I departed just as she did all those years ago – in somewhat surreal silence.

Sadie was uncomfortable with Mother's presence and couldn't fully understand her reasons for appearing out of the blue. In fact, she had to ask her to leave after only one week. Mother was making a nuisance of herself by drinking in local pubs and sending numerous begging letters to my father. He didn't even read them but just threw them straight in the fire.

I would never see Mother again and she died the following year. It would be 20 years before I would visit her unmarked grave in Hawks Hill Cemetery in Saltcoats on the west coast of Scotland. She had found solace to some degree in the company of an uncle in Stevenston but died alone of a drug overdose and lay undiscovered for some time in a house in Saltcoats. Her brother James from Newtownards paid for her funeral and her uncle supplied her burial plot. My father refused to assist with the funeral costs and chased her family from his door.

No one will ever fully understand the hurt and pain my mother went through in life and I cannot hold her fully responsible for the hardships we endured as children; my father was just as guilty. She was never an evil woman, she was psychologically damaged and we all suffered as a consequence. It was only in later life that I was able to stand at her graveside and forgive her. I also thanked her for the gift of my life, which resulted in her two grandchildren, Robert and Cassandra.

Agnes and I were now growing closer by the day and making up for lost time. After starting back in my previous job, I struggled on, biting my lip at my father's temper. Not only was I heading away from Agnes's home in the Scrabo Estate each night blessed with her love and devotion but I also had a clean shirt and a packed lunch tucked under my arm ready for the next day. Like two sides of a zip on a well-worn jacket, we found ourselves being inextricably linked into a life together. We weren't in control; instead other forces were pushing us together at a pace faster than we would have wanted – we both knew we should have waited longer but we couldn't. Agnes had her own family problems and very good reasons for wanting to get out of the family home. Eric, her father, was a kind and good man but he was fond of a drink. He also smoked the highest-tar brand of cigarette available and had the heaviest, most productive cough I had ever heard. It sounded as if it was wrenching at his very soul as he tried to get it up while at the same time gasping for breath. This was an affliction that would ultimately claim his legs due to blockages, and end his life prematurely.

His drinking drained the coffers and as a result his family would often have to do without: there was never enough money to go around by the time he brought home his plundered pay packet, and Sarah and their eight children would ultimately suffer. The only difference Agnes would concede in comparison to my own circumstances was that at least they always had food on the table and the love of both their parents.

Between the two of us, we managed to make all the arrangements for our wedding and our reception, which cost the princely sum of £128, in the Orange hall in Newtownards. Seeing that Agnes was only 16 years old at the time and I had just turned 18, we had all sorts of well-meaning advice thrown at us. For example, when we turned up at the manse to discuss the wedding details with the minister, he was shocked at our obvious youthfulness and was very gracious as he tried to talk us out of marrying so young. Nothing would change our minds, however, and the date was set for 17 August 1974 in Regent Street Methodist church in Newtownards, one week after Agnes's 17th birthday.

Our wedding day was very special and will live with us forever. Yes, we were very young but we knew what true love was. We gazed into each other's eyes as we took our vows and understood the path we had chosen in life. I loved Agnes so much and could see a reflection of her love for me in the tears that ran down her cheeks. So convinced were we about what we were doing that it was easy to ignore the whispers of 'It'll never last'; 'They are so young'; 'I give it two years.'

After the reception, we headed off in our little Hillman Imp for our one-night honeymoon in the Londonderry Arms Hotel in Carnlough on the Antrim coast. When we saw that we'd been given a room with two single beds, we really thought that our secret destination had leaked out. Either someone had phoned the hotel requesting a room change as a joke, or, more realistically, the staff, on seeing how young we were, decided in their wisdom to keep us apart; I pushed both beds together, though, and the rest is our business!

We arrived home the next day and moved into Agnes's family home for a short time while we searched for a place of our own. My father was furious, as he hated the thought of Sarah and Eric being so close and treating me as their son. What made matters worse was that, during his father-of-the-bride speech, Eric had referred to me as his son and he meant it from the heart. My father was fuming, and loudly blurted out, 'He's not your son, he's my son.'

Sarah eventually found us a little house in West Street belonging to Mr John Smyth the butcher, which would only cost us 90 pence per week. It was a small, very run down cottage at the rear of his shop. It consisted of a living room, downstairs bedroom and a kitchen. There was a bedroom upstairs but this was totally uninhabitable due to the dangerous condition of the floor and the serious mouse infestation. We lived and slept downstairs after doing a little decoration and were unconcerned about the state of the place, as this was our own little hideaway.

The mouse problem was so bad that we could smell them. We would lie in bed each night and watch them running all over the bedding and pillows. They would scratch all night long in the cavity between the wall and the window. Initially, it was unnerving but as time wore on we somehow grew accustomed to the nuisance and fell asleep. We were just so happy in those days. After a year, we managed to get out of that mouse-infested little house in West Street and move into a cosy upstairs council flat in Rathmullan Drive, two doors away from her mother, but I was beginning to feel like we were stuck in a rut. I was now working as a van driver for a paper packaging firm called Ferpak in Newtownards but I felt that I needed to do something drastic if I was to provide the future I thought Agnes and I deserved. I had reached another milestone in my life.

Late in 1975, I decided to join the police. I had no role model who had inspired me to become a policeman, no member of my family was on the force and in fact no member of our family had ever held down employment other than driving or manual labour; I just knew I was capable of better things. I wanted to join the Royal Ulster Constabulary, so tentatively went through the selection procedure and to my great surprise I was accepted. I remember being stunned at just how easy this procedure was. I had to attend Bangor RUC station on a given date for a basic test in mathematics and general knowledge followed by a short medical. The recruiting sergeant then made a short visit to our home to conduct an interview and to supervise me as I composed a short essay in his presence. I was told with a wink and a nod that I was in.

At that time there was heightened disorder in Northern Ireland and there was a shortage of policemen on the streets. The Ulster Workers' council strike in 1974 had fuelled some of the worst riots Northern Ireland had witnessed for many years and it was clear that the RUC had to adopt the primary role in dealing with street disorder in the Province, using the army as back-up. As a result, there was a call for a radical increase in police numbers and I felt that I had been caught up in this desperation as I was cakewalking into the force. The statistics for this period reveal what was going on: male part-time Reserve constables were increased from 2,000 to 4,000. Four hundred full-time Reserve women constables were recruited and their male counterparts were increased from 350 to 1,000. The increase to the ranks of the regular force was just as strong, with their numbers increasing from 5,000 to 6,500.

The timing of my date to report to Enniskillen for training could not have been worse, however, as Agnes now informed me that she was pregnant with our first child. I was over the moon but the police training process involved 14 weeks away from home and Agnes did not really want to be left on her own for such a long period of her pregnancy. There was also the worry that I could be posted to some strange corner of Northern Ireland after I passed out, so I had no choice but to postpone my place in the police and carry on with my work as a storeman/driver in the paper packaging company.

On 20 March 1976, my son Robert arrived into this world. It was undoubtedly the proudest day of my life: I had a son. He was born prematurely and rushed to the Ulster Hospital at Dundonald, where he was placed in an incubator for some time. I was overwhelmed at his arrival and Agnes still complains to this day that I neglected her somewhat in favour of my son. Though this was by no means intentional, I was overwhelmed with a sense of responsibility towards Robert that was almost too much to bear. When he was taken from me and placed into the care of someone else, horrible images of my past came flooding into my head and caused near panic. I could not lose him; I was so afraid and could not leave his side. A few short weeks later, he was released into our care fit and strong. I would sit beside his cot and stare at him for hours, while at the same time praising Mother Nature for providing me with her ultimate gift of new life. Robert was my flesh and blood, and no one in this world would take him away from me. Agnes and I were now living through the happiest times of our lives. We enjoyed not only each other's company but also the love and affection that can only be derived from a child. We had decided over many hours of discussion to have our children young; I wanted my kids to play along with me, not push me in a chair.

In 1978, our daughter Cassandra arrived and our family was now complete. I cried long and hard in private about my good fortune. Cassandra was beautiful, a beauty known only to a father. I was determined not to make the same mistakes my parents had made while I was growing up and I showered on my children the love and adoration I had been deprived of. I had no role model to guide me through this task. I relied on my own instincts and the guidance given to me by Agnes. I now had a son to help me, a daughter to admire me, and the love of a good woman.

I was so lucky to find Agnes and I only wish my other siblings had all been so blessed. Our broken and traumatic childhood continues to impact on us as adults. Most of my brothers and sisters have made grave errors of judgement in relation to their marriages as they sought comfort and solace in the first suitor to come their way. This practice has proven destructive in the long term and resulted in a litany of broken vows and a string of lonely children. My eldest sister Sadie has two broken marriages behind her, with two adult children to her second husband. My deceased elder brother John had two broken marriages in Australia, with six children to his two wives. Mirroring his own childhood, he left behind him a trail of deprivation and abandonment. His alcoholism and need for money would ultimately reflect upon his home life and everyone would suffer as a result. In the end, he had to go his own way in life. He disappeared from the face of the earth while my sisters employed the services of the Salvation Army to help find him after he was lost to us for nearly 20 years.

Cherie is the latest to join our long list of broken marriages. She recently separated, citing her misjudgement in choosing the wrong husband 20 years ago just at the time when she was crying out for the security of a loving relationship. Again, her two children have been made to divide their loyalties in their teenage years.

My younger brother Tom is presently in his third marriage, and has three children from his two previous failed relationships. The only one who has not been divorced is my youngest sister Irene. She and her husband moved to Australia three years ago, taking with them their three sons. Like me, she seems to have retained a close relationship with her first love.

The psychological scars of neglect and abuse still run deep within us all, even if some of us won't admit it. We invariably put the reasons for failure in relationships down to other factors without realising the true cause that is rooted in our childhood. It is their children I now feel sorry for. But, unlike us, they have love, warmth and food available – and also the knowledge that at least one of their parents will always be there for them.

CHAPTER 9

WE WERE CANNON FODDER
AND WE KNEW IT

In 1979, my young sister-in-law was the victim of a very serious assault in Newtownards. Totally shocked and stunned, she confided in me, as she was too afraid to go to the police station alone. I immediately took charge of the situation and reported the matter to the police. A full investigation commenced, resulting in the offender being convicted and sent to prison. After seeing justice done that day, my interest in joining the police was rekindled and within a week I had re-applied to join the RUC. This time, however, I first wanted to experience service in the part-time Reserve force to test the water with a view to joining the regular force at a later date. After another very simple selection procedure, I was accepted and in April 1980 I was posted to Comber RUC station only three miles away. I loved it. I was now a policeman in Northern Ireland, a step not taken lightly in this part of the world, even if I was only on the fringes as a part-timer.

Part-time Reserve constables in the RUC were men and women who worked in civilian jobs during the day, then at night donned the uniform of a police officer and carried out security duties in support of the regular force, thereby releasing more experienced officers for duty on the street.

Part-timers had to attend a monthly night class in a nominated police station to study basic police procedure. They were paid monthly for every hour's duty they performed.

This then evolved into the full-time Reserve. Full-time Reserve constables were engaged on three-year contracts, again to carry out a supporting role for the regular force. Men and women, many of whom had failed to reach the required standard for the regular force, were employed on the same shift system as the regular force. Their training at Garnerville ran separate to and was less comprehensive than that of the regular force.

Both part-time and full-time Reserve constables had the prefix 'R' in their epaulette numbers, denoting their standing within the organisation, and they could not attain promotion. Some members of the regular force treated part-time members with disdain and seemed to resent us, as if we were in some way depriving them of lucrative overtime. But then again, some Reserve constables also considered themselves equal to regular officers even though they were not employed or trained for that role.

From the first day you put on that green uniform, you set yourself upon a pedestal, ready to be knocked off. Others seem to see you differently and some friends distance themselves and become reluctant to share details of their day-to-day lives. I felt that many RUC officers adopted an overbearing air once in uniform. The more immature among them adopted a new and disconcerting 'them and us' attitude, considering themselves somewhat superior to the normal working man on the street. This became more pronounced at the height of the Troubles as, by necessity, policemen detached themselves from the rest of the community as a defence against attack. They adopted different daily patterns and only frequented known safe establishments, thereby only mixing with fellow officers to the exclusion of past friends.

I served in Comber for the best part of one year and volunteered for extra duty as I soon realised that I was deriving real enjoyment and satisfaction from police work. But Comber gave me a false impression of what it was like to work in the RUC. Manpower in the area was being maintained at an unnaturally high level due to the fact that the new Chief Constable, John Hermon, lived only a few miles away in the little townland of Ballydrain.

Senior officers were trying to create a good impression with their new boss by swamping the area with police uniforms. Regular or part-time officers, it didn't matter, they just wanted tangible results. Residents in similar towns and villages throughout Northern Ireland were crying out on a daily basis for any police at all to patrol their troubled streets and yet here was this very safe little village at full manpower, and then some. I naively assumed that the situation was the same in every town.

I struck up a very good working relationship with a senior constable whom I admired and looked up to. Constable Smith was instrumental in my decision regarding the future and encouraged me at every stage to consider policing as a career. Based on my experiences in Comber, I applied to join the regular force in October 1980. Again, after an even simpler selection procedure, which I felt was based on my initial 1975 application, I was accepted for service. Due to my inherent lack of self-confidence, no one was more stunned than I was when I was accepted to be a full-time policeman. Looking back now, I still find it hard to believe that I was not questioned about my troubled past during the selection process.

As a result of the increased street disorder and the escalating terrorist campaign at that time, there was a big push to get men onto the streets as fast as possible. I now feel that the selection procedures were diluted somewhat and standards were dropped. Some will say that was the very reason I got in so easily and I would accept that. But then again, many men with links to loyalist organisations also slipped through the net and into the ranks of the RUC; there they stayed, polluting the force for many years to come.

Agnes was not pleased about my decision, to say the least. Though she never openly opposed what I was doing, she was aware of the campaign of hatred being directed against the police and army in the Province and knew it was always much worse for policemen than soldiers. During their tours of duty in Northern Ireland, soldiers returned to the security of their heavily fortified bases after their patrols were over. Their families at home on the mainland were under no threat at all. Policemen in Northern Ireland, on the other hand, had to return to their homes where they often lived alongside the very people who were out to kill them. This situation caused enormous stress and would have put a strain on any relationship.

Unsurprisingly then, Agnes wasn't too happy when the time came for my 14-week training period in the depot in the old garrison town of Enniskillen in County Fermanagh. My mind was made up though, and I headed off after lunch on Sunday, 22 March 1981 in my old Morris Marina, stopping off to give another new recruit, Stuart Montgomery, a lift. I knew Stuart from my service in Comber. He was a really good lad from a great family with police connections going back some time. He was progressing into the regular force from the police cadets, a background that ensured he was to get a lot of friendly ribbing from the rest of the squad.

The depot in Enniskillen is an imposing building from any angle and once inside there is an uncanny regimental aura about the place. It is as if the ghosts of a thousand loyal soldiers line the battlement walls observing the new batch of defenders of the realm being put through their paces. As I passed through the gates, I was overcome by a sense of immense achievement and pride about being chosen to play my part in serving my community.

Once training started, it seemed to me that too much time and effort was devoted to rehearsing the marching set piece for our passing-out parade. On the first full day we drilled for hours to the beat of 'Killaloo' roaring out from the loudspeakers. We were constantly being roared at by the drill sergeant as we struggled to remember our steps, and it seemed that our successful performance on that final day would somehow prove his worth. Looking back, I now realise that he was trying to instil in us the important discipline of working in harmony as a close-knit team: something that would be essential when we got out onto the streets.

Our rooms were constantly inspected for dust and dirt. Men would skate about the highly polished floors on remnants of old carpets called 'skids' to avoid marking them. We also had to parade each day in front of our instructors and often the commandant, and if we were found fault with in any way, we had to go through a 'show parade' again later in the day. Every other member of my squad, all 74 of them, had their collars felt at some stage by the drill sergeant and I thought I was about to escape until they set me up. I was standing in perfect formation on the final morning as the sergeant inspected the lines. Unbeknown to me, the lads behind were throwing handfuls of dust all over the back of my tunic and even on my cap. The sergeant knew full well I was being set up and took great pleasure in ordering me to show parade at 5 p.m. that evening. The rest of my squad then all burst into fits of laughter at the sight of my reddening complexion. It was all done in good humour, though, and we toasted the event that night in the bar. The show parade never took place, as the sergeant found it too hard to keep a straight face.

There was always a very high terrorist threat outside the depot, so it wasn't safe to leave the sanctuary of those walls. Luckily, there was a student bar adjacent to the toilet block. The most popular tipple was a 'Mrs B's special' – a pint of red lemonade with a dash of beer. Mrs B was the formidable lady who was in charge of the bar and she would soon let the commandant know if she saw you drink more than you should; we feared her more than the drill sergeant!

The depot was, without doubt, the perfect establishment for creating the policemen and women required to combat the terrorist campaign in Northern Ireland. Its imposing high walls and stout gates created the necessary atmosphere in which essential military discipline could be absorbed by all within. Since 1986, however, training has been carried out at Garnerville in Belfast, after the Chief Constable John Hermon felt his recruits were under very high threat travelling to and from Enniskillen every week and sought permission from the Secretary of State and the Police Authority to move the training centre. In my opinion, things have never been the same since that date. The atmosphere at Garnerville is much more relaxed. Discipline was left behind in the old regimental barracks in Enniskillen that had been witness to so much history.

My training in Enniskillen started very well and I soon settled down into my studies and physical training. As the days passed, however, there seemed to be a dark cloud hanging over me. We were being constantly assessed and the training staff and the commandant reported that I lacked confidence and suffered from very low self-esteem. This troubled me greatly, as I remembered the same thing being reported at my initial interview prior to joining the force. The anxiety I felt affected my grades and they dropped from an initial high 90 per cent to a low 70 per cent as a result.

At my mid-term interview with the commandant, I was again made aware of the very same complaint. I was really confused at this stage because, although the same criticism was being made, I was given absolutely no help, encouragement or even advice about how to overcome my problems. My final report from one of the instructors, a female sergeant, ran along the same lines and was the worst I had ever had. After this, I was really concerned and even considered quitting the force. It seemed my childhood was haunting me again, as I was still saddled with a sense of inferiority. But instead of walking away at that point, I decided to continue on in the hope that the situation would improve once I settled into the job. There was a huge financial incentive for me to do so, as I was earning four times the amount I had taken home whilst working as a van driver. I really saw a career in the RUC as the best way of providing for my family and I was determined to stick it out.

As we prepared to pass out from Enniskillen, the Troubles had taken a turn for the worse due to the hunger strikes being carried out by republican prisoners in the Maze Prison, who were demanding that their political status be restored. On 5 May 1981, Bobby Sands was the first hunger striker to die and over 100,000 people attended his funeral, reflecting the strength of feeling in the nationalist community. Normally placid members of society came out in their droves to protest against Margaret Thatcher's political intransigence. There was very serious violence and street disorder in the Province and, as a result, a severe shortage of policemen on the ground. The pressure of the situation in some ways took the heat off me, as there was a desperate need to get men out on the streets. In any other force, I believe I might not have made it through, given my poor final report.

I remember looking around at my squad mates during a quiet moment in the depot canteen and wondering how many of us would die in our first year on the job; I just knew our chances were not good. Twenty-five people had died since the start of the year as a result of terrorism (thirteen security-force members and twelve civilians) and so many armoured vehicles were being damaged in riots that the police workshops could not keep pace with the repairs. We would religiously watch the television news each night to keep abreast of exactly what was happening to our senior squad, which had departed some weeks previously and was now in the thick of it on the ground.

I had been informed at the halfway stage in my training that, upon completion, I was to be posted to the Belfast Divisional Mobile Support Unit (DMSU). I would be assigned to Number 4 unit, the Ebony section, at Castlereagh, which was a mobile unit of thirty men in five armoured Land-Rovers engaged in confronting and quelling serious street disorder in Belfast. I had no choice in where I was sent and to tell the truth this news had filled me with utter dread. I wasn't entirely sure what the role of the DMSU was but I had watched them on the TV news, right in the midst of some of the most serious riots I had ever seen. I had previously believed that in order to join these specialised units you had to serve your time on ordinary duty. But it seemed that someone, somewhere, had a different view and selected mature and mostly married men for this type of duty. When I joined the police, I had hoped to be given a posting somewhere locally, where I could become a community policeman, and then at some later date make my own decisions with reference to specialised units. This was not to happen.

I now realise I was totally unprepared psychologically for this posting, but as a young raw recruit trying to hang on to his job by his fingernails, I was afraid to complain. The prospect of my complaint becoming common knowledge among the rest of my squad also worried me so I decided just to get on with it.

It was about this time that the slight distortions in relation to the information I was giving Agnes started. She was young, relatively naive and fearful, and didn't really understand what my posting to No. 4 DMSU at Castlereagh entailed, so I told her that we were ordinary policemen but we travelled about in large numbers. I think in a way she was happy with that.

My passing-out parade was to be at noon on my 25th birthday on 24 June 1981. I was about to embark on, according to Interpol, the most dangerous policing job in the world and I felt uneasy to say the least. The parade went off well enough with Agnes and my father witnessing the customary throwing of forage caps in the air. After the pleasantries, the whole squad was told to report that evening to Garnerville in Belfast for further training in public order, to be followed by weapons training at Sprucefield and driving school at Lisnasharragh. The married officers were now separated from the single; those with no spouses locally were dispatched off to the Ballykelly army base outside Londonderry. We didn't even get the weekend off – welcome to the RUC!

In the weapons training room of Sprucefield, the other recruits and I were issued with our first piece of police equipment. In any mainland force, it would be your notebook, whistle or truncheon. In the RUC, it was a Ruger .357 Magnum revolver with massive soft-point bullets that would rip an arm or a leg off and with a recoil that many men were unable to handle. (The ammunition would be removed from service five years later for being too powerful.) Our guns were brand new and still in their boxes, so we had to de-grease them before heading outside into the yard to test-fire them. The instructor laid on a little demonstration to show the force of this gun and ammunition. He found an old one-gallon paint can, filled it with water and placed it on the wall of the range. He paced back and loaded the much less potent .38 special bullet that was later standard issue to the force. He fired and it made two nice little holes in the tin, through which little jets of water spurted out. Then he reloaded, this time with one Magnum round. He took aim and fired.

'Good Christ,' I shouted out as the tin blew apart. Water shot up into the air and the tin nearly ended up in the shopping centre next door. 'God help anyone who's ever hit with one of these rounds.'

My own personal gun was perfect. With shot after shot I was hitting the centre of the target; I seemed to have the knack for this. The recoil was massive and many of my fellow recruits could be seen firing with their eyes closed, anticipating the bang and therefore missing the target completely. Rounds were ricocheting right and left down the range, one of them even shot the light out. But after a few hours we were all classified as competent to shoot and headed back to Garnerville.

Later that afternoon, we stood in sombre mood in the assembly hall of Garnerville, anticipating what our first operational briefing would hold in store. The inspector introduced himself and explained that we were being formed into what were to be known as 'Amber Serials', which were groups of ten recruits, one sergeant, a driver from the driving school and a rear gunner from the firearms training unit. Our names were called out in alphabetical order and we were placed into teams. I was the last of the first batch and headed over to join what would become my 'serial' for duty on the street. I looked at them all closely and in a way was quite pleased with my colleagues: they were all about my age and included an absolutely gorgeous WPC by the name of Wendy.

After the remainder of the recruits were assigned to their teams, Derek, an instructor from the driving school, was designated as our driver. He was a mature, middle-aged man with a rugged look that was testament to his having served many years on the force. This reassured me that at least it was pretty unlikely he would get us trapped up some blind alley. I then heard the inspector call out the name 'Albert McDade'. Albert, from the weapons training unit, was to be our tail gunner. Again I was well pleased with Albert, as he radiated an air of confidence and was clearly very competent in his chosen field, but on hearing his name I also couldn't help feeling that it was strangely familiar.

After the formalities, we mingled with the other members of our new crews. Albert was the last person with whom I shook hands and as I looked him in the face and grasped his hand I felt as if someone had walked over my grave. I don't know what it was but 'Bert', as everyone called him, also thought there was something familiar about me. As I couldn't think of any other explanation, I put it down to maybe meeting him in Enniskillen or even Sprucefield when I was engaged in my handgun training and thought no more of it.

Within the hour we were in the car park outside, getting familiar with our Ford transit minibus and being told what would be expected of us in the coming months. 'Who has done the SMG [Sterling sub-machine gun] course?' Bert shouted out, looking at us all for a show of hands. No sooner had he asked than I had my hand in the air. As I had been in the part-time Reserve, I had already been trained in most of the weapons available to the force.

'Good, Eddie, you'll sit at the rear doors with me. I'll be carrying the Ruger rifle.'

After a couple of hours packing our vehicle with long shields and first-aid kits, we were stood down from duty and allowed to head home after getting a start time of 8 a.m. for the next morning. We were told that it would probably be a long day but, understandably, we weren't told where we were headed.

The next day, I arrived as keen as mustard – my first full day in uniform had arrived. Well, technically speaking, anyway, I kept telling myself. We were, after all, still recruits and not yet fully trained. After a quick coffee in the canteen, we headed out to our vehicles. Bert and our driver were already there.

'Right, lads, mount up. We have to get going now,' the driver shouted from the van.

Everyone bundled in the best they could. Most had to sit on the floor between the shields. I perched nervously opposite Bert at the rear doors with my loaded SMG sitting on my lap. 'Thank God I volunteered for the SMG, I think we have the best seats in here,' I said to Bert.

Then we were off. No sooner had the rear door closed than we were heading out of the gate and onto the streets of Northern Ireland as policemen for the first time. Recruit or fully trained, it didn't matter. If you were wearing the uniform, the public still expected you to perform perfectly in every way.

'Where are we heading to, Bert?' I asked him quietly, leaning forward to do so as if it was all some kind of secret.

'Castlewellan, Ed. We're going to a Prod march and rally.'

'Oh, right,' I replied, though it didn't mean much to me. The whole van was then briefed by the sergeant sitting in the front.

'Well, cub, what station did you get?' Bert asked as we drove along, referring to which station I was to report to after training.

'Belfast DMSU, the Ebonys,' I replied, only to hear him take a sharp breath.

'What?' I asked him. 'Is that not a good move?'

'Yeah, it's OK. I'm only keeping you going,' he replied, laughing out loud. 'Where did you grow up?' he then asked.

'Newtownards, then I lived in Belfast for a while.'

'Where in the city?' he went on.

'Oh, here and there, we moved about a lot. Dover Street, Clifton Park Avenue, you know, all those classy areas,' I told him, deliberately keeping my voice low so as not to be overheard, knowing full well these could be considered the more run down areas of Belfast.

Bert appeared quite puzzled, as if trying to work something out in his head.

'When were you in Clifton Park Avenue?' he asked as he turned his head slightly to one side.

'Oh, '67 or '68, I think.'

'What does the Eddie stand for?' he went on.

By now, I was getting puzzled by all these questions but I whispered 'Edmund.'

'Edmund Gregory?' he exclaimed in a slightly raised voice. 'Christ, now I know where I've seen you before. Think back to Clifton Park Avenue and the police car outside your house.'

'Oh, Christ,' I mumbled quietly. 'Now I know you, too. You were the policeman holding me in the car.'

God, I could have cried there and then. It's hard to explain the emotions that washed over me but I was overjoyed to see him again.

Bert knew I was stunned and gave me time to catch my breath. I was in a bit of a daze as I cast my mind back all those years.

'I'll not ask you any more, cub, but I assume you're OK now. Are you settled well?' he asked.

'Yes, thanks, married and two kids now,' I replied, smiling at my new-found comrade.

'More power to you, cub. You certainly have dragged yourself out of that gutter,' he said in a sincerely kind voice, but after that I heard no more about it. I guessed he felt he had awakened too many ghosts as it was.

These first operations were pretty terrifying. We were not even real policemen at this stage and yet they were sending us out to patrol some of the most hate-filled streets imaginable. Terrorists or thugs baying for blood wouldn't stop to ask if you were a real policeman or a recruit, they would try to kill you just because you were wearing the green uniform. We were cannon fodder and we knew it.

I was to be involved in my first serious incident on a July day in 1981 and it would have grave repercussions. While we were travelling home from another very troublesome Orange parade in Castlewellan, a gunman shot at us from houses in the village of Drumaness. This was a classic example of republican terrorists exploiting the RUC's tendency to stick to predictable patterns: they knew this would be the route we would take on our return trip to Belfast and thus were able to organise an ambush. We were all shattered that night after hours spent restraining Catholic residents as Protestant bands were happily marching through their town. Stones and bottles rained down as we pushed and shoved our way through that hostile crowd and by the time we were relieved by other units we were filthy, sore and covered in spit.

We all collapsed into the rear of our minibus and headed back to base at Garnerville for what we hoped was stand down and home. Most of the crew was sleeping on that journey back and I was really struggling to keep my heavy eyes open. Then, just as my head was about to loll against the side of the van, two distinct pings made me sit bolt upright. I hadn't a clue what the noise was but then the driver shouted out, 'Heads down, lads, we've been shot at.' One bullet from a high-velocity weapon had hit the windscreen of the minibus and passed through one of the plastic side windows in the rear. As the minibus was packed, it was only by the grace of God that no one was hit. I sincerely believe our lives were spared that night because, rather than sitting bolt upright, some men were lying on the bench seats and others on the floor.

As soon as we turned the next bend in the road, we stopped and were ordered out of the vehicle, and told to take cover as best we could. I was still a bit dazed after my rude awakening. It was pitch black and I wandered about in bewilderment looking for non-existent cover. I heard what I thought were another couple of shots and then with a mighty tug I was pulled to the ground and pushed into cover by Bert.

I remember lying there for what appeared to be ages, not even sure that where I was lying would be safe ground, as I couldn't see a bloody thing. No one was sure where the shots had come from, so we didn't move as our gunners scanned the area with image intensifier night sights attached to their rifles.

While lying there in the dark, I did a quick body check for injuries. I had noticed a sharp stabbing pain in my right side just under my ribs and there was the warm feeling of sticky blood on my fingers as I groped inside my tunic and shirt.

'Christ! I don't believe it. Bert, I think I've been shot!' I shouted out.

Bert called out for the first-aid kit while maintaining his scan of the houses towards the village.

I lay there wondering if this was the time when trauma takes over after being shot and you no longer feel the pain. I was getting colder by the minute and was scared. Thankfully, my life hadn't yet started flashing in front of my eyes, for I'm convinced that as soon as the movie starts playing, that's when I'll know it's curtains.

We couldn't use torches, as we were still very vulnerable to attack, so one of the lads held up an overcoat while Bert struck up his lighter to try and see my injury. After he tore open some of my clothes, we discovered that the wound had been caused by the protruding cocking handle of my Ruger Magnum revolver digging deep into my side as I fell on it. It had torn my tunic and made a pretty puncture wound in my side. Phew, what a relief!

'Fuck sake, Eddie, you scared the shit out of me then,' Bert exclaimed, clearly delighted I was OK as I took cover again.

I now had my revolver out, not really knowing what to do with it, while it was ascertained that everyone else in the unit was OK. The thought of firing this bloody gun filled me with trepidation. When using soft-point .357 Magnum bullets, it had enormous recoil and a short flame escaped from its barrel; in the inky darkness of night this could be seen for miles and our location would be easily spotted.

After a short while and still in total darkness, we all jumped back in the Transit and made off at high speed for the nearest police station at Ballynahinch to check for damage. Christ, this was like something out of the Wild West. There was a neat hole in the windscreen and another in one of the side windows at the rear about two feet from where my head had rested. I got cleaned up the best I could in the toilet and wiped the blood off my gun. The bleeding had now stopped, so I removed the field dressing we had found in the first-aid kit. Bert was so concerned: a really great old-timer who was not afraid to be seen helping someone in need. It didn't take me too long to realise that he had now saved me from harm on two occasions. His concern was genuine and I am certain he would have felt the loss of one of his 'cubs' deeply.

After a somewhat sombre journey, we arrived safely back at Garnerville and were eventually stood down. I couldn't believe how nonchalant the staff were about this potentially fatal incident. We had just had a near miss with death and yet they seemed to be so blasé about it all. No one spoke to us about what had happened or even asked us about how we felt. We were detailed a starting time for the next day and sent home as normal – that was it! I was a nervous wreck and all I wanted to do was sit in a darkened room and gather my thoughts. I wondered whether I was just going to have to get used to this kind of thing happening regularly or whether this show of bravado helped the officers deal with the stress of the attack. I soon began to realise that the act of laughing it off or having a few drinks was the chosen way in which well-established members of the RUC dealt with their demons. Many men drank to excess and gambled so much they ran into serious debt – more than likely their way of dealing with the horrors of the job.

I sat in my car at Garnerville for what felt like ages that night before I calmed down enough to drive home to Newtownards and face Agnes. When I arrived back, I decided not to tell her about what had happened. How could I? It would have put her through hell, sitting there every night worrying where I was and which incidents I might be involved in. For weeks afterwards I was yearning inwardly for someone to talk to about this episode in order to get it off my chest. There was no one to whom I could turn, though, so I bottled it up and placed it into the imaginary little chest of memories I had created deep inside my head.

Things progressed as expected for the next few months. I attended firearms training and driving school, interspersed with periods of duty with the Amber Serials at the many scenes of major public disorder and the funerals of the hunger strikers. Ten hunger strikers in all would die in the Maze Prison. Some police officers, including myself, were quietly astonished by their sheer courage and determination. On the other hand, many policemen openly gloated at their deaths, taking every opportunity to laugh in the faces of passing republican sympathisers.

I thoroughly enjoyed my time at driving school. It was now based at newly acquired premises on Montgomery Road in Belfast, one of the most important bases in the city in relation to counter-terrorism. Within its imposing walls resided the observation squads, anti-racketeering squads and counter-terrorism units, all ready to be deployed where required at a moment's notice. As we were receiving our driving instruction 'on the hoof' and because the school cars had no radios, we had to make sure we returned to Montgomery Road every half an hour to look up at the window of the driving-school office. If there was a red sheet of paper in the window, it meant we had to head to Garnerville for duty with the Amber Serials. If it was green, then it was OK to continue with the driving instruction. 'What a way to run a driving school,' I thought, but it worked and we all passed three weeks later.

It was while performing crowd-control duty with my fellow recruits at a Royal Black Institution parade in Londonderry in August 1981 that I first set eyes on Inspector X, who at that time was in charge of No. 4 DMSU, the company I was about to join. I was introduced to him during a lull in the parade but while we were talking he turned round to remark to a sergeant with him that I looked far too young to be in the DMSU. He wondered out loud what the job was coming to and then walked off, leaving me in mid-sentence.

What a boost for my self-esteem that was as I prepared to join the frontline.

CHAPTER 10

I NOW FOUND MYSELF
IN THE LION'S DEN

On Monday, 17 August 1981 at 5.30 p.m., I reported to Castlereagh RUC station in Belfast for duty with No. 4 DMSU, otherwise known as the Ebonys. My first day as an operational policeman had arrived. As a result of the very serious public disorder due to the ongoing hunger strikes, the RUC had now been placed on full alert. We were to work 12 hours on and 12 hours off duty, and all non-essential deskbound officers were to be mobilised onto the streets.

All the preconceived ideas I had of being a respected member of the community's police force were about to be cruelly and mercilessly shattered. I now found myself in the lion's den. I was young, raw, keen and strove to uphold the important principles of police work – courtesy and honesty. As it was only a matter of months after my passing-out parade, I still retained the most important definition at the forefront of my mind – that of courtesy:

> Courtesy is an essential quality and one which will smooth many a
> path. The public have a right to expect it, and with it, its

complementary quality – good temper. It should be remembered that an angry man is quite incapable of exercising the judgement and discretion so often needed in the performance of good police work. A policeman should be careful to avoid giving any justification for complaints of over-zealousness or the causing of unnecessary embarrassment to any individual. The confidence of the public should be retained by exercising courtesy, discretion and common sense in carrying out his duty.

Over the next few years, I was to find myself in the impossible position of trying to stick to this code as I was moulded into a policing role not of my choosing.

Castlereagh RUC station first opened in February 1960. It has been radically extended since then and there is now hideous green fencing on the original low red-brick wall as a precaution against terrorist attack. There are massive concrete sangars (sentry boxes) at every vantage point on the wall and these are permanently manned due to the high threat this base has been under for so many years.

Castlereagh has a controversial history in relation to the fight against terrorism in Northern Ireland. Nestling behind the main building is the purpose-built holding centre – a self-contained unit of cells and interview rooms. Until 1999, when the centre was closed following the recommendations of the UN and the Patten report, this was the site of the main interrogation centre for terrorist prisoners from the Belfast area and sometimes further afield, depending on available space. It was safe to assume that most terrorists with a record had at some stage been through the gates of this station.

The holding centre was totally independent from the normal police station and it was adjacent to our DMSU vehicle park. From the rear yard, I could see the air vents protruding from each cell wall and this close proximity allowed us to get a little of our own back on the hardened terrorists imprisoned inside. As we loaded or unloaded our Land-Rovers in the dead of night, we would deliberately make as much noise as possible, ensuring they would get little rest.

Some of the practices at Castlereagh left a lot to be desired: for example, the procedures followed when prisoners were being released from custody. In the company of a member of the holding centre guard squad, usually a full-time Reserve constable, the prisoner was walked straight through our car park as they made their way to the front gate and freedom. After numerous complaints from us about the way in which this compromised our security, it became apparent that our own thoughtless authorities were sanctioning the practice. Unbeknown to the prisoners, there was always a photographer planted in the dark recesses of the front sangar, who made full use of this opportunity to photograph suspects as they were leaving the compound. Although we could take photos of them while they were in custody, they would tend to alter their expressions, making it hard to get a good up-to-date picture of them. Photographs taken without their knowledge offered a better chance for us to be able to identify them when they were back on the streets. It was, however, crazy to think that, as they passed by our parked private cars, they could be making a mental note of the registration numbers for their next job. The dangers were all too real, as I was to find out in 1985, when, on the advice of Special Branch, I had to sell my beautiful Volvo 244 as my car registration number had been found scribbled on a piece of paper during a house search in West Belfast. The IRA always had the wherewithal to find our home addresses from these numbers.

On my first day of duty, I arrived a few hours before I was required so that I could get my locker and kit sorted out. Our station sergeant issued me with the extra kit I needed and then showed me around what was to be my workplace for the next five years. 'Old Nat', as we called the station sergeant, was a character indeed. He had undoubtedly seen a lot of service before being put out to pasture in this desk job. Swinging back on his rickety old chair, he told me of his times as a peeler in Londonderry during the very early days of the Bogside riots, 'when men were men,' he said. Whenever any of us wanted to go off sick, or returned after a spell of absence, he would throw his leg up onto the desk, pull up his trouser leg and point out the severe burning on his shin caused by a petrol bomb during the Battle of the Bogside in 1969. He would point to it and say, 'Sick, son? That's sick.'

Starting time arrived and we made our way out of the very small room that the Ebonys occupied on the first floor. There was no way it could accommodate a briefing of 30 men, so we all headed into the adjacent room and took up our positions around the two full-sized snooker tables. Right from the start, I formed the impression that we in the DMSU were always going to have to make the best of what was available to us. We didn't even have a locker room for our use; we just stripped down and changed in the main corridor, where our 30 lockers stood against the wall. I didn't mind, for I wasn't too shy in those days. Even when some of the more excitable young typists regularly appeared for the end-of-shift strip-down, we just carried on regardless, much to their amusement.

As I stood at the far end of one of those big tables, I noticed that one of the old hands started to slowly roll a few snooker balls down the first table towards the briefing sergeant, just hitting his duty sheet board. I was somewhat puzzled by this until I found out later that it was his way of seeing what mood the sergeant was in. If the sergeant was feeling shitty, he would castigate the officer there and then, but if he was feeling reasonably good, he would play along and return the balls even harder than they were sent. This silly little game may not mean an awful lot to anyone outside police circles but in this unit you had to be able to gauge the spirits of your fellow team members, as we all depended on each other for our very survival.

The DMSUs were the dragon's teeth of the RUC: 3,500 men trained, fully armed and ready to be deployed anywhere in the Province at a moment's notice. They were attached to most divisions throughout Northern Ireland and existed to provide back-up for ordinary divisional policemen as and when they were required. Each unit consisted of one inspector, four sergeants and twenty-four constables – the usual term used for operational planning purposes therefore was a unit of, '1, 4 and 24' – and included at least one WPC. A deskbound sergeant was detailed as operational planning sergeant and his role was the day-to-day running of the unit.

The tactics of the DMSU were drawn up by street-hardened officers with many years of experience behind them, and other UK forces were now copying the RUC 'street disorder manual', such was our expertise. The key to our tactics was our vehicles. They were used in tight-knit groups to break up and drive back rioters. We pushed burning vehicles and barricades aside to keep arterial routes open. Once inside the riot zone, we used our federal riot guns (FRGs) to thin the crowd, thus allowing the safe use of snatch squads to make arrests.

It was vitally important to understand and fully use the protection offered by our vehicles. Before this point, soft-skinned Land-Rovers had been used but we were now seeing the introduction of the prototypes of the Hotspur Land-Rover, which had a single-skinned armoured plate covering the sides, back doors, roof and engine bulkhead. It was still very basic inside but better than no protection at all. All praise must go though to the men who built these monsters, as without doubt they saved many lives. I can testify to their strength, having sat inside many times observing rioting mobs only to hear the pinging and bangs of rounds hitting the armour plate. I tried not to think about the terrorists getting hold of armour-piercing rounds. The deafening roar from the relatively small petrol engine, combined with the discomfort of constant condensation from inside the steel plate painted with fireproof black paint, made the working day seem like a week. Later on, workshops started to install a simple air conditioner behind the front seats. This was a godsend – and I can speak from experience, having had to endure some very hot summers and even hotter rioting while sitting inside with four other policemen crammed in like sardines. I spent every day of my working life for five years on patrol inside one of these vehicles. It is no wonder that so many policemen have bad backs in their later years.

The glass in the windscreen, side windows and rear doors of the Hotspur was fully armoured and nearly two inches thick; they could take a number of direct hits without shattering. Having said that, the front windscreen was damn near impossible to see out of on dark, rainy nights due to the acute angle at which it lay in its frame, which caused a mass of reflections. To make matters worse, in the event of serious stone-throwing we had a front grille at our disposal that could be lifted up from its resting place on the bonnet in an instant by pulling on a steel cord hanging above the two front seats. This obscured the view from the windscreen even more and while driving I literally had to peek through the thick bars in order to see where I was going. One time, when I was chasing rioters in the Ardoyne, I very nearly came to grief with the grille up when we had to take evasive action to avoid a burning car. While driving over some waste ground, I struck a bollard that just appeared from nowhere. No real harm was done, though, as the tons of armoured Hotspur just ploughed on regardless. The final problem with the windscreen was a novel fire extinguisher, which was supposed to put out a petrol-bomb fire on your windscreen. While it would successfully douse the flames, the smears it left behind meant you then couldn't see out at all.

Specialised training was somewhat rudimentary in those early days of 1981 when I joined the DMSU: it consisted of basic instruction in the use of baton guns, the long riot shield and embussing and debussing from our heavily armoured battleship-grey Land-Rovers. The equipment available to us was also pretty poor: there were none of the fireproof suits or overalls that would be considered essential today. All our crowd-control duties were carried out in normal tunic and trousers with a black open-face motorcycle helmet and a pair of leather gloves for protection from the bashing of other riot shields and bricks.

Most of my essential training had already been completed prior to joining the Ebonys, during my months with the Amber Serials. A few weeks earlier, during riot training in one of the massive hangars at Aldergrove Airport, we had been instructed by the Operational Training Unit (OTU) in the use of the long riot shield. One of the instructors had a crazy sense of humour and gathered us around him as he showed the effects of burning petrol. He doused a riot shield with petrol, threw a match at it and, 'whoosh', up it went in a ball of flames. The heat was intense as we all stepped back, reeling from the smell of melting plastic. For the next part of his party piece, he picked a timid-looking recruit out from the crowd and made him stand next to the smouldering shield. He told another instructor to stand by with a fire extinguisher just in case. Unbeknown to us, he had a jar containing weak tea hidden beside him which he then threw at the trousers of the recruit, pretending that it was petrol. He immediately started throwing lit matches at him, cursing as they failed to ignite. The recruit was petrified. He really thought he was being set alight as the smell of petrol still lingered from the previous attempt. He ran off screaming as everyone fell about the place in stitches laughing, including myself. Later, however, when I thought about the incident more carefully, I was very concerned about the long-term effect it could have had on that young lad and what the consequences might have been when he had to face that same danger for real out on the street. Believe me when I tell you, there is nothing more frightening in a riot than fire. You have absolutely no control over it as you are being pelted with petrol bombs from all directions. You don't have to get a direct hit to suffer, as splashes work just as well. In the early years, rioters would mix sugar with the petrol, so when it ignited it stuck and burned furiously. The number of extinguishers was limited and it didn't take long in the heat of battle for them to run out of their essential gas. We only used water if acid bombs were being thrown.

Here in Castlereagh, I was no longer among fellow recruits but in the midst of some of the toughest-looking men I had ever seen. Most of them had already served in the city for many years in the old Special Patrol Group (SPG), an infamous band of hardened police riot squads whose dubious reputation was now being glossed over. The SPG had been much smaller, more localised and somewhat more select in appointing potential members into their ranks. They only wanted like-minded men who, it was felt, would tow the 'unionist-thinking' line. From what I could tell, though, the duties of the new DMSU were not that far removed from those of the old SPG and it seemed that it was just a public relations renaming exercise – my first ten pay cheques still had 'Number 4 SPG' printed on them, referring to my station.

The faces of those men in the snooker room had that look that only came from close contact with some of the most horrific sights that Belfast had to offer. I was immaculate standing there on my first parade and I felt so out of place among all the well-worn shirts, the dirty trousers and tatty boots that were the hallmark of this type of frontline street work. The pungent stench of stale cigarette smoke and alcohol was all too prevalent from the men around me. They were a strong-looking bunch, though, and it was obvious to me that this was a tight-knit team, so my biggest fear was whether they would accept me as one of them. My worries seemed unfounded, however, as I was never left out of the conversation and banter that continued even in the presence of all the sergeants and the inspector. I felt at home right away as the briefing commenced.

After the formal introductions, I was placed as a member of Ebony 2, with Sergeant C in charge, and detailed to carry the SMG and the FRG. The rest of the men were also given their duties, which ranged from driving to carrying the other weapons. We had a wide range of weapons available to us at that time, but no cushy modern kit here. There were two ex-army self-loading rifles (SLRs), four M1 Carbines, two Ruger rifles with night sights and ten SMGs, most still with weld marks clearly visible on the safety catches. This dated them back to the '70s, when the RUC was first disarmed then prohibited from carrying automatic weapons due to the recommendations contained in the Hunt report. The welds put on at this time were ground off to make the weapons semi-automatic again when the order was rescinded some years later.

The whole unit was detailed to patrol the area around the Woodburn RUC station in West Belfast, a hardline republican area in the notorious B division. This didn't mean an awful lot to me at that time, but I soon learned that there were certain areas that were particularly dangerous for us to venture into and this was one of them. It was the type of place that made the hairs stand up on the back of your neck and you instinctively knew that you shouldn't be there.

My first tour of duty with the DMSU was to be a baptism of fire. You could almost taste the atmosphere of hate on the streets. The hunger strike supporters loathed the RUC with a passion and within two hours of starting my official police career I was heading straight into a riot.

I will never forget the emotions I experienced on that relatively short journey through the city centre of Belfast as we listened on the police radio to what lay in wait for us. I had seen a lot of the disturbances in this area on the television news over the preceding days but this was the first time I had ever been there in the thick of it. I was literally quaking in my boots and anyone who tells you they wouldn't have been frightened either doesn't have a clue what they're talking about or is a bloody liar!

As our armoured Land-Rover drove slowly in convoy with our other vehicles towards Andersonstown, we all leant forward trying to get a clearer view out over the heads of the sergeant and the driver. I could see a lot of activity, with petrol bombs being thrown at the vehicle in front. People were standing all along the road as we passed, wanting nothing more than to witness our destruction. The situation in the Province was not the same as the riots in Toxteth, or indeed the miners' strike, where the rioters just wanted to make their point. In Northern Ireland, if the rioters successfully stopped your vehicle and you had to get out, they would try their best to kill you. Terrorist guns were always present at riots in case such an opportunity presented itself.

Tourists mingled with members of the press, their cameras waiting for the action shots that would make their holiday. It was widely believed in those days that certain members of the international press who were running short of footage and about to fly home would pay local thugs to arrange a serious riot for them to film, only they wanted an exclusive – they wanted blood. One such 'staged' event was broken up by one of our other crews behind the DeLorean car factory in Dunmurry and resulted in exclusion orders being served on two German cameramen.

Then, suddenly, it was our turn to come under fire and with a mighty thud we were hit on the side of our vehicle by a petrol bomb. Another immediately followed it on the same side. The heat inside the vehicle was intense and the smell of burning petrol and paint was overpowering. Smoke was stinging my eyes and sticking in my throat. I could feel myself descending into panic but fortunately I regained control of myself.

I wasn't a hardened policeman who had already served several years on the force like the rest of my colleagues. I was Joe Bloggs, an ordinary guy stuck into an RUC uniform and sent into a riot. I was completely unprepared and this was the first time in my life I had ever been exposed to such vitriol. What made it more frightening was that I was in the company of men who looked upon this as 'payback time' – their turn to 'get back at the Fenians', as they put it. They were egging the crowd on with gestures and taunts through the sliding hatches on each side of the armour plate.

We were then hit again but on the other side of the vehicle. This time some of the petrol found its way through gaps in one of the baton gun ports and started a small fire inside the Land-Rover. It was very quickly put out with our extinguisher but one of the lads shouted out angrily that his brand-new waterproof coat had been the first casualty, with third degree burns to its back. They were laughing and joking at this but I was frozen, not knowing what to do. Then the sergeant shouted out to get the baton gun ready. He told me that when it was safe I was to open the port and fire it at the petrol bombers. Out of earshot of the sergeant, one of the other lads whispered to me to take the batteries out of my torch and stuff them up the barrel of the gun as well: an all-too-common practice at that time and something that caused horrific injuries. I ignored him and his disappointment was obvious.

The baton ports on these vehicles were made of sliding steel plate and therefore we couldn't really see what lay on each side of our vehicle. The front-seat passengers had a good view but in the back we could see bugger all. It was all very well for the sergeant to tell me to open the port and look out to identify the target, but with petrol bombs raining down, would you want to?

I tentatively opened the port, half expecting to get an eyeful of burning petrol. I could see a few youths at the corner of some houses 50 yards away, getting another petrol bomb ready; they lit the fuse and ran towards us. Just at the very moment one of the boys lifted the petrol bomb above his shoulder to throw it, I took aim and fired the baton gun. Christ! I hit him on the shoulder. He dropped the bottle beside him and it smashed as he fell to the ground. With his legs in a ball of flames, he was dragged away by his mates, kicking and screaming.

The lads in the wagon were ecstatic at the hit and were already making up nicknames for me, such as 'Eddie the one-hit wonder'. I felt uneasy but had to keep firing, as some other lads were getting ready to throw more petrol bombs. This exchange of fire lasted for some time until all our vehicles were out of the ambush zone and we could beat our retreat. At each junction we were pelted with bricks, bottles and petrol bombs. Obviously the press corps was expecting this show of strength. Their numbers had now swollen as they danced all over the road in front of us, slowing our progress.

I guess I must have fired at least ten or twelve rounds during that incident and I found myself wondering 'What the fuck am I doing in this job? This is not what I wanted, I want out!' I was choking with the cordite smell of the rounds I had fired and the petrol fumes that had now filled the vehicle. My nose was blocked up and my eyes were streaming with soot. I don't know if it was the acrid smells inside the Hotspur or the shock of my first hit on a human body but I was finding it really hard not to be sick and had to swallow back the bile a few times. Before joining the RUC, I had had visions of myself as a bobby on the beat helping out the members of the local community, but I was now on the frontline of the fight against terrorism and, whether I liked it or not, I was deeply involved. I had crossed the line and was a policeman who had inflicted pain on another human being. If that young lad died, I would have to accept full responsibility and I wasn't sure whether I could cope with that burden. I couldn't afford to let the rest of the crew see that I was so upset, though, as they would no doubt have viewed it as weakness and I had to continue working with them.

We got out of the area as soon as we could and headed for Woodburn RUC station to take stock. After we entered the station and parked up, I headed straight to the toilets and threw up before I could reach the bowl. Thank God none of the other lads saw me, as this would definitely have been regarded as behaviour unbecoming of a member of the DMSU. I reported to Sergeant C that I had hit someone with a baton round but he was busy listening to the radio and keeping track of what was going on outside the gates. Nobody seemed particularly bothered and they just told me not to worry about it.

There was no reporting system for fired baton rounds during the early years of the Troubles and this was a gaping loophole that needed to be closed. I did find during my years of service that there was generally a lot of abuse in relation to the use of these guns, but when they were required on occasions like this, they were a very effective tool indeed. When a petrol bomber was coming at you with murder in his eyes, he didn't want to spit in your face, he wanted to throw that petrol down your throat and watch you burn. He wanted to kill you and all your mates with you. Faced with such an enemy, it was vital that the security services were able to defend themselves, and it was the very success of the baton guns that made them so unpopular with the republican movement, which is still arguing today for them to be banned.

We had a cup of coffee in the canteen and I calmed down somewhat. Then the sergeant looked over towards me. I had the baton gun beside me on the table and he screamed out in horror as he spied a white plastic baton round up the spout. This was highly dangerous, as these guns had no safety catches. After all the turmoil, I had committed the cardinal sin of forgetting to unload. He never let me forget that serious lapse of concentration; little did I know but he was to be my sergeant for the next 21 years!

We then returned to our base station at Castlereagh, where we finished duty at 2 a.m. after a full night of dealing with other riots and being hit on various other occasions in and around Andersonstown. I couldn't believe what I had experienced. This was my first day on duty as a policeman and I was scared stiff. I had never felt so alone in all of my life. I eventually arrived home in the early hours of the morning and Agnes was waiting up for me. She must have known something was wrong, as I was filthy with black stains over my face and shirt, but I couldn't tell her what I had been through.

No matter how hard I tried, I could not turn off that horror movie that was playing over and over inside my head and it was not until later in life that I finally came to terms with my actions that night. After seeing what a vicious, hate-filled crowd like that had done to two army corporals, Derek Wood and David Howes, in March of 1988, I realised that I had only done what was necessary to survive. The two corporals were both pulled from their car when they got caught up in an IRA funeral, then stripped, tortured and shot dead in front of a baying crowd. It is likely that the other members of my team and I would have met the same fate if we had been immobilised and forced to leave the safety of our vehicle. I had been protecting my life and those of my mates, and once I realised this, I was able to put that ghost to rest in my chest of memories. That first night, though, the only solace I could find was with my old friend Pierre Smirnoff.

The next day it was to be the same 5.30 p.m. start at Castlereagh. I had listened to the radio news all day, hoping not to hear any news of injuries or death from baton rounds in that area. Thankfully, there were none.

NOT WAVING BUT DROWNING

On 7 September 1981, while we were having dinner in the canteen at Castlereagh RUC station, the television news reported the horrific deaths of two young policemen outside the village of Pomeroy in County Tyrone. Their patrol car had been caught in an ambush on a country road and they were literally blown to pieces by a massive bomb. No further details were being released as to their identities, as no doubt their relatives were still to be informed.

Sadly, news like this no longer came as a total shock to us. No one made any obvious display of emotion; instead, we raged inwardly. I wondered what the reaction would have been if the same explosion had occurred on a country road in Kent or Surrey and two English policemen had been blown to pieces; surely there would have been a huge outcry. It seemed that we in the RUC had become somewhat hardened to the death of our own colleagues, a situation that probably stemmed from the dangers that we faced every day on the street and the fact we felt that no one really cared outside our own circles.

Later in the evening, I found out to my utter horror that one of the dead lads was my young mate from my depot days, Stuart Montgomery. During our 14-week training course, Stuart and I had become close friends as we drove up each week to Enniskillen together. We had helped each other through our studies, even reciting the dreaded definitions, of theft, burglary, etc., on the long journey back to the depot each Sunday night after a weekend at home. We had a passing-out parade party after we left Enniskillen, getting totally blocked in the process, and that was the last time I ever saw him alive.

Stuart was only 19 when he was killed, one of the youngest RUC officers to die during the Troubles. He was on his very first patrol from his first station at Pomeroy, having started duty only an hour before. He had been involved in another training course since leaving the depot and had just arrived at his station. He was travelling with his partner, Constable Mark Evans, in the second of a two-car patrol when a landmine exploded beneath them on a deserted country road. They both died instantly, with bits of their bodies being found up to 150 yards away. Such was the force of the blast that it left a crater 50 feet deep by 50 feet wide. Although two men were charged with their murders, the charges were later dropped when two witnesses withdrew their statements.

I was devastated by this news and what made it all the more galling was that the explosion had taken place less than two miles from the home of hunger striker Martin Hurson, who had died two months earlier. The thought of his supporters revelling in the death of my friend made my blood boil.

I attended Stuart's funeral in Comber and was immediately greeted on the steps of the church by his father. I felt so guilty and could not hold back the tears. In full uniform, I was given pride of place at the head of his cortège and helped carry his coffin to the graveside just outside the village. Even to this day, when I meet his father he treats me like a son, although I can detect that vacant look stemming from his loss all those years ago. Stuart's mother died shortly after his murder; she just appeared to lose the will to live and departed, no doubt due to a broken heart.

Stuart's death hit me really hard and again made me question my future in the police. It would be nine years before I could muster the courage to visit his grave, such were my deep feelings of guilt that I had survived. I worked for a few days after the funeral but it was all too much for me and I had to take a couple of weeks off to get my head together. Even at this early stage in my career, I was showing signs of the problems that would eventually lead to serious illness.

Agnes and I were at this point still living in the two-bedroom council flat a few doors up from her mother in Newtownards. Things were pretty cramped now that we had two children, and as we were eligible for a bigger house from the Housing Executive we decided to move. Policemen in Northern Ireland cannot live wherever they want, however. Before they either buy or rent a house, they have to apply in writing to the local divisional commander and request his permission. As there are only a very limited number of areas that are considered safe, the vast majority of policemen live in private developments. I didn't feel able to make such a big commitment, though, as I felt so unsure about whether I would continue with my career in the RUC. So, after months of pleading our case, and after involving the police welfare department, we were allocated a new council house in the Bowtown Estate in Newtownards. We were delighted and Robert and Cassandra were excited at the thought of having their own bedrooms.

We moved in a few months later and started decorating our new house exactly the way we wanted it. As this was the first phase of the development, ours was the only cul-de-sac completed, therefore only a handful of families were moving in beside us. By and large they were hard-working people and, like me, they were only interested in making a better life for themselves and their families. As a small community, we set about making our neighbourhood a decent place to live.

After we had been there for a few months, however, as in so many other working-class areas in the Province, the criminal element moved in and started to ruin the neighbourhood. They were moving out from their ghettos in Belfast, bringing with them the baggage of criminal ideals and loyalist extremism. Flags started to appear on every lamp-post and loyalist murals were daubed on gable walls. Things were now beginning to turn ugly, especially for a policeman living in their midst. While not openly hostile to our presence, they did observe my every move. Certain individuals would be seen around my car at night, in the back garden, and our coal was even being stolen from the bunker. I feared that this was only the start of a campaign to get rid of us. I would see groups of adolescent thugs gathered on street corners at night on my way to work and worry about the safety of Agnes and the kids. I believed it was only a matter of time before the guns appeared or they burned us out. Agnes was totally unaware of what was happening. She was quite naive about what was going on with regard to the criminal element in Northern Ireland at that time, so how could I tell her? It would only have caused her more worry. Rightly or wrongly, I decided it was better to keep this to myself for the moment.

While the local divisional commander had approved my move to the Bowtown Estate, he now received word from a Special Branch tout that a policeman was going to be burnt out of the estate if he didn't move of his own accord. I was called in to see him in his office in Newtownards the next day and it came as no surprise to hear that I was the policeman that they were referring to. Thankfully, the commander was very supportive. He seemed to be genuinely concerned about my situation and offered me some valuable advice. He put me in touch with a financial adviser with whom I had an interview one hour later and I walked out of his office with the funds to buy our first home, just off the Bangor Road in Newtownards.

I was still worried about making such a big financial commitment but the safety of Agnes and the children had to come before everything else. The Special Branch tout was informed of my plans and I was granted a 'stay of execution' until we moved out.

I was furious that these loyalist thugs had forced us out of our home and it made me reflect bitterly on something that had become patently obvious to me even at this early stage in my police career – the one-sided nature of our duties. We were being constantly bombarded by reports from Special Branch concerning the movements of leading figures in the republican camp but we very rarely received information about the other side to the problem in Northern Ireland – the hardline Protestant thugs. This really alarmed me, as I knew without a doubt, and from personal experience, that the loyalists were out there committing murder and robbery but little effort seemed to be made to stop them. There seemed to be a great deal of empathy within police circles towards the Protestant community, while, in contrast, I was shocked by the overt displays of hatred shown by some members of the RUC towards the nationalist community. To their credit, the majority of my colleagues exercised great restraint in very demanding circumstances but some men lost all self-control. Perhaps they justified their actions to themselves by stereotyping all Catholic members of society as potential terrorists. I was still proud to be wearing the green uniform of the Royal Ulster Constabulary but at the same time I was beginning to feel deeply ashamed of the actions of some of my fellow officers.

To give an example of the kind of thing that was going on, upon the death of each hunger striker, Sinn Féin called for a show of solidarity and arranged what was called a 'Black Protest'. Hundreds of women and children holding black flags would form a line stretching for miles. They would stand silently for hours in the middle of the Andersonstown Road in Belfast. Some policemen considered it great fun to harass the protesters by driving their

Land-Rovers at speed very close to them while the men in the back cursed and spat at them from the baton-gun ports. There were even stories circulating of members of other Belfast units spraying urine at the protesters from kiddies' water-pistols.

It was no surprise that I started to drink and smoke heavily as I tried to deal with all that was happening around me on a daily basis. It seemed to work and made the situation more bearable at times but gradually my home life started to suffer due to my massive mood swings. I would come home some days feeling OK, then something would trigger off a swing. Great credit to Agnes, though, she always knew when I was about to snap and gave me a wide berth, thereby letting me come out of the mood on my own. A lesser woman would have packed me in a lot sooner.

CHAPTER 11

THE WATER HID MY TEARS

For the next few months or so, things went on much the same. I was now dealing with all kinds of incidents, such as bomb scenes, rallies, shootings and riots. It would take an encyclopedia to catalogue them all and there is certainly not scope within the confines of this book. But there were also periods when time would pass excruciatingly slowly as things were so quiet. I would often sit for hours in the freezing cold at the open rear doors of our Land-Rover with my loaded Ruger rifle or M1 perched on my knee as we patrolled every nook and cranny in the city. My hands and feet would be so cold that they would have been useless in any emergency. The boredom would sometimes be intense and I would resort to lighting up a cigarette, which seemed to be the magical cure.

At that time in the early '80s, on most nights of the week there was an eerie calm in the city centre of Belfast after 8 p.m. Nothing much happened on the streets at night except the usual drunken fights at chucking-out time. This unnatural tranquillity was no doubt due to the fact that at the height of the disturbances over the hunger strikes people were afraid to socialise in the city centre, preferring instead to frequent the pubs and clubs out of town. Every morning, fresh corpses would be found by the early patrols in the dark alleyways of the Shankill and Falls roads, and people were very afraid to move around. On those nights, Belfast would resemble a ghost town and would be saturated with police and army patrols all hoping for that lucky break: catching gunmen or bombers on the move.

Trouble in Northern Ireland seemed to come like buses: all at once or rarely at all. As a result, we were constantly on a very high state of alert and sometimes needed a safety valve to let off steam. On those quiet nights when there was rarely a car to be seen on the road, I would head up to the top of the Ballysillan Park for the 'freewheel'. This was our only entertainment during those very long shifts and something at which I became quite adept.

At the top of the hill, I would shift the Land-Rover into neutral and freewheel as fast as I could to the junction of the Ballysillan Road. Without using the brakes, I would screech around the corner with blue lights and siren on, nearly up on two wheels as the boys would shift over to the other side to provide some counter-balance. We would then immediately turn left and onto the Oldpark Road. We would have lost some momentum but it was all downhill from there on. With skill, and still without using the brakes at all, I would manage, much to the delight of all on board, to arrive slowly at Clifton Street before coming to a halt two miles down the road outside the chapel. I think that record, for the distance which the vehicle could travel without losing momentum, still stands and it would be nearly impossible to beat due to the volume of traffic nowadays.

Many nights we would patrol the city streets so slowly at times that I would be permanently in first gear. The Land-Rover would happily chug along on its own without me having to use the throttle. Here we would relieve the boredom by swapping positions with each other. The call would go out and the driver would jump out and run around the rear of the crawling vehicle while at the same time the gunner would jump out and take up the driver's seat. This went well until one time I was driving and duly jumped out to run around the rear only to find that the gunner was laughing his head off as he closed the rear door. I had to run double quick to assume my position as driver again. As you can imagine, this went down really well with all on board, especially the sergeant, who by this time was in stitches.

To the layman, this type of behaviour may seem childish and immature but you have to bear in mind that these were not normal times we were working in. We were constantly under enormous pressure. Two Hotspur Land-Rovers had already been blown apart within the previous few months with improvised grenades fired from home-made launchers. Home-made 'drogue' bombs made out of old baked bean tins filled with Semtex explosive with a tail attached were also being used to target the police. They had to hit the vehicle square-on to explode and so, to improve accuracy, the terrorists attached a length of string and a black plastic bin bag to stabilise the bomb in flight. Another home-made explosive was made from nitrogen fertiliser and we spent a lot of time searching cars for component parts of a weapon almost as deadly as the gun – the seemingly innocuous coffee grinder. When it is spread on fields, ammonium nitrate is a benign fertiliser which helps produce bumper crops. Mix it with fuel oil, however, and it becomes the kind of inexpensive deadly bomb the IRA hungered for. Coffee grinders were used to break up the coarse fertiliser pellets into a finer and more efficient powder, making it easier to mix with diesel oil. Anyone found with such equipment would be treated as a terrorist until they could prove otherwise. A number of policemen had already died on these streets as a result of the various tactics employed by the terrorists and there was always the underlying fear that we were to be next.

But, however quiet some periods would seem to be, the one thing we could be certain of was that the peace would eventually be broken and it was not always as a result of terrorist activity. In the winter of 1981, at 1 a.m. on one of the coldest nights for years, we were about to head back to base and then home when the radio came to life: 'Ebony Four from Uniform [Uniform being our radio controller].'

'Ebony Four from Uniform,' the radio crackled out again.

Sergeant P replied, 'Uniform from Ebony Four, go ahead.'

'If you are still in the Lisburn Road area, then go to the junction of Lisburn Road and Windsor Avenue, very serious traffic accident.'

'Roger, Uniform, we are on our way, be there in two minutes.'

'Ah, for fuck sake,' we all cried out in unison. We were bloody freezing that night and just wanted to go home, yet here we were being sent to a call which could take us hours to sort out.

Before we had time to complain further, we arrived at a scene of utter carnage. Belfast was having one of its coldest nights in living memory – it was -5°C at this stage and the River Lagan had frozen over at Shaw's Bridge. The roads were treacherous and there were accidents happening all over the city. There in front of us was a car that had ploughed into an enormous tree; a few more feet to the right or left and there would have been no serious impact. It seemed fate had indeed played a big part in this one.

Four youths were trapped in the car: two boys in the front and two girls in the back. One of the two boys in the front was clearly dead, while the other and the girls in the back were very seriously injured. The front seats had been moved back in the impact and nearly cut off the girls' feet. None of them had been wearing their seatbelts. When I crouched down by the rear of the car, one of the young girls opened her eyes and smiled; she didn't seem to be in too much pain and so we talked for a while.

'I told him not to steal the car. I just wanted to get the bus home,' she told me.

I was struck by just how pleasant she was and was deeply saddened when I realised the full extent of her injuries. Blood was pouring from her ears and it was obvious that she was dying in front of me. I had initially thought that the steam coming from the car was emanating from the burst engine pipes but it was actually steam rising from warm blood. As the fire brigade arrived with their cutting equipment, I had a closer look inside the car and by then the floor was under about two inches of blood.

Two kids, including that beautiful young girl, died that night in a stolen car in a total waste of young human life. While it was terribly sad, this accident had been caused by sheer bad judgement or bad luck, and policemen and women have to deal with scenes like this every day all over the world. I could deal with the trauma of accidents like this, but the bloodshed caused by terrorism was another matter.

The worst atrocity I have ever had to deal with was a bomb explosion in Rugby Road, Belfast, late on 2 June 1982. There was a booby-trapped motorcycle parked up against a hedge outside the church in Rugby Road.

Underneath the petrol tank was a bomb with a tripwire attached to the fence wire and intertwined through the hedge. The Irish National Liberation Army (INLA) placed the bike there in the hope that a police patrol would find it, think it had been stolen and try to recover it. Unfortunately, at 11 p.m., a local boy, 16-year-old Patrick Smith, found the bike and tried to move it, for reasons known only to him. The bomb exploded immediately and he was literally blown to pieces. The two friends who were with him were also very seriously injured.

I started work the next day at 6.30 a.m. and our crew was detailed to take part in a search at the scene of the explosion. This was considered routine for the DMSU, as our training included a comprehensive search course, but at that stage I hadn't realised exactly what we might be looking for.

I had never ever seen a sight like this before. There was blood and guts everywhere, like something out of a horror film; I felt really sick. Don't get me wrong: I am not normally squeamish. I have seen dead bodies and post-mortems, and dealt with serious accidents, all of which I can cope with. This was totally different, though; this was the body of a young boy blown apart by a bomb placed by men who just wanted to cause death.

The bulk of Patrick's remains had been removed by undertakers before we arrived that morning but CID had to wait for first light for us to collect all the rest. The local cats and dogs were having a field day and there were seagulls perched on every vantage point. The stench of death hung heavy in the air.

Reserve Constable C and I were each given a large clear polythene bag and told by the CID officers to go around and pick up as many pieces of his body as we could find; unfortunately, there weren't even any gloves left for us to use. I have never done anything so gruesome in all of my life and I believe that I should not have been used for this without volunteering. I was sickened, really sickened and upset, but we had to get on with it as there were camera crews filming and the press were taking photographs. I wasn't given a chance to object as I was a policeman and I had a job to do.

'For Christ's sake,' I shouted out. I was picking up bits of a 16-year-old boy from the ground, from the nearby trees and even a large piece of his skull with hair still attached from the grounds of the Theological College opposite. I had to scrape bits off the white painted church wall; the stains were dreadful, as if someone had thrown a bucket of blood all over it. I looked over to Davy, my partner, to witness him crying and heaving up into a corner. Davy was one of the longest-serving members in our unit and had seen a lot in his time. He was a mountain of a man and I was deeply affected by his suffering.

Someone from CID came over a few hours later with a very worried expression on his face; he had just realised that part of an upper arm was missing. He had been collecting the bags all morning and doing a rough reconstruction on paper, trying to work out if all body parts were accounted for. Many were missing. I called for the fire brigade to inspect the high roofs of buildings around the blast scene but I was overruled. There was no way they would come out to look for human flesh.

We finished at the scene around lunchtime as the Department of Environment Road Service hosed the area down the best they could and opened the road to traffic. No sooner had the white tape been removed from the lamp-posts than cars were being parked on the bloodied street where that young boy had met his death. It appeared so irreverent but that is just typical of Northern Ireland – life is cheap.

We were signalled over the radio to 'Romeo Tango Bravo' (return to base) and the rest of that day I was fit for nothing. There was no debriefing and no one to talk to about the horrors we had seen, no one to help me deal with my emotions. I cleaned my uniform the best I could but the stains of blood were etched into its fabric. Certainly there were people in the RUC an incident like this would not fizz upon. In fact, some I know would have positively relished it, but not me. I stood in the shower for hours and when I finally let my emotions out, I almost collapsed onto the floor of the cubicle, the water hiding my tears. I couldn't control this torrent; all that was required was a moment away from the gaze of my peers and a reminder of the carnage I had just witnessed. Like a safety valve on a steam engine, this release of emotion was unstoppable until my mind attained a safe working pressure again. The next day brought it all back with a bang, as I was featured on the front page of the *Daily Mail*, crouched over in the middle of the road with my clear plastic bag as I picked up pieces of that young boy from the ground. I felt sick again and really dirty. Some of the lads in the unit tried to console me by saying he was a bit of a 'gouger', a term we used to describe habitual offenders, and that he deserved it. But that didn't make any difference to me and to this day I still get very upset at the mere thought of that incident, especially if ever I have to pass the scene. There is still a large hole in the hedgerow. Even after 22 years, it seems Mother Nature herself was deeply wounded that day and refuses to allow new growth to cover the site.

While armoured Hotspurs and bullet-proof vests are very valuable pieces of equipment, they did not protect me from the psychological damage inflicted by repeated exposure to events that I found hard to stomach or comprehend. The sights I was forced to witness as a result of terrorist atrocities will, I fear, stay with me forever.

CHAPTER 12

DOUBLE VODKAS ALL ROUND
FOR BREAKFAST

From this incident onwards, my overall health and well-being went downhill very badly. I was drinking and smoking more as I tried to shut out all that was hurting me deep inside. I was so low at this stage that I even looked to smoking cannabis as the solution. There was never any problem getting a joint at that time: if none had been quietly confiscated or found during a house search, you always knew who to turn to for one. But it wasn't for me. Yes, the immediate effects were very pleasant and it relaxed me for a while, but I usually felt much worse after it had worn off.

At home, I would use the excuse of a slap-up meal to down a bottle or two of wine without appearing too dependent on it. Barbecues were an excellent way of disguising a session and amid the cover of a family group I could get well and truly plastered, thereby achieving my goal. I stopped physical training and had lost interest in most things in my daily life, including my family. Robert and Cassandra ran the gauntlet of good days and bad, both seeming to possess that knack of knowing when Dad was having a bad one and avoiding him. I became very domineering and intolerant, for example dictating that they turn the television off as soon as I retired to bed, as I could stomach no noise from downstairs while I was trying to sleep. What I failed to realise at the time was that the bad days were becoming more and more frequent and I was turning into my father!

Agnes complained many times that I was getting very moody at home and was spending a lot of time on my own rather than with the family. Looking back now, I can see how worried she must have been, as I divulged very little about my everyday work to her, thus leaving her to imagine that the problems were a result of things going wrong between us rather than with my job. Nothing could have been further from the truth, as I loved her so much and honestly believed that I was sheltering her from worry by refusing to share anything about what I was going through.

On some occasions, I would disappear all day on my motorbike, touring the countryside rather than going to work. I would find a phone box and report in sick, as I was having serious problems coping with the very thought of having to put on that green uniform again. Unlike the rest of the lads in the unit, I seemed to be dwelling on events too much. Everybody is different, thank God, and some people can cope with carnage better than others. The lads in the unit were aware of my suffering to a certain degree and helped out the best they could with parties and daytrips away to the north coast for some sea fishing, but all this was only painting over some very major cracks that were starting to appear in my brickwork. From the outside, my walls appeared to be OK but the foundations were dodgy to say the least.

In my highly charged emotional state, it felt very strange to be patrolling as a policeman the same dark and dreary streets in North Belfast where I had once scrounged as a boy. I felt as though I was looking at the scene from the other side of the fence, though I wasn't sure whether I was any better off now.

North Belfast was probably the most bitterly divided area of Northern Ireland. Of the 3,703 murders carried out during the Troubles, almost a quarter took place here, along the area's notorious sectarian interfaces. I was now on 'hard patrol', running from street corner to street corner while wearing full body armour and carrying a rifle, and taking cover in the dark corners of the Shankill Road that had been my old childhood stomping ground. Memories of our dire poverty came flooding back as I stopped where 100 Dover Street had once stood and looked up at that old, green, cast-iron gas lamp still there after all those years. I could picture us as kids, swinging from a rope I had tied to the ladder-rest at the top of the lamp after clambering up like a monkey.

Never in my wildest dreams as a boy, ducking and diving for survival, did I ever think that one day I would be working in that same area as a policeman or that my life would be saved on the very street where I had played as a child.

It was the day of the judge's summing up in the supergrass trial involving UVF man Joseph Bennett in the Crumlin Road courthouse in April 1983. Fourteen hardline members of the UVF were found guilty on his evidence and sentenced to a total of 200 years. The evidence in the trial had been so weak that they had all believed they were about to be freed. So when they were convicted, they went crazy. Our unit had been involved in ensuring order in the courtroom when they were sentenced and we had had to force the prisoners back into their cells by the use of batons until they could be transferred through the tunnel that leads under the Crumlin Road to the prison. The ensuing street disorder outside the courthouse necessitated our retention on duty and we were heavily involved in trying to control serious rioting outside the building as friends and relatives of the convicted went on the rampage. All hell broke loose and the anger flowed out onto the streets of the Shankill Road and surrounding area. Roadblocks and barricades went up at a moment's notice. Rioting started and went on well into the night, eventually erupting in most Protestant areas of Belfast.

The Shankill Road was ablaze with burning barricades, and flaming cars were being rolled towards our lines at the junction with Agnes Street. Shots were being fired all over the city as attacks on police and army escalated. I took cover at the corner of Agnes Street and a wry smile came to my face when I found my name still carved on the street sign all these years later. We were then forced back into the Land-Rover and pushed back to Craven Street, where we reversed our Hotspur into its junction to monitor the Agnes Street crossroads. I was sitting in the rear in my position as gunner that night, with a fully loaded M1 Carbine on my lap, and as I peered out of

TOP LEFT: My mother, Trilby, pictured as a young girl.

TOP RIGHT: The author aged six at the
Model Primary School in Newtownards.

ABOVE: Childhaven in Donaghadee: the first of many welfare
homes in which I would stay during my childhood.

ABOVE: At Marmaine Children's Home in Holywood, County Down. From left to right are John, Irene, me, Cherie, Tom and Sadie.

BELOW: Allworthy Avenue: just one of our many hovels in Belfast.

TOP: Although the original cast-iron sign upon which I scraped my name is gone, this one still marks the spot on the Shankill Road to which I was drawn as a child.

ABOVE LEFT: The façade of the Shankill Road Mission. I found sanctuary within its hallowed walls.

ABOVE RIGHT: Agnes on our first full day together.

TOP LEFT: My passing-out parade on my 25th birthday in 1981.

TOP RIGHT: The traditional throwing of forage caps into the air to signify the end of RUC training at the depot in Enniskillen.

ABOVE LEFT: About to go on patrol with No. 4 DMSU based at Castlereagh in Belfast.

ABOVE RIGHT: The early type of armoured Hotspur Land-Rover in which I spent five cramped years.

TOP: Clearing riot debris off the Shankill Road. (Pacemaker Press)

ABOVE: The author amid the chaotic scene in which Sean Downes died.
(Pacemaker Press)

TOP LEFT: Dundonald RUC station in Belfast,
home to the Close Protection Unit.

TOP RIGHT: Irish President Mary Robinson's visits to Northern
Ireland always proved controversial and necessitated a high
degree of close protection from the RUC. (Pacemaker Press)

ABOVE: The current Irish President, Mary McAleese, was generally
more popular than her predecessor but the Close Protection Unit had
to adopt a background role to her Garda protection officer at many
nationalist venues in Northern Ireland. (Pacemaker Press)

TOP: One of the very few husband-and-wife teams at Westminster. Peter Robinson is MP for East Belfast and his wife, Iris, is MP for Strangford. Trying to follow in his father's footsteps is their son Gareth. (Pacemaker Press)

ABOVE: In 1998, Peter Robinson's DUP constituency office in Belfast was daubed with the slogan 'DUP = LVF' during a heated election campaign.

TOP: After the carefully orchestrated handshake with Gerry Adams, US President Bill Clinton made his way down the Grosvenor Road towards Belfast city centre. I was driving Tony Lake, his National Security Advisor, three cars behind; the second limo was a decoy. The building to the left is the Royal Victoria Hospital where a room had been secured and fully equipped – just in case! (Pacemaker Press)

ABOVE LEFT: The author partaking of some stress relief by racing at the World Police Road Racing Championships at Donington Park in 1996.

ABOVE RIGHT: Meeting up with my brother John in Australia after 24 years. He died a few years later.

the very small square of bullet-proof glass in the rear door I noticed a lot of activity going on some distance away at the other end of this small street. I made the rest of the crew aware and the sergeant swung the spotlight around to find out what exactly they were up to. We couldn't reverse, as the street was blocked by debris, so it was decided that we should go back out on foot and investigate. To be quite honest, this idea didn't thrill me at all, and just as I was about to step out of the half-open rear doors, Reserve Constable X shouted out at the top of his voice, 'Stop!' I slammed the heavy doors closed again and looked at him in total amazement. He had obviously spotted something that he didn't like.

Reserve Constable X was not someone prone to panic and was, without a doubt, the best person to be with in a situation like this. Some of the men in the unit, including myself, looked upon him as a bit of a hero as he had actually shot and injured a terrorist gunman a few years previously. He was the most efficient policeman in our unit, very knowledgeable and had only been refused entry into the regular force due to his lack of height, an unfair situation that would be remedied by the introduction of equal opportunities legislation in the future. On this occasion, his quick thinking and razor-sharp responses undoubtedly saved my life, as when I looked back out of the tiny windows I saw a gunman taking up position on the corner behind. Before I could say anything, we were hit on the rear doors a number of times. If Reserve Constable X hadn't spotted the gunman, there was no doubt that he would have got a clean shot at me.

The rounds were now coming thick and fast, and in a situation like this, there was no way we were going to open the hatch to return fire for fear of letting one in. In an all-steel vehicle, the bullet would have ricocheted around many times, deforming before hitting someone with tragic results. We moved off immediately and informed other crews to stay away from the area. Sometimes this was the only course of action as it was just not worth risking lives in the pursuit of a gunman whose intentions were to entice you out of your vehicle. He would make good his escape long before we could get to him.

While we retreated from the scene, I reflected that it was from a roof here in Craven Street on 12 October 1969 that a loyalist gunman shot towards

Unity Flats and claimed the first RUC victim of the Troubles, Victor Arbuckle. Ironically, those responsible for his death were not the republican sworn enemies of the RUC; he was shot by a member of the Ulster Volunteer Force protesting at the fact that the B Specials were being disbanded and also about the disarming of the RUC recommended by the Hunt report. It would also be loyalist terrorists who would fatally injure the last policeman to be killed in the Troubles, Constable Frank O'Reilly, at the Orange Order protest at Drumcree on 6 October 1998. The press officer of the Portadown Orange district, David Jones, said the RUC officer's death was a tragedy, but unbelievably he also saw fit to add that the Orange Order would continue its protest at Drumcree, saying, 'Unfortunately, when you are standing up for civil liberties, sometimes the cost of those liberties can be very high.' His comments were described as 'a deplorable insult to a brave police officer' by Pat Armstrong, chairman of the Police Authority.

As well as the Bennett case, we were heavily involved in most of the other supergrass trials that were ongoing throughout this period. Men such as loyalist Budgie Allen and republican Raymond Gilmour were, for their own reasons, coming forward to supply the police with sworn statements as to their own, and hundreds of their comrades', involvement in murders, shootings and bombings. In exchange for their testimony, the supergrass prosecution witnesses were promised immunity for their own crimes, a new start abroad with their wives and children, and false identities. Others who had confessed to serious offences did not get immunity but were given assurances they would get more lenient sentences in exchange for their testimony and then a new, safe life abroad. Although there was always talk of vast rewards, this was inaccurate and over-inflated by opponents of the supergrass system; the supergrass just received his keep, lodgings and pocket money from the authorities.

Back in August 1982, before the Bennett trial, one day out of the blue we had our duty changed. This in itself was not too surprising, as we were forever having our shift times altered in order to police various protests and rallies. But on this occasion, we heard through the grapevine that all other Belfast DMSU units were also having their shifts changed in order that everyone would start at 5 p.m. the next evening. Something big was coming up: that was the consensus of opinion among the more senior men within the unit, but even the sergeants and our inspector were not told the reason for the change at that stage.

At home that evening, I told Agnes that I might be late home the next night. I couldn't explain to her why, as I didn't really know myself, but I guessed it would be an overnighter judging by the amount of equipment and food we had packed in the Hotspur.

When we gathered for duty the next day, there was a palpable air of excitement among the members of my team. It was always great fun to get away and do something out of the ordinary, even when we didn't know where we were going. We paraded at 5 p.m. around the crowded snooker tables and were detailed our vehicles and guns, then told to be fuelled and loaded up ready to go ASAP in the yard. The atmosphere was electric as we ran around getting our kit sorted. We took extra baton rounds, just in case: we had learned from past experience that it was always far better looking at them than looking for them. The inspector jumped into his flagship Hotspur – he always got the newest and most up-to-date vehicle with the best heater – and with a wave of his arm, we were off.

The buzz of excitement continued inside the crowded Hotspur as we all tried as best we could to get comfy. One of the lads even volunteered to lie on top of the portly policewoman we had with us. The second word of her reply was 'off', but you could do and say things like that to the WPCs then without running the risk of disciplinary action. In the early years, by way of initiation, new policewomen at the station would habitually be up-ended and then have their bare arses emblazoned with the station stamp. Some liked it, some didn't. This kind of behaviour has now all but been stamped out, if you'll forgive the pun.

As we headed out of town and up the M2 motorway, we just knew we must be heading for Londonderry – where else could we be going in such numbers? There were literally hundreds of Land-Rovers making their way along the motorway, as it had now transpired that all DMSU units throughout the Province were to be involved in this operation. We headed towards Coleraine to turn off towards Londonderry. This was the safest route, away from the notorious Toomebridge and Glenshane Pass, scene of so many attacks on police and army in the past. My excitement at this stage was now turning to trepidation as the sheer scale of the exercise we were involved in began to unfold. I couldn't help but wonder what the night would hold in store. Even some of the very senior men in our unit were expressing their concerns; they, too, had never seen anything like this before.

There were Land-Rovers nose to tail all along the road from Coleraine to Ballykelly. To relieve the tension, we would from time to time open the rear doors and pelt the following Hotspur with hard-boiled eggs, tomatoes and anything else we didn't like in our issued lunch packs.

By means of a secure radio, our inspector had now learned where he was going and led us to the disused airfield at Ballykelly army base not far along the coast from Londonderry. As we made our way through the gates of this imposing base, there were soldiers at every junction, directing us to the pre-planned and marked parking slots along the main runway. We all looked at each other in stunned silence. I even made the comment that this could be the disbandment of the RUC, seeing that every vehicle in the fleet seemed to be here in this one base at the same time. It also appeared that every heavily armed police officer was here. Although most of my colleagues scoffed, my comment seemed to strike a chord with some of the lads, including our sergeant. A soldier informed the inspector that all senior ranks were to report to a large hangar at the end of a taxiway. After about an hour, he returned and asked us all to follow him back to the hangar and bring all weapons with us. Some of the men were now starting to give my suggestion a little credence, as this was surreal.

We entered the hangar through a slight opening of its massive steel doors and joined about a thousand other police personnel and army wallowing in a pungent stench of pigeon shit. Some time later, when it was apparent that no other units were to arrive, the doors were slammed shut with a mighty bang. Soldiers then took up a sentry position and it was clear that nobody was going to be allowed to leave until whatever business we were there for was concluded. It appeared to me, as it did so many times in the course of my career, that the army didn't fully trust the RUC: no doubt they were afraid of some of us leaking information about the impending operation. I caught the eye of my sergeant and we both shrugged our shoulders in disbelief. This was a very major operation indeed: nothing on this scale had been seen since 'Operation Motorman', when the republican 'no-go' areas of the Province were cleared in 1972.

All became clear when the briefing by the army brass and our own very senior officers commenced. All they wanted us to do was to hit 98 houses throughout Londonderry city at the exact same time of 05:45 the next morning and arrest 100 terrorist suspects who had been named by a supergrass: easy or what?!

What a logistical nightmare that operation must have been. All routes to the various houses had been researched in advance and timed at a normal speed. The DMSU teams, each with an accompanying CID man, were to set off in staggered formation, those travelling the furthest distance leaving first, the shortest last. We had to hit all the houses at exactly the same time so that no warning calls could be made. Our crew, with Sergeant P in charge, was to go to a house in the notorious republican Shantallow Estate and arrest the person named on the warrant.

After the briefing, we all settled down, comfortable in the knowledge that our future in the RUC was secure for the time being at least. We laughed and joked with all the other crews and there was little chance of anyone getting their head down with the noise that was reverberating through the hangar. Throughout the night, the soldiers supplied us with steaming hot soup and sandwiches, and at the appointed hour the mighty door was opened and the first teams were away. We were next away five minutes later, so we picked up our CID man and made our way to our truck.

We drove calmly through the quiet, damp streets of Londonderry towards our objective. There was no hurry, as the run had been timed at normal patrol speed. Any sign of haste would have caused great suspicion and possibly given a warning in the Bogside, the first republican area we passed through on our way to the Shantallow. The streets were deserted and, considering the vast fleet behind us, this was indeed a marvel of planning. It was a weird sight in the misty still of dawn: so many armoured police Land-Rovers heading into the city across the Craigavon Bridge, with some travelling on the upper deck and some beneath them on the lower deck, depending on where in the city they were headed.

Fifteen short minutes later, we were holding back before entering the Shantallow, as we were just a bit too early. Then over the radio the order from the control room was 'GO!' We screeched up to our target house and all the doors of the Land-Rover were flung open. I took up my position with the rest of the lads and started giving cover as I scanned the surrounding area using the image intensifier sight on my Ruger rifle. I was to run around to the rear of the house and cover the back door. If anyone were to come out, I would have to detain him or her at gunpoint. All the lights in the neighbourhood came on and all hell broke loose; they could sense police activity in these ghettos, as many of those living in this area had something to hide.

Some of the more aggressive of the residents were now coming out in their nightwear and starting to bang dustbin lids in the well-used tactic of warning all other neighbours of a police or army presence. I saw the upstairs light of our target house come on and after what appeared to be ages I got the call to retreat to the vehicle. 'Thank God,' I said to myself, as some irate neighbours across the street were beginning to get a bit more active. I jumped into the Hotspur and slammed the door shut without even checking if everyone was aboard, as we were starting to get pelted quite badly. 'All OK,' I shouted out as we headed out of this now awakening cauldron of hate. I then looked at our new passenger and thought what a pathetic-looking creature he was. Just out of his bed and in a filthy state, he was stinking. It looked to me as if he had been out on the town the night before and just collapsed into bed wearing the same clothes.

The call was made over the radio to the control room that we had scored a hit. Thinking we were dumping the prisoner off at Strand Road RUC station in Londonderry city, I settled down for the five-minute journey. Then the news came in that we had, in fact, got one of the top IRA men in this area and he was to be conveyed straight to the holding centre at Castlereagh.

'Jesus Christ,' I shouted out. 'That will take us hours and there's not even a bloody window we can open.'

That was the longest journey of my life, sitting opposite that hardened terrorist. Obviously well schooled in counter-interrogation techniques, he was able to maintain eye contact for unbelievably long periods of time. It's damn near impossible to win this type of contest without losing one's rag completely, so I always tried to avoid getting into the situation in the first place. I later found out that it was alleged that he might have been involved in the murder of two soldiers and one policeman, not just killing them but also mutilating one of their dead bodies. This practice was widespread along the South Armagh border in the early '80s. The IRA would torture a soldier or policeman until he died of his injuries, then disembowel him. According to FAIR (Families Acting for Innocent Relatives), 'many had their genitals cut off and forced into their mouths'. They would then pack the body with explosives, sew it up and clothe it again, all in an attempt to blow up the army/police recovery team.

At Castlereagh, we dumped our prisoner at the holding centre and I went for a much-needed shower. We then headed into our cramped little room, signed off at 10.30 a.m. and cracked open the bottles by way of toasting a job well done: double vodkas all round for breakfast!

It turned out that we had been following up on the information provided by Raymond Gilmour. Gilmour was, in fact, an RUC agent. After secretly infiltrating and destroying the smaller terrorist group, the INLA, in Londonderry, he had penetrated the Londonderry IRA Brigade's Active Service Unit. The information that he had passed on to his RUC Special Branch handler had compromised several IRA operations and resulted in the detention of many of the top terrorists. When his cover had finally been blown after the seizure of one of the IRA's prized M60 superguns, he had agreed to turn supergrass and provide evidence against his 'comrades'.

When those arrested were finally placed in the dock at the Crumlin Road courthouse in Belfast late in 1984, you could feel the hate in the air. Again I was engaged in internal security within the courtroom. I was positioned up in the gallery armed with a high-powered rifle, watching for any escape attempt or attack on the judge or supergrass. As he gave his evidence, Gilmour would nod over to identify each terrorist that he mentioned. He seemed ever so cool and had obviously prepared well for this important task. Human nature being what it is, I found myself gloating at the downfall of these terrorists. The tables had truly turned, I believed, and, at long last, it was payback time. For too long we had been on the receiving end of attacks by this rabble and it was great to feel we were getting our own back to some degree.

My satisfaction was to prove premature, however, as on 18 December, after about six weeks of evidence, Lord Chief Justice Lowry suddenly called a halt to the trial and dismissed all the charges against the suspects. I have to admit that, after hearing some of the flimsy evidence that had been presented, I wasn't completely shocked to see the trial collapse, but I was enraged to see these men and women walking free from court, having got one over on the forces of law and order.

This was in stark contrast to the jubilation I had felt the year before at the conclusion of the Christopher Black supergrass trial, also in the Crumlin Road courthouse. The Christopher Black case had begun in December 1982 and he spent three weeks in the witness box in January and February 1983, giving his evidence against the 38 people that he had implicated. The trial ended in August after 120 days – the longest and, at £1.3 million, the costliest criminal trial ever held in Britain or Ireland. It had taken place in crazy circumstances, with the most dangerous of the accused, in the prison officers' judgement, in the dock and the rest seated on adjacent benches, surrounded by my unit and prison officers. Members of my own unit, who were fully armed, were positioned in the public seating area and from time to time high up in the spectators' gallery. Some men even sat on the bench adjacent to the judge. We changed position daily as it was felt by all that the monotony of constant observation could lead to complacency.

Altogether, 35 people were convicted as a result of Black's evidence, 4 receiving life sentences for the murders of a part-time member of the Ulster Defence Regiment (UDR) and the deputy governor of the Maze Prison. Sentences totalling more than 4,000 years were passed.

After the collapse of the Raymond Gilmour trial, however, all subsequent supergrass trials were dismissed and in 1986, 18 of those convicted on Christopher Black's evidence had their convictions quashed.

CHAPTER 13

WE NOW HAD A BOMB
ON OUR HANDS

The supergrass system had seemed to us in the RUC to be a great way to get some of the most hardened terrorists off the streets but even during the months that all these suspects were in custody, the killings in the Province continued. One tragedy that hit me really hard was the death of my good friend Micky Dawson from Newtownards. He had always been the life and soul of our squad during my training days in the depot at Enniskillen. He was a big lad with that imposing stature so rarely found in policemen these days. He always had time for a chat when we bumped into each other in and around Belfast; he was a tower of strength and someone I had a lot of respect for.

In the early hours of 12 April 1984, a suspicious red sports bag was reported to have been found in the front garden of a house in University Street in Belfast. Micky was a member of a local police patrol tasked to investigate it and, as he stood talking to the householder, the UVF device exploded without warning. He was declared dead shortly after arrival at the nearby City Hospital. The householder and mother of eight children, Mrs Margaret Whyte, a 52-year-old Catholic, also died.

NOT WAVING BUT DROWNING

The Whyte family had been subject to a reign of terror for many years. A year earlier, a bomber had lost his leg while attempting to plant a bomb at the family's house. On that occasion, Mrs Whyte had looked after the terrorist by placing a pillow under his head, trying to make him as comfortable as possible until the police and the ambulance arrived. He was later convicted for this attempted attack.

After hearing of Michael's death on the local television news, I reeled in utter horror: not only did an innocent woman die that day but also one of the most efficient and untarnished policemen I had ever met. I attended his funeral, which was held with full police honours at Movilla Cemetery in Newtownards, but wore civilian clothes and watched from afar. For some reason, I always felt guilty at policemen's funerals: as if they died playing in some game I was also part of and, in an inexplicable way, I felt I had somehow contributed to their death. It would be some years before I could muster the emotional strength to revisit his grave. I felt scared at the very thought of it, as if my presence there would somehow release the demons in my head. I was consciously trying to keep a lid on my chest of memories and each time I was reminded of some horror it would open slightly; self-preservation therefore took over and I deliberately avoided situations like this.

Agnes knew very well there was something wrong with me at that time but, again, I told her nothing. As far as she was concerned, this was just another poor unfortunate policeman who had lost his life defending the community. Here in Northern Ireland, we have become somewhat hardened to such deaths. During the Troubles, such incidents were reported daily on the television and radio, and somehow they lost their ability to shock. For me, however, this death was different. Michael was a friend and I was haunted by what had happened to him. Unable to talk about my feelings, I felt myself sliding back into despair and, as had happened to my mother, the only escape I could find was at the bottom of a bottle.

A few weeks later, just as I was beginning to emerge from my depression, I was faced with another horrendous incident: one that was to cause me lasting physical harm. Our crew was on city patrols when a call came over the radio to be on the lookout for a brown Housing Executive van that, according to information received, was supposed to be carrying a huge bomb into the city. We raced from our location on the other side of Belfast and managed to intercept it as it was being abandoned outside the showroom of R.E. Hamilton's Ford car dealership in Linenhall Street. The bombers jumped into another car and sped off before we could apprehend them. We couldn't give chase in our slow Land-Rover, so it was someone else's problem; we now had a bomb on our hands. We immediately cleared the area and the bomb squad was tasked with making the device safe. All the streets were taped off and buildings cleared, although some very stupid people would not heed our advice and had to be strongly warned to leave their offices. I was in Clarence Street when I noticed that some idiots were still in one of the buildings and were looking out of the windows directly at the van. If the bomb had exploded, they would have been killed or maimed for life. I managed to get them out within a few minutes and directed them to safety.

As I returned to check for anyone else who might be left, the bomb exploded with a deafening thud and, almost instinctively, I fell to the ground. I lay there covering my head for what seemed like ages until the dust had settled, hoping desperately that nothing hard was on its way down from the buildings high above. I was being covered in fragments of glass from the windows and prayed that no large shards were going to hit me next. I had lost my breath momentarily. When a bomb goes off, a massive vacuum is sometimes created, depending on where you are caught in the explosion. The next breath is always the hardest as you are enveloped in a cloud of smoke and dust; you can taste the grit and feel the dust finding its way into your eyes and lungs.

Thank God I was just around the corner and did not receive the full force of the blast, although a large chunk of the van's body did fall beside me, ripping my trousers as it settled. My right ear was ringing very badly and I had blood on the collar of my shirt. I was nearly completely deafened but I was not immediately concerned as I thought that maybe the blood was from a cut to my head as I fell to the ground. We gathered ourselves together and, after checking for injuries, we handed over control of the crime scene to the local station patrols for forensic examination.

NOT WAVING BUT DROWNING

I was dazed for a while and started to feel worse as the day wore on. I felt as if I had the flu, as I was aching all over and chilled to the bone. I think I was in shock but the consensus of opinion in the unit was: 'You're in the DMSU, lad – you'll get over it', and the solution was back to Castlereagh, brush off the dirt and dust, have a few drinks and home!

I was shaking for days and there was no help available in overcoming any fears or problems I may have had in relation to this or any other events I had been involved in. In fact, in all my five years in the DMSU, we were never once made aware of any help or counselling even after witnessing some of the most traumatic incidents in the Troubles. I was a realist, I wasn't looking for some secret potion that would relieve me of all my woes but it would have been good practice to have someone we could turn to for advice. I had never heard of Post-Traumatic Stress Disorder at this time, but now I realise that I was already suffering on a chronic scale.

I attended my doctor the following week, as the ringing in my ears had not stopped. After a thorough examination, he found no serious damage except for a slight perforation but the constant ringing has never ceased, even after 20 years, and I will suffer from tinnitus for the rest of my life.

After this very frightening episode, things really started to get the better of me. I now found myself looking for ways out, thinking of excuses to get out of certain duties and I began taking many more days off on the sick. Smoking and drinking seemed to help block things out but I was only fooling myself. At that time, we were at the forefront of the fight against terrorism in Belfast. We weren't sitting in some comfortable chair in a secure office but were out on the streets day after day, under constant threat of attack and death. Living under such strain for a protracted period almost inevitably leads to health problems and the fact that I had carried over serious trauma from my childhood had obviously reduced my ability to deal with the pressure I was now under.

I was to reach breaking point on Sunday, 12 August 1984. I paraded for duty at 2 p.m. and it started out just like any other day in the Belfast DMSU as Sergeant C detailed us for duty. At that time in the Province, we had a very unwelcome visitor by the name of Martin Galvin, an American lawyer. He was head of NORAID, a USA-based organisation set up to raise funds for the families of republican prisoners. Many of its members openly supported the IRA. Galvin had been refused a visa and had entered the country illegally. Our instructions were to police a rally in Andersonstown at which he was expected to appear and attempt to arrest him. I was to carry the M1 Carbine and FRG. It was made clear at the briefing that our attempts would be resisted and that we would probably end up in hand-to-hand combat with the nationalist community. On hearing this, many of the men got openly excited at the prospect of getting in some 'Paddy bashing'.

We arrived outside the headquarters of Sinn Féin at Connolly House on the Andersonstown Road at approximately 3 p.m. and I took up a defensive position facing the St Agnes chapel on the corner of St Agnes Drive. For the third time in my life, the name 'Agnes' was to prove significant but on this occasion, in a way, it also led me into a false sense of security.

A Sinn Féin anti-internment rally was approaching us from the direction of the city centre, led by people carrying numerous banners. To rapturous applause, they arrived in front of Connolly House and proceeded to raise their banners, thereby forming a screen in front of the offices in an attempt to hide someone or something from our view. It could only have been Galvin that they were trying to hide and, according to our orders, we now had to arrest him. It was obvious to me, however, that this was neither the time nor the place for such an act of bravado. The area was thronging with women and children, who would undoubtedly be put at risk by the reaction that would follow such a high-profile arrest. Sometimes I really did question the wisdom of many senior officers in the RUC. I felt they habitually churned out half-baked decisions resulting in widespread chaos that the men on the ground had to clear up.

At the appointed moment, a great cheer went out as Gerry Adams announced Galvin, who then appeared on the stand behind the wire of the Sinn Féin office. You could feel the air of excitement in the heaving crowd. After all, Galvin was one of their heroes.

We were told to get ready. I wanted to shout out, 'No way, get a grip!' But the police snatch squad headed straight for Galvin and had to fight a running battle to get to the front, crashing through all the women and children who were sitting on the road and creating a physical barrier to our progress. All hell broke loose. This was one of the most stupid operations I have ever seen in all my time as a policeman and one that I am not afraid to say filled me with deep shame. Women and young children were baton charged, hurt and trampled on, and for what – a feather in someone's cap?

We now started to get pelted quite badly from behind. The stones and bottles raining down were largely missing us because of the defensive cover of our vehicles. Instead, they were hitting the women and children involved in the peaceful rally. I saw one young girl, about ten years old, being hit full in the face by half a brick. I was unable to help as blood poured from her tiny face. I knew her nose was broken as I could see white bone showing through the torn flesh and blood. It was obvious to me that this child and the older woman with her were in deep trouble. At the end of the day, they may have hated my guts but I was still a member of their police force, supposed to help them and keep them from harm. But here I was, on the other side of the fence trying to beat them into subjugation: something was terribly wrong! The crowd, no doubt, would have killed me if I had broken ranks, such was the understandable hatred shown toward us that day, and there would have been a furore within RUC ranks if I were seen helping what they generally termed a 'Fenian' protester.

Galvin, on seeing what was starting to develop, escaped into Connolly House and the snatch squad soon gave up their pursuit, no doubt under orders from HQ after seeing just how ugly a scene was starting to develop. 'What was the bloody point? This is fucking stupid,' I remember angrily shouting out to one of the other members of my unit.

We were now being hit by stones thrown from the roof of the shops behind us. Petrol bombs were raining down, hitting the vehicles beside me. I took up my position as riot gunner and aimed at the rioters throwing from the corner of the chapel. At that time there were new instructions in relation to the use of plastic bullets. Before you could fire them you had to get the OK from your sergeant or senior constable, wherever he was. Permission granted, I picked out the main throwers and started to fire. At no stage did I make a conscious effort to hit any of them. After the events of my first day on duty, I had vowed to myself I would never again take deliberate aim at another person. My actions were, therefore, an attempt at keeping their heads down and it was working.

I appeared to be the only one exercising any degree of control, however. Baton rounds were being fired indiscriminately into the crowd and people who were not threatening us in any way were being hit. There was mass panic, people were running and screaming, and I genuinely started to fear for our own safety as some of the crowd started to break up individual metal railings to use as spears. We were now caught in a bottleneck created by the protesters hiding behind our Hotspurs and the furious mob in front. We had no choice but to sit and take the hammering, while I could see the injured being carried away from the front of the crowd at Connolly House. I ran out of ammo and had to bang on the Hotspur door beside me for more plastic bullets. The hostile crowd realised I was out of rounds and made a run towards our line. White with fear, our bloody driver locked himself inside the vehicle and refused to open the door until the sergeant ordered him to do so. I grabbed the bag myself and fired off a few rounds to beat the crowd back to the corner.

The riot went on for most of that day and well into the evening, and we never fully regained control until reinforcements arrived from the city patrols. The fresh DMSU took up position behind the rioters and, by using their snatch squads to make numerous arrests, they removed the sting from the rioters' offensive. When it was quelled somewhat, we departed and headed for a well-needed break at Grosvenor Road RUC station.

It was only then we heard that a plastic bullet had killed a former republican prisoner by the name of Sean Downes. I went cold. At that stage, no one knew who had fired the fatal shot. Visions of my first day's duty and the hell I went through came flashing back. I was having real problems composing myself and had to go off for a while to have a smoke in a quiet corner of the yard and gather my thoughts. My mind was racing as I experienced a glut of emotions: relief at still being alive, fear, dread, trepidation and exhaustion. I mentally recalled all the shots I had fired, trying to eliminate myself, but I knew full well these things are so bloody inaccurate that the fatal shot could have been anyone's. To make matters worse, as the shot had apparently been fired at point-blank range, it could be construed as murder.

While I was at Grosvenor Road station, I had to fill out a form relating to the rounds I had fired. No real detail was required at that stage; it was just a matter of filling in the blank spaces on this official document. There were only six baton gunners present at the scene and we were all under suspicion. I was appalled by the way our authorities were commencing a witch-hunt, apparently not giving a damn about what we might be going through. In the corridors of power in Grosvenor Road station, the midnight oil was burning in every head of department's office as they hunted for some poor sod to crucify. At the end of the day, our authorities must have known they had fucked up big style and no doubt wanted a scapegoat to deliver to the press.

Among the many critics of our actions on that day was the Catholic Bishop of Down and Connor, Dr Cahal Daly. He said:

> The display of force and the use of force by the police cannot be said to have been justified by the behaviour of the crowd, or to have been in proportion to it. Widespread indignation has been aroused even among moderate and peace-loving people who are totally opposed to paramilitary violence.

The Economist declared:

> This has given the IRA success beyond its wildest dreams. Police officers either panicked or went on the rampage, firing off plastic bullets in contravention of their own rules. Sean Downes died on camera and the IRA gained a fresh martyr.

We returned to base at Castlereagh and finished late that evening. Everyone pissed off home straight away, no doubt feeling – as I did – ashamed and in no mood for a crew drink to a job badly done. There was no debrief, no advice and no one to talk to. Jesus Christ! I just needed to get this off my chest. I was heaving inside and found it hard to compose myself enough just to make it home. I didn't even change out of my uniform; I just put my jacket over my filthy green shirt, not caring that I was putting myself in danger of becoming an IRA target.

It was the journey home that represented the greatest danger for policemen. Republican terrorists were astute enough not to attempt to follow an RUC man to his home in one journey, as this practice would have attracted the attention of even the most inept officer. Instead, they would wait in the shadows, breaking the journey into sections over the following few days. Many members were followed to their homes in this fashion only to discover an under-car bomb the next morning. Unfortunately, several policemen failed to discover these devices and paid with their lives.

A small bomb strategically placed under the car's floor pan beneath the driver's seat or behind the driver's side front wheel can do a lot of damage. This, without a doubt, has been the terrorist's greatest weapon in their sordid arsenal. The device can be made quickly and packed into a small plastic lunch box with a small amount of commercial high explosive, a detonator, battery and timer all taped up to a large magnet. A couple of seconds is all that is needed for the terrorist to get it in position and make their escape. The timer would usually be set for some minutes as a safety device to ensure the safe attachment to the target car before the circuit would become live. Premature explosions caused a considerable number of deaths of republican activists. After the bomb was planted and armed, any movement of the car would trigger the mercury tilt switch and it would explode.

The ironic thing was that these devices were very easy to spot. We were all shown how to find them and it was stressed that we should always look under our own cars before getting into them. It could be done very easily and as cover you could deliberately drop your keys and have a look while you were picking them up again. Human nature being what it is, though, complacency often set in and for some officers it became a bit of a chore to check every time they got into their cars. I have to admit that I also fell out of the habit of carrying out that vital search.

Some years later, all police personnel were given the opportunity to have their own personal cars fitted with a simple device under the carpet that would detect a bomb placed under the car. It was a magnetic detection unit wired up to a series of lights that were hidden from pedestrian view and would show if your car had been tampered with. These units worked very well but then the old enemy of the peeler set in again – laziness. The units had to be removed each time the car was due a service or was being sold on but in many cases they weren't. The terrorists soon learned about these devices: again the Ulster policeman shot himself in the foot by his own carelessness.

Another precaution we could take was to change our car number plates. We simply had to apply in writing to our authorities and we would be supplied with bogus numbers that did not check out to our home address. An even simpler measure was just to change our routes and times of departure from our stations. Gary, a good friend of mine who worked in the border station of Rosslea, sometimes varied his route so well that he even crossed over into the Irish Republic and rode his motorbike through Monaghan on his way home to Newtownards – though his authorities frowned upon this practice, it perhaps saved his life.

On my way home that night, I called into the Fox and Hounds pub in Newtownards and got really drunk in the company of another policeman I met there. He was stationed in Bangor and was fully aware of the mess in Andersonstown. He had the greatest sympathy for me but his words of encouragement didn't help me at all as he said, 'Sure, the Fenians deserved it.'

When I eventually arrived home, Agnes was visibly shocked at my appearance. She had heard about Downes' death on the news and wanted to know if I had been there. I was so ashamed that I hadn't the heart to tell her that potentially I had been involved in his death, so I said I had been there but in the background and then told her that I had met an old friend for a drink on the way home.

I reported for work reluctantly the next day, knowing full well what was in store. It was patently obvious our authorities were looking for some poor sod to hang. I felt this was to be a public relations exercise: a character assassination of a policeman who had done wrong in the eyes of the public would take the heat off headquarters about the events that day. I was crapping myself: a man was dead and I was really scared that they might try to pin it on me.

I had no sooner signed on duty than I was told to see my inspector in his office. 'Shit! This is it,' I thought. I was half expecting handcuffs and an escort to Grosvenor Road station for interrogation.

Our inspector was not the best man-manager in the world and, to be perfectly honest, not even the best police inspector. He had an uncanny knack of avoiding trouble. It appeared to all within our unit that he just wanted to reach his retirement as easily as possible with no problems. When he was on patrol and calls would come over the radio, his crew would cry out in exasperation as he ordered the driver not to respond and leave the call for some other crew.

He informed me that there was to be an investigation to identify the baton gunner who had killed Sean Downes. My heart sank and I went cold. He informed me in a condescending voice, totally devoid of emotion, that there were two detectives from B division coming later that evening to take a statement from me under oath. I got the impression he wanted me to make an admission there and then to get him off the hook.

The detectives arrived at the appointed time and I have to admit that they were very sympathetic about the situation I was in and put me at ease straight away. They were, after all, only doing their job and I had no problem with them. I was questioned for three hours and had to report on every single shot I had fired the previous day: at whom, what were they doing, what were they wearing, did they go down, etc. It was without a doubt the most severe grilling I had ever received, even compared to the witness box of the High Court. Once it was over, however, I felt I could relax a bit, as it was now all down on paper and not a muddled mess in my head. I had explained my role and actions, and felt much better for it. On paper, my defence looked good. Before leaving, they warned me that my statement would be checked to make sure that it tallied up with what was recorded on the 'heli-telly' (the camera pictures taken by the army helicopter), which, unbeknown to us at the time, had recorded the whole incident on film. Just when I thought it was all over, having given my statement, I was going to have to wait even longer to be cleared. The rest of the evening I was useless and didn't go out on duty at all. I was exhausted.

The next day it was reported on the news that a Reserve constable in the Royal Ulster Constabulary was being questioned concerning the death of

Sean Downes. My first reaction was one of relief but then I felt sorry for the poor sod. The officer involved was eventually acquitted in 1986 of a manslaughter charge but those two years had taken their toll on him.

As far as I was concerned, however, this incident had been the final straw. I had had enough. I had to get out of the DMSU, as I just couldn't take it any more. There were a lot of men in DMSU units who positively thrived upon the very situations that were troubling me so deeply. They seemed to openly revel in the hurt and harm they inflicted upon the Catholic community: a mindset that was alien to me. As far as I was concerned, I had never chosen to become a member of the DMSU and I don't think I would ever have applied to join. I am of the opinion that my authorities back in 1981 made a very grave error in sending me to that unit straight from training. I was not suitable at all and feel it ultimately denied me the opportunity to become an effective policeman.

CHAPTER 14

BEING AT THAT LEVEL OF STRESS FOR SO LONG HAS ITS PRICE

Even though my decision was made, I still had to carry on as usual for nearly a year after that fateful day. I performed all duties required of me while also trawling through the weekly force orders (vacancy bulletins) in a concerted effort to find another department to which I could transfer – anything to get me away from this living hell on the street. I felt I had reached breaking point. I was so low I even contemplated packing the whole job in there and then after the Downes' investigation.

Then, all of a sudden, I had a stroke of luck. No! I think it was divine intervention.

I was driving a Land-Rover around Belfast late at night patrolling the D division interfaces – notorious trouble spots between Catholic and Protestant housing areas just off the Antrim Road. During a quiet spell in the evening, Sergeant P, sitting beside me, asked: 'Eddie, have you ever thought of doing the advanced driving course?' Well, what a shock that was. In all my time in the police, I don't think I had ever come across an advanced police driver. They were a rare and elite breed in those days and only ever seen in the traffic branch or other specialised units. Those lads who were not yet sleeping in the rear of the wagon were in stitches at Sergeant P's suggestion. 'Piss off, sarge. He's a bloody awful driver' and 'Has he got a licence at all?' were some of the milder pieces of banter they threw at him.

'Why, skipper? Do you think I could do it?' I asked him.

He replied, 'Without praising you too much, Ed, you're a bloody good driver.'

Something inside told me that this was my passport out of the DMSU.

Sergeant P was one of the best and most able sergeants I ever came across in the police in my 20-odd years of service. He had the uncanny knack of knowing exactly what was going on within the minds of his men and was always there to help his crew, day or night. I think, in a way, he knew just how low I was getting and wanted to help me in the best way he could. I only wished I had worked with him more often, as I am sure he would have noticed the difficulties I had been having sooner and been of more help to me in the early years of my RUC service.

This off-the-cuff remark set me on a roller-coaster. Over the course of the next few days, he made a call to his mate Jimmy in the driving school and sorted me out with a place on the next advanced driving course. Normally, this process would take some months, if not years, but I think he knew it would be best to get me off the streets as soon as possible.

Now I was crapping myself again but for very different reasons. This was, after all, the ultimate course in relation to driving standards within the police. I don't think I had ever looked forward to anything more in my whole period of service.

My big day came at last and I reported to the RUC driving school at Lisnasharragh on 9 September 1985, feeling like a kid on his first day at school. I was in for a shock, however. Before I arrived I was pretty confident that I was a good driver; I soon found out that I was hopeless!

On the first morning, I was taken out on an assessment drive and shown all my inherent flaws. I had apparently developed some pretty bad habits since passing my basic course four years previously. They started me as a complete rookie and in the space of four weeks turned me into what I would describe, without wanting to sound egotistical, as a very good driver. I attained, at the first attempt, an advanced grade 1 pass: the highest it is possible to achieve. I was therefore entitled to drive any of the fastest cars in the force. Mind you, I really had to work very hard for it and put in maximum effort. My final drive was at over 120 mph in a Ford Granada 2.8i along the Ballygowan Road outside Belfast while giving a running commentary as to what was going on around me and the state of the road ahead. You would have thought I had won an Olympic gold medal to see me that night as I relaxed over a celebratory meal with my fellow students. I was then invited to join the Institute of Advanced Motorists.

After this success, it was back down to earth with a bang. I had to return to the DMSU as there were no vacancies for me in traffic branch or any other units at that time. I continued my role in the DMSU as before, but at least now I had some hope of eventually getting out. I was just putting in time.

Before I could escape, however, things were starting to turn really ugly on the streets of Northern Ireland due to the signing of the Anglo-Irish Agreement at Hillsborough on 15 November 1985. Co-signed by the British Prime Minister, Margaret Thatcher, and the Taoiseach, Dr Garret FitzGerald, the document was by far the most wide-ranging political development since the opening of the Northern Ireland Parliament by King George V on 7 June 1921. It committed both governments to a closer working relationship in the affairs of Northern Ireland.

For the RUC, the result of the agreement was that not only were we faced with the ongoing republican threat but we also now had to contend with something that would prove even more serious, especially for RUC men living in relatively safe Protestant areas – the loyalist backlash.

After the signing of the Anglo-Irish Agreement at Hillsborough, the Chief Constable Sir John Hermon briefed his senior officers about its contents and issued a message to the wider force dispelling some of the rumours circulating about the agreement's implications for the RUC. 'Politics is not the business of the RUC, our business is policing,' the statement said. He went on to assure us that the RUC would remain the RUC, complete with its green uniform and existing badges. He pledged that the force would remain free from political interference and explained how he would work, under the terms of the new agreement, to improve cooperation across the border with the Irish police.

In an effort to bolster morale, he expressed his pride that the RUC had remained steadfast in spite of the heavy burden it carried and went on to say that other decent people outside the RUC shared that pride. He believed that the majority of the people of Northern Ireland had great confidence in the RUC and assured them that his force would do all it could to prove worthy of that confidence and increase it. He concluded by stating that our future lay in our abiding dedication to serving all the people of Northern Ireland impartially and justly, without fear or favour, without regard to religion, class or creed.

None of these proud words could do anything to prevent the backlash that was heading our way. On 23 November 1985, a vast crowd, approaching 300,000 strong, gathered at Belfast City Hall to protest at the agreement. I was on duty with my unit and was standing at the corner of Donegall Square North and Donegall Place observing what was happening. Thank God the event passed off without serious incident, as we were outnumbered by thousands to one.

The loyalists went into another paroxysm of rage in December when the first meeting of the new Anglo-Irish Conference took place in Belfast. The sight of the Irish Foreign Minister and his officials flying into Stormont by army helicopter was just too much for them to bear. Several arrests were made among the assembled hostile crowd of protesters as the police defended a barbed wire fence erected around Stormont Castle. Hundreds of workers from the Shorts Aircraft factory and Harland and Wolff shipyard downed tools and marched in protest to the new Anglo-Irish Secretariat at Maryfield. They pulled the security gates down with their bare hands but the police beat them back with baton rounds. In all, nearly 40 police officers were injured in clashes that afternoon. The following Saturday, protesters marched again on Maryfield. Trouble broke out and a police car was overturned and set on fire; another 23 RUC officers were injured.

A few days later, there was a meeting of nearly 400 concerned policemen in the Police Federation's social club at Kilroot outside Carrickfergus. I attended this packed meeting, along with many men from my unit who were interested in the way forward for the force. There was a growing atmosphere of suspicion throughout the force at that time and we felt that we were slowly but surely being sold out by the politicians. Unbeknown to us, a secret tape recording was being made of the meeting and this was played at a news conference a few days later by one of the Rev. Ian Paisley's friends, the Rev. Ivan Foster. Once again, the personal views of policemen found their way to Paisley's door to be used for his own political ends, delivered no doubt by another unscrupulous officer who had infiltrated the force.

Foster was clearly excited by two speeches by sergeants, which were greeted by whistles and applause. One of the sergeants was heard on the tape asking our Federation chairman, Alan Wright:

> Are you prepared to convey from this meeting tonight the complete disgust which the members of the Police Federation have both in the Police Authority, their political masters and the Chief Constable for their recent collaboration in the system that has rendered the RUC a political puppet in the eyes of the people of this country?

Wright lambasted the recording as 'an irresponsible betrayal of trust' and the Police Authority said: 'The views expressed in no way reflected the attitude of the majority of RUC officers.' But they did. We, the men on the ground, were furious at this stage at what we saw as betrayal by our authorities. They appeared to be acceding to the wishes of the politicians while the men under their command were under ever-greater danger both out on the streets and at home. Attacks on police houses had started again and continued to increase both in number and ferocity. One such arson attack was on a family who were watching television when petrol bombs were thrown through their living room window. A part-time female Reservist and her mother escaped from their home with their clothes on fire after their door had been battered down and petrol bombs thrown, only to be greeted by a jeering crowd in the street. Another Reservist was shot in the hallway of his North Belfast home. Other officers woke to find their homes ablaze or full of smoke and had to run for their lives. It was now common to see daubed on gable walls: 'Join the RUC and come home to a real fire'. 'Buy and die' was also painted on many homes abandoned by police families.

While we were out fighting on the ground, we were now also burdened by concern for our families at home, as they were very vulnerable. The camaraderie within the RUC saw us rally to protect those at risk. Many men, including myself, patrolled like vigilantes after work in an attempt to ensure the security of neighbourhoods of serving members who were on duty. The Loyalist Day of Action on 3 March 1986 could be seen as the breaking point in relation to the confidence, whether real or imaginary, between the RUC and the unionist cause, and it was felt by many in the loyalist camp that the RUC was no longer 'their' police force.

While these problems were ongoing, I continued to look for a way out of the DMSU and one day I received a strange request from Nat, our station sergeant. It appeared that a branch called the 'VIP escorts' required a grade 1 advanced driver for the day and he wondered if I would be interested.

'Who the hell are the VIP escorts?' I remember asking Nat. He told me that they were a group of plain-clothes policemen based just around the corner at Lisnasharragh RUC base and they escorted and protected all the VIPs in their charge. 'Jesus, I was five years in this bloody job and I never knew they were there,' I said to him.

With some trepidation, I agreed to the request and reported to the VIP escort branch for duty. I dusted off the only suit I had to my name and it was like a de-mob suit from after the war. In fact, I think it was the very suit I was married in. Wine-coloured and complete with ultra-wide lapels and flared trousers, it looked hideous but, seeing it was only for one day, it would have to do.

Wow! What a first day that was. I was detailed to drive a Rover 3.5 V8 as tail car to Lord Lowry, the Lord Chief Justice. This was a 'hell for leather' drive all the way from his home in Crossgar to the law courts in Belfast, boot to the board, horns and lights at every slow driver blocking our path. We would make a third lane where one didn't exist up the middle of the white line, flashing our lights at other drivers who were in fact on their own side of the road. 'Christ, this is crazy,' I said to the lad beside me.

In those days there certainly was a high terrorist threat to the lives of senior members of the judiciary but I was now of the opinion that there was far more chance of them being killed in a car crash. Then I thought to myself that maybe this little bit of showboating was for my benefit, as the old hand driving the lead car was obviously trying to lose me. I later found out that this branch was indeed rife with such seasoned officers with chips on their shoulders. They felt they had nothing to learn, as they had been there and done all that in relation to their police service.

Somehow we arrived safe and well at Chichester Street and delivered the Lord Chief Justice to his chambers. What a baptism of fire that day was, but I thought I could get to like it. Security was very tight in this unit. I had been in the police for five years now and yet these bodyguards were still very cagey, telling me no more than I needed to know. In later service, I would come to understand this secrecy myself and became very coy about telling others what I was doing. I had thoroughly enjoyed this VIP escorting, though. I knew this was the type of work for me and I wanted more but unfortunately I was only a relief driver and that's all I would be for the foreseeable future.

Things at home had improved a lot due to my new-found goal in life. I began to appreciate Agnes more than ever and Robert and Cassandra formed new bonds with their previously elusive father. Family days out and holidays, once so rare, were now common occurrences. Cassandra still talks about her enforced trips to museums and castles around my favourite retreats in Scotland. In the past, I had been away from home during all the daylight hours and they saw precious little of me. Now, I was enjoying more time off as more reinforcements were being drafted into the DMSUs, providing welcome relief to very hard-pressed men. The war was by no means over but at last it seemed as if it was going our way.

Things also seemed to be going my way when I was made aware of an imminent force order looking for men to join the VIP escort branch. I could not believe my luck. I think I was the first to apply and after a while I was granted my interview board at the RUC training centre.

As anyone who has ever sat a board will understand, you never ever know what you will be asked during the interview but luck was on my side that day. As I sat in the waiting room passing time before my turn, I picked up a newspaper and nonchalantly perused a short article concerning the proposed merger of the SDP and the Liberal Party. After some questions on basic security measures, the remaining questions were on current affairs and the political scene, focusing on the merger. I think the chief inspector on the selection board thought he was being very smart by asking me questions on such an obscure topic but I showed him. I waffled my way through the advantages and disadvantages and the expression of total confusion on his face said it all; I had no doubt that he had expected to catch me out!

I was selected. All I had to do now was pass a physical and firearms assessment at a later date, both of which I found very easy. I had been training in preparation and was again at a high degree of physical fitness, and was also very competent with a gun, having won the title of DMSU Marksman in 1983, taking the William Pollock Cup. This award was in memory of a sergeant who died in a Hotspur crash in the city some years earlier and the trophy was awarded to the DMSU member who attained the highest aggregate score at all weapons-training sessions throughout the Belfast units in that year. After these assessments, there was the intensive and physically demanding three-week bodyguard course and I was in! I was moving to the VIP escort branch as a police bodyguard based at Lisnasharragh; I was out of the DMSU. Thank God – I could now forget all that had happened before, or so I thought!

Subconsciously, my entry into the VIP escort branch felt like I was running away from uniform service on the street but then I also felt that I had spent five years at the coalface and therefore had done my bit. My sentiments matched those of my ex-Chief Constable, Sir John Hermon, who said in his autobiography: 'Being at that level of stress for so long has its price, a price I feel will have to be paid in future years.'

The VIP escort branch, as it was known in 1986 when I joined its ranks, was fairly disorganised. It had been established in 1974 to provide police bodyguard protection to certain 'high-threat key figures' in society and was, by and large, manned by more mature officers who had been drafted into the ranks at its inception. In 1990, the branch was renamed the Close Protection Unit (CPU), after its move to Dundonald RUC station. Each VIP was assigned two bodyguards, who took it in turns on a daily basis as driver or protection officer. I was shocked to see that many of these bodyguards were grossly unfit and lacked the polished appearance that one would expect from a unit dealing with such a high level of terrorist threat here in Northern Ireland. I think I had expected them to look like the members of the US Secret Service I had seen in films, while the reality was very different. I formed the impression very early on that many men were behaving more like butlers and chauffeurs than bodyguards, and I could immediately see that this would have serious security implications. Many men were openly pandering to the foibles of their judges and government ministers rather than drawing a line in the sand in relation to their security duties and what was expected of them. All around, I detected a nepotistic, almost Masonic influence in the day-to-day running of the VIP escort branch: some men could do no wrong. Like the 'Three Legs of Mann', they always landed on their feet no matter how they fell!

Many of the already established officers were opposed to change of any kind and it was therefore with cheerful insincerity that new members were welcomed into the branch. Some old hands even went to the extent of changing newcomers' duties to suit their own selfish needs. This happened right in front of my very eyes but the arrogant offender changed his tune and re-altered the duty sheet when it became apparent I was not to be trodden on.

Money, or more precisely overtime, seemed to be the driving force for many of them and all methods were used to 'bump up' their figures, including claiming for non-existent duties and meals. The stories of men signing on in the morning and then heading off to the golf course or boat club, only returning to sign off again that evening, were rife and it was a standing joke that men could not get in the gate to start work in the morning because of men leaving after having signed on. If you didn't go along with the schemes that were in place, you were sent to Coventry, labelled a 'firm's man' or even worse – a tout.

For my first year, I was placed on what was termed 'the float': I would move from crew to crew on a daily basis, filling in for absent members. This was very good practice in that it gave me great insight into what was to be expected from each member of the team and, indeed, the VIP, otherwise known as the 'principal'. But as there were only 36 men in the unit at that time it meant that we had to work very long hours indeed. On average, I was consistently working well over 100 hours of overtime per month and my home life began to suffer again as a result. The guilt of being an absent father dogged my everyday thoughts and the vows I had made regarding my own children's upbringing were now being broken daily as I spent less and less time at home.

Another negative point in the VIP escort branch was that there were so many personality clashes that teamwork was almost non-existent. There was not the same *esprit de corps* that had existed in the DMSU. If you asked someone to do something for you, even if it was of a trivial nature, you usually received the standard reply – 'Fuck off!'

There were some good lads in the unit who did their very best in the circumstances in which they found themselves. They kept their noses clean, were punctual, well turned out and carried out their role with some degree of professionalism. On the other hand, many were non-receptive to new ideas and to different approaches in relation to their duties, appearing to me to be stuck in a bit of a rut. This, I have no doubt, stemmed from the fact that they had spent far too long in that one branch. They had become egotistical and snubbed the ordinary uniformed policeman on the ground. I would hear complaints about this all too often and feel embarrassed as I was now being tarred with the same brush. To give an example, tales were rife that many VIP escort squad members were treating the uniform branch with utter contempt upon entering secure areas or while being stopped at vehicle check points (VCPs). These allegations were raised by a new chief inspector on his first day in the unit and, to my utter horror, he was lambasted there in front of the whole unit by one of the constables who called him a liar. As the offending officer was protecting a senior judge at that time, nothing was done about this blatant disrespect and it was brushed under the carpet as usual.

In an attempt to counteract this problem, a few men were transferred out to uniform duty for a period of approximately six months. By and large, it did bring them back down to earth and for a while upon their return to the unit they were almost human again. But, as is always the case in life, some slipped through the net and it was usually the worst offenders.

Despite these problems, there was fun was to be had. One incident that really sticks in my mind was when an old-timer we affectionately called 'Brains' tried to take some horse shit into work. After getting quite drunk, for some unknown reason Brains decided it might be a good idea to put some shit onto the inspector's desk. So he headed out in the middle of the night and borrowed a horse from a nearby field. He rode it bareback the length of the Castlereagh Road and, unbelievably, in through the gates of the high-security RUC Lisnasharragh base, past the dumbstruck guard squad. He tried as hard as he could to get the animal to go through the door of the inspector's office, as he wanted it to shit on his desk and then stay there to welcome the inspector in the morning. The horse decided he was having none of this, however, and the plan failed. As I have said, Brains was a good old-timer but when working with him I always had to retain the keys of our armoured car, as he would drive off to do his shopping at a moment's notice, leaving me high and dry with my principal by my side.

I think this would maybe be a good point to dispel some myths about being a police bodyguard in the Royal Ulster Constabulary, as there is nothing romantic about it at all. Whitney Houston does not sing 'I Will Always Love You' (the theme from *The Bodyguard* movie) each time you open your locker door, although I'd swear some of the more impressionable young officers can just about detect a distant echo! Most of the time, close protection duty is quite boring. You have to spend many hours sitting outside some dingy office or walking countless golf courses in the pouring rain or, worse still, shopping. If you are detailed to protect a judge, you will find yourself sitting in a stuffy courtroom all day listening to a mountain of legal jargon, most of which sails right over your head. When out in public, you are constantly aware of being scrutinised.

I doubt very much if any member of the CPU will ever dive and take a bullet for anyone. As one of our older men told the former government minister Richard Needham: 'I am the man who shoots the man who shoots you.' While the American President's Secret Service agents would undoubtedly lay their life on the line for their principal and be assured of a folded flag, here in Northern Ireland the situation is somewhat different. We have government ministers and politicians on short-term loan and with many I felt they were not even worth a cup of tea, let alone risking my life.

Many RUC men transferred into the RUC traffic branch because they wanted to specialise in traffic law. Many moved into CID because they wanted to investigate crime. Men wanted to get into the dog section because they loved working with dogs. But some men transferred into the VIP escort branch for nothing other than money. Tales of virtually unlimited overtime spread like wildfire throughout the force and we attracted men for all the wrong reasons.

After several months on the float, I was moved to a crew providing protection to Geoffrey Foote, a barrister or, more precisely, a Queen's Counsel. His claim to fame was that he had served as prosecution counsel on a number of highly sensitive terrorist trials, including some of the supergrass cases, and our authorities had seen fit to upgrade his threat status and supply him with permanent police protection. He was granted the protection of two bodyguards and an armoured Ford Cortina.

I now settled into a well-ordered life in the VIP protection branch. I believed that the horrors of the past had been consigned to history and the hinges of that now little-used chest of memories were clearly showing signs of rust. Nothing more was being stuffed under its bulging lid as I was out of uniform and away from harm on the street. I was feeling good about the world and myself, and had a sense of detachment from all the hurt and hatred spilling onto the streets of Belfast – it was now someone else's responsibility to clear up the mess.

This situation couldn't continue indefinitely, however, and just as I was beginning to feel that I had laid some of the trauma of past experiences to rest, I was confronted by even more death and destruction. I was horrified by the savage killing of the two army corporals, Derek Wood and David Howes, on 19 March 1988, and as Geoffrey Foote was directly involved in prosecuting the killers I had to sit through all the gruesome evidence in the courtroom during the preliminary hearings. I found this extremely traumatic and even to this day I shudder at the very mention of that event. Those two men were the victims of animalistic bloodlust and that incident was without a doubt one of the most visually shocking of the Troubles. Four television camera crews and an army helicopter camera captured the two plain-clothes soldiers being stripped and slaughtered. The combined video footage used in the subsequent trial was considered so inflammatory that the Lord Chief Justice banned it from ever being shown in public.

It was at times like this that I felt the horrors of the past haunt me again and I found it difficult to avoid breaking down. And yet I still considered protecting Geoff to be very good respite. He would be in the courts on an almost daily basis, thereby establishing some routine in my life. While socialising in the evenings, he would be relatively unknown without his wig and gown, and we could blend in very well with the rest of the crowd in the pubs and restaurants in the centre of Belfast. I protected this principal for nearly two years but by the end of this period I was starting to get a little bored. He was not at high risk and once his socialising increased, meaning a lot more unpredictable evening work, I started to look for a move onto another, more challenging crew.

CHAPTER 15

IT WOULD BE IN MY BEST INTERESTS IF I WERE TO PLEAD GUILTY

In the summer of 1988, I therefore secured a transfer to a crew protecting the Rev. Martin Smyth MP. I was excited about this appointment as it meant I would be able to exercise more of my new skills. Martin was an instantly recognisable public figure, so we always had to be on our toes. As head of the Orange Order, he had to attend many Orange Order parades around the Province. Tension on both sides of the sectarian divide was high, making it stressful work, and I have to admit that at times I did find myself questioning the use of policemen for blatant partisan protection! On dozens of occasions, I would have to walk along the side of the road during the marches, protecting him from a distance, as policemen, whether in uniform or on plain-clothes duty, are not allowed to be seen walking as part of an Orange parade, and rightly so. This 'distance' protection worked well until the time in Ballymena, not long after I had started working for him, when a bystander launched an attack on Martin. The attacker lunged forward at him using his umbrella as a cudgel. Quick as it happened, I managed to get between them and sent the brolly flying through the air. Uniform police then arrested the assailant and after questioning it transpired that he was not the full shilling and had a long-running grievance because Martin had signed his expulsion from the Orange Order for disreputable behaviour.

It was quite unnerving walking with the Orange lodges all over the Province. I suppose it would have been different if I had actually been a member of a lodge, as then I could have involved myself in the celebratory aspect of the journey. Every man on the parade knew exactly who I was and what I was doing there, and I never heard an angry word spoken, in fact quite the opposite. They would go out of their way to look after 'Martin's man', as they called me. But, then again, I was a policeman and therefore I was one of them in the sense that they were sure I must have been a Prod. At mealtimes, we were always fed with him at the head of the table and the obligatory prayers were always for the safe return of Martin and his men to their respective homes that evening. Such touches did little to dispel my discomfort, however.

Our authorities were going through a period of penny-pinching at that time and on one occasion this led to a threatening situation arising for Martin. Martin and his wife were returning to Northern Ireland after a holiday and were to board the ferry at Stranraer in Scotland for the sailing back to Larne. I met up with them in Scotland as arranged and, after securing his car on deck, we headed up to the motorists' lounge to settle in for what I thought would be an uneventful and peaceful crossing. There should have been two bodyguards with Martin at the time, but, as I have said, our authorities were trying to cut back and would not allow the extra expense for that journey. The driver was to start later that day and meet us upon docking at Larne.

To my horror, as we sat quietly in the lounge, all hell broke loose as coachloads of defeated Celtic football supporters boarded the ferry shortly after us. Celtic supporters were, by and large, from the working classes of the Catholic community in Northern Ireland and many were filled with hatred towards policemen and anything Protestant. Initially, we managed to escape their attention, as we were tucked away in the motorists' lounge, which was off limits to foot passengers. But it wasn't long before we were spotted.

Martin at that time would definitely have been a hate figure amongst hardened Catholics in Northern Ireland as, being the head of the Orange Order, he represented the leading edge of unionism. Some of the more placid among the Celtic fans did no more than make gestures and hurl verbal abuse at us. They knew full well that I was his police bodyguard and any stupid actions would have instant repercussions for them. But the drunks among them wanted their pound of flesh and taunted us to such a degree that other passengers were now starting to get concerned and move out from the lounge to seats elsewhere. Another passenger beside me identified himself as an off-duty police officer and offered his assistance if required. I asked him to get the purser, as there was no way I could leave Martin on his own.

Before he could move, however, the captain arrived, as by this stage the purser and other staff had moved the growing number of angry supporters to the most stupid place imaginable – the bar at the front of the boat. The captain offered us the use of his cabin and Martin thanked him but declined, saying that it would not be very diplomatic for him to be seen hiding from thugs and giving them the satisfaction of having us on the run, and in a way I agreed with him.

I have no doubt whatsoever that if it hadn't been for my presence on that crossing, those supporters would have thrown Martin overboard, such was the hatred that they showed. From that time onwards, after I filed a report telling my authorities I was no longer prepared to carry out that duty alone, no more one-man trips were allowed.

From my first week with Martin, I was puzzled by his many predictable and downright dangerous visits to a house just off the Antrim Road in Belfast. These visits always occurred when he had just returned from London after a day in Parliament and a clear pattern was being set. As he settled into the rear seat of our armoured car at Aldergrove Airport for what I thought was to be the journey home, I would instead hear the muffled instructions, 'Go to Evewilliam Park, please.' On arrival in this quiet cul-de-sac, the house would be in darkness save a dim light in the hallway. On my first night, I accompanied him to the door, as would normally be the case with any of our VIPs. But he then instructed me not to follow him again; in future we would drop him off at the bottom of the driveway. It struck me as being very strange that two highly paid police bodyguards were risking their lives and the life of a Member of Parliament unnecessarily. Even though the house nestled on the fringes of the republican stronghold of the Limestone Road, I could deal with the short-term terrorist threat; what concerned me more was the clear and predictable pattern of his visits – it was very bad practice. We were setting up a routine. Each night he was there, I could not relax at all. Rather than sit in the armoured car awaiting an attack, I would walk to the end of the cul-de-sac to stand guard beside some hedges or in the alleyway across the street with a Heckler and Koch machine gun tucked inside my overcoat. But the rear of the house was totally unguarded, a gaping loophole in VIP security that would never be closed. No one else had ever thought of the security implications: once again the greatest enemy of the policeman – complacency – had raised its ugly head. Any time I would suggest a change of pattern, I would be told in no uncertain terms to mind my own business but I wasn't to be swayed and took every opportunity to change the routine. Martin was, after all, the elected Member of Parliament for South Belfast, a minister of religion and the head of the Orange Order in Ireland: qualifications that would undoubtedly have made him a prime target for the IRA or any other republican group. Some years later, and after many more visits to Evewilliam Park, the friend he had been visiting moved to the other side of the city. This I thought was the end – indeed not. We carried on just where we had left off – only sitting outside a different house, this time in Carryduff.

On another occasion, I had to deliver Martin to one of the most vandalised and dilapidated Orange halls I had ever seen. It was very close to the Irish border in South Armagh and it was felt by the divisional commander that a whole DMSU from Newry was required to ensure our safe passage that night. It took ages to get the operation set up properly. At the nominated time, I met up with a police scout from Newry RUC police station, whose duty was to guide us to the hall. I have always found during my service in the police, and especially in this branch, that if you need something to be done, you should do it yourself. The scout on this occasion was so incompetent that he got us well and truly lost.

My driver and partner on that night was one of our more senior men. He sort of knew his way about this bandit country, thank God, as by now I was on the radio with the waiting unit who were getting very concerned by our delayed arrival. They tried to talk us through the route but we appeared to be coming from a totally different direction. I felt like throwing the scout out onto the road, as he was making wisecracks from the rear seat and seemed to think the whole thing was some great big joke. I lifted the loaded Heckler and Koch with its twin clipped magazines up from its resting place beside me and set it on my knee. I decided if we ran into an IRA roadblock, a common occurrence down that way, I might have to bail out with Martin should we find ourselves immobilised in any way.

Suddenly, I realised that things were worse than I had thought. 'Fuck! What are those yellow signs doing there beside the road? Christ, we're in the South,' I yelled at the driver as he stared out through the thick armoured glass, trying to figure out where the hell we were. Martin gave one of his usual little coughs from the rear seat just to remind us that he was still there and could hear my profanities. Frankly, I thought it was unavoidable in a situation like this.

I looked over at the driver and said, 'What the hell do we do now?' I couldn't believe the fact that we were in the South of Ireland with a fully loaded machine gun and two side arms: a situation that could find us in a local Garda police cell all night trying to explain. Thankfully, however, the driver was able to laugh at my concern as we then swung straight through the gates of the Orange hall just 100 yards back into the North.

'How did you do that, you big bluffer?' I asked him with a huge grin on my face.

'Short cut, my boy,' he replied, as if he had known where he was going the whole time. Maybe he did but I had never been so glad to see an Orange hall in my life!

The young sergeant in charge of the DMSU unit came running over to us straight away with a face like thunder and said, 'I didn't see you come over the border, OK?' I think he was scared stiff of getting into a paper war with his authorities over this impromptu border incursion.

'Yeh, no problems, skipper,' I said as I lit up a fag. 'I'm only glad we got here at all. Will you guide us out to Newry when we leave?' I then threw the scout out of our car and arranged for the DMSU to drop him off where we had picked him up.

We were starving, as we had been on the go all day, eating on the hoof as best we could. The Orange lodge members had the tea on and, while they were having their secret meeting behind locked doors in the main hall, we polished off a whole tray of buns and cake washed down by copious amounts of tea.

This duty with Martin only lasted for about 18 months, thank God. To be quite honest, I think that's long enough for any man to be at that stress level without risking fatigue and therefore problems later on. It was always more relaxing if he was working at his constituency office on the Cregagh Road in Belfast. He would spend hours at work there and I would get stuck into a good book as I sat in the reception area. But when he was out of the office and in town, we were constantly walking a tightrope.

It was at about this time that a new chief inspector arrived in the unit from an outside station. Within a short time of his arrival, he had made a very good and accurate appraisal of the unit, deciding that we needed more training to bring us up to a better standard of physical fitness. We had, in recent years, grown fat and lazy, as there was no official refresher training regime in place. Without someone in authority cracking the whip, it was sometimes hard to motivate men. He carried out a full report and instructed the firearms and physical training teams to prepare a course for us to complete to their satisfaction. I had no problems at all with his approach and carried out the training to the best of my ability.

The course, spread over a period of four weeks, was very hard indeed. Although it has to be said that I am no athlete, somehow I managed to scrape through, but some of the other members of our unit were shown in a very poor light. Some were so unfit and overweight that they had real problems in completing their set tasks. There were constant complaints of sore sides and shin splints. One of our older members found the physical preparations for the course so hard that it was generally thought to have led to him having a premature heart attack. He collapsed one morning while sitting in the armoured car about to go out on duty from our new base at Dundonald. His crewmates rushed him across the main road and into the Ulster Hospital but to no avail, as he died a short time later.

On the whole, however, this new regime had a very positive effect on the unit and it was encouraging to observe the men starting to work together as a team. Some members decided it would be a good idea if they were to meet up at base one hour before starting duty in the mornings for the purpose of physical training. This was a great idea and thoroughly enjoyed by all who participated, though quite frankly I found it bloody difficult to get myself out of bed at that time of the morning. The routine was to head out of base and run to the vast wooded and beautifully landscaped parkland surrounding Stormont Buildings, where exercises would be carried out at various stages on the run around this estate in the crisp morning air. This proved so popular that our authorities, on seeing so many 'dinosaurs' within the unit at least making an attempt, dubbed it 'Jurassic Park'. Never were there so many brand-new trainers and tracksuits seen running around the grounds of Stormont with their price labels blowing in the wind.

Late in 1989, I was moved to another crew, this time looking after a county court judge. At that time he was sitting at Craigavon and Armagh courts and I found it really interesting to listen to all the evidence and make my own judgements about the guilt or innocence of the accused. He was a notoriously difficult principal to work with, however. As a former Second World War pilot, he was a very independent man who rarely took advice from anyone, let alone a policeman. He was so independent that he would drive his own car to court on a daily basis; we could only follow. This might not sound so bad but we had to permanently tail him to ensure his safe arrival – and you just try doing this in rush-hour Belfast!

I had to be very tactful to avoid friction and therefore conflict. I was even praised several times by my authorities for being a somewhat steadying influence on the judge. I managed to do the job without the need for constant supervision, while his previous bodyguard had worn a path to the chief's office with all manner of trivial problems he could not deal with himself.

The Close Protection Unit had a great record in the protection of its VIPs. That is, if success can be measured in the fact that we didn't suffer any losses while they were in our care. On the terrorists' part, this was not for the want of trying, though. In the background, the terrorist groups were continually collecting information and planning attacks. Members of the judiciary in Northern Ireland have always been under serious threat from terrorism and, as a result, most of them have round-the-clock security. This is all well and good, but sometimes the system breaks down and single-mindedness takes over, resulting in total chaos. I feel such a breakdown led to the bleakest day our branch ever suffered; I openly cringed upon hearing the news while on duty in Belfast.

On 25 April 1987, one of Northern Ireland's most senior judges, Lord Justice Gibson, and his wife, Lady Cecily, were killed by a 500 lb IRA landmine outside Newry at 8.30 a.m. as they crossed the border after a holiday. They had just left their Garda escort in the South and were about to pick up the escort team from our branch as they crossed the border into the North. They had earlier returned to Ireland on the Dun Laoghaire ferry and as their names reportedly appeared on the passenger list it was suggested that this was how the IRA had learned of their travel plans.

The team from our unit due to meet them at the border was late in arriving at the crossing point, but in any case they could not have saved their lives as the bomb was well hidden. One of their permanent bodyguards was off duty that day, so the other man and a temporary member of the team were due to meet the judge at Killeen crossing point just outside Newry. These two men were later transferred out of our unit for some years and in fact one of them went back to his roots in England and never returned to the Province.

Even after such an atrocity, the judge I now worked for often failed to adhere to common-sense procedures in relation to his travel arrangements. But procedures within our unit were radically tightened up in relation to security and some, including myself, even questioned the wisdom of informing the Garda of advance movements of VIPs. All VIPs now travelled under pseudonyms agreed in advance with our unit and HQ. All movements, even on a daily basis, were logged in advance in writing and a permanent record kept by a desk-bound member. Scrambler telephones were installed and more secure radios requisitioned. Despite these measures, a year after the attack on Lord Justice Gibson, another bomb exploded at the very same spot. A similar device killed three members of the Hanna family who were travelling from Dublin Airport after a holiday in America. The family had no security connections whatsoever; the IRA mistook their Jeep for one owned by High Court judge Eoin Higgins, who was also returning from the United States. They had observed his every move since stepping off the plane at Dublin Airport; details were passed to another IRA volunteer at the border who then targeted the wrong vehicle.

The year 1990 was to be a particularly bleak time for me in the Royal Ulster Constabulary. One morning in March, I was driving one of our armoured cars to collect the judge when I was involved in a minor traffic accident on the Bangor Road just outside Holywood. For a few weeks before this event, I had been complaining of feeling unwell, suffering frequent bouts of nausea and tiredness, accompanied by occasional dizziness. I had already taken some time off work trying to get rid of whatever it was that was ailing me and I knew I should not have been driving that day. On the morning in question, I collided with a car in front of me. I didn't really remember the facts of the accident clearly and had to dig very hard indeed to find a reason for it. It wasn't a particularly serious accident, there was just some damage to the bumper and lights, and no one was injured. I was driving an everyday Ford Sierra saloon car that had the added weight of over half a ton of armour plate and glass, something that causes serious difficulties in relation to your overall braking distances. But, then again, I should have been driving within its capabilities, thereby being able to stop in the event of an emergency. I genuinely thought I had stopped just in time before being struck from behind and shunted into the car in front. I was so sure of this that it formed the basis of my official statement under oath to the investigating police sergeant from Holywood station.

A few days later, I was hit by a bombshell when I was told that my travelling partner on that day had submitted a totally contrary statement to the investigating sergeant, which made mine look like a farce. When pushed for a reason as to the obvious conflict in relation to his evidence, he would not divulge his reasons. He then lodged a claim for injuries based upon his statement. Even the sergeant was baffled about the discrepancy but had no option but to include it in his report. I was totally confused and quite concerned by this string of events, as it was putting me in a difficult position.

One week later, I had my driver's authorisation card removed and was suspended from driving pending the outcome of the case. This upset me greatly as I really felt I was not guilty and was now being driven around by the very man I felt was attempting to feather his own nest. Many of the other officers in our unit were horrified by his total disregard towards a fellow officer. Eventually, I was informed to my utter horror that the Director of Public Prosecutions was proceeding with a case against me for careless driving based on the evidence of this man. I was totally shocked and went into a fit of rage. I demanded I be removed from this crew, as I could no longer work with him. My request was denied, so in rage I went on leave for one week to cool down. I was even refused access to see his statement by the investigating officer in Holywood station.

When I returned to duty, I still had to work with him on a daily basis. He would be all sweetness and light, acting as if nothing had ever happened, as he tried his best to maintain some degree of normality in the crew. It got to the stage, however, where I couldn't even be in the same room as him. The atmosphere was horrendous and the other members of the unit had bought him a one-way ticket to Coventry.

On 6 July 1990, at approximately 9.30 a.m., while I was sitting at home having a cup of tea prior to attending the court case at Bangor courthouse, I received a very strange phone call. The caller's voice was totally unknown to me and when I pressed him for his identity, all I was told was that he was a senior officer from my own HQ. He told me in a somewhat stern voice that it would be in my best interests and those of the branch if I were to plead guilty. He did not want all the details of this case and details of the branch dragged through the court. He added that if I did this, my future in the unit would be secure. This was all he said before putting the phone down. I was puzzled and concerned, as I was not totally sure who it was on the other end of the phone. For all I knew, it might have been someone acting on behalf of the other man. As I arrived at the court, this turmoil was going around inside my head. I knew full well that my position within the branch was untenable and as a convicted driver I would have to be re-tested at a later stage to ascertain my competency to drive again at the police advanced grade.

With this advice in mind, and the fact that the magistrate was totally puzzled that there was no further evidence to submit, I changed my plea to guilty and was fined the token sum of £25. I knew from the expression on the magistrate's face that he too was disgusted this had come to his court at all. 'Such a waste of the court's time,' I overheard him whisper to the clerk of the court.

I was devastated. I now had a record for careless driving. My faith in human nature and the police was now totally shattered. I felt a crowbar fill my hands as I started to lift the lid on that old dusty chest of memories that had lain closed for so long in a darkened corner of my mind.

CHAPTER 16

'SOME COPE WITH STRESS BETTER THAN OTHERS'

As a result of that court case, my faith in the system was gone. I took a few more days off work and returned the following week but my self-respect was shattered. The lid of that chest of memories was now open to the elements and, try as hard as I could, I could not get it to close again – demons were spilling out all over the floor. I headed off alone on my motorbike to tour the coast of Donegal, maybe as some sort of escapism but more than likely just to get my head showered. Almost in a trance, I found myself drinking in a disgusting harbour-side pub in Killybegs, totally unconcerned about my safety even though it was fairly obvious I was an off-duty police officer. Terrorist assassination, I felt, would have been a blessing in disguise. I was in a mess. I didn't give a shit if they blew me away; inside I was heaving with anger at the whole bloody world. As the day wore on, I became more detached from reality. I was in a different world, especially after downing a few pints. I was as low as I could get.

The RUC was by now more aware of the effects of stress on its officers and was taking steps to deal with it. The Occupational Health Unit had been established in 1988 at the RUC's storage depot in Seapark and almost immediately began recognising Post-Traumatic Stress Disorder as a legitimate and debilitating condition, but it was still very difficult to detect those in need. 'We are all human beings,' said Deputy Chief Constable Blair Wallace. 'Some cope with stress better than others.'

After that day in Killybegs, I realised I wasn't coping at all. I was depressed and scared about what I might do, and having received information about the new OHU, I decided to try to reach out and contact someone who might be able to help me deal with my feelings and turn things around before it was too late. I made the call for help from a telephone box on the Holywood Road and the nurse I spoke to immediately put me at ease. She was very concerned about whether or not I was armed with my personal-issue gun but I had left it in my locker at work out of harm's way. I guess she was afraid I would use it on myself and I have to admit that the thought had crossed my mind many times. As we talked, she became so worried about my state of mind that she volunteered to drive across the city to collect me but I was able to make my own way over there. When I got to her office, I broke down completely. It was obvious that I was in need of professional help and I was signed off work immediately. I was on sick leave for the next eight weeks and, after a few sessions with the nurse at Seapark, I was informed that I was exhibiting the classic symptoms of Post-Traumatic Stress Disorder. It was a relief to find out that there was a name for what I was going through, and to realise that I wasn't alone in my suffering, but unfortunately the only help I was offered was an audiotape on relaxation techniques. I had thought that I might go through some kind of counselling process but maybe it wasn't available at that time.

To be fair, the relaxation methods on the tape did help in the short term. They included muscular relaxation exercises, breathing exercises, meditation, instructions on stretching, yoga, listening to quiet music, spending time in nature, and so on. And I also sought new ways myself to relieve the tension. Some positive recreational work and activities helped distract me from my painful memories. My new-found artistic flair for painting in oils became a way of expressing my inner feelings in a positive and creative way. This was very helpful as a means of improving my mood, limiting the harm caused by PTSD and rebuilding my life. But these distractions alone, I felt, were never going to facilitate recovery. I now believed I had to actively come to terms with the trauma I had faced in the past – I had to face my demons head on.

I ended up going back to work before the eight weeks were up and the reason for my premature return was simple. I had a surprise visit to my home from a sergeant from the CPU. He informed me that if I wanted to return to my position within the unit, then the person causing the conflict would be moved off the crew if I so wished. I wasn't really happy with this idea, as it would have marked me out among the rest of the men as a moaner, even if they detested the man themselves. I was unsure about just how much the sergeant knew of my case or indeed who had sent him. I trusted his words, though, and decided to return the following week. This was the first and only visit from anyone during the whole time I was off sick and it left me feeling quite odd: I kept getting the impression he knew more about my condition than he was letting on.

The prospect of returning to work filled me with utter dread and I felt all the good work of the past seven weeks slipping away. I was getting stressed out again at an alarming rate. Though I was able to get on with my work when I went back, I still could not muster the emotional strength to carry my personal-issue gun past the gates of Dundonald RUC station and home: I didn't trust myself any more. I knew that if at any time in the future I again found myself feeling so low, I would probably use it to kill myself.

Eventually, however, the cause of my professional demise was unceremoniously kicked off the crew and after that things started to improve. I even received more sympathy than I had expected from some of the other men. I re-sat my driving test on 24 October and gained another grade 1 pass, again at the first attempt. Once this hurdle was over, I started to feel better and was able to throw myself back into the job.

If the VIP to whom we were normally assigned left Northern Ireland on holiday or business, our responsibility for him or her would end after we delivered them to Aldergrove Airport outside Belfast. Due to our high security clearance and possession of passes, we would bypass all security measures and escort our principal straight to the departure lounge. Once we had seen the plane airborne, we could relax to a certain degree, safe in the knowledge that their security was now out of our hands – some other police protection team would meet them at the other side. While they were away, our operational planning office would re-detail us to other duties, usually filling in for absent members of other teams. On a summer's day in 1991, I was detailed to work with the Lord Chief Justice Sir Robert Lowry. As one of his regular minders was on holiday, I was designated to work with his permanent minder, 'Archie', as driver.

Lord Lowry, now deceased, was a golfing enthusiast and at every available opportunity he would make his way to Royal Portrush Golf Club on Ulster's north coast. While we in the RUC had our own idiosyncratic methods of curtailing the damaging effects of stress, the Lord Chief Justice took his anger out on a little white dimpled ball. Being a non-golfer myself, I could never fully appreciate the benefits of the game but it must have worked as we drove a totally different and stress-free man back home again after his round.

The links course at Royal Portrush is physically demanding, to say the least, and while the Lord Chief Justice may have been short in stature, he certainly made up for it with his powerful drive off the tee. His protection team would normally take it in turns to walk by his side for nine holes each. At this time, he was under very serious threat and his security was under constant review, so it was also deemed proper to provide us with a two-man tail car as back-up.

The crew providing protection to the Lord Chief Justice was generally considered by other members of the CPU to be unorthodox, to say the least. It seemed to all within the unit that they had complete freedom and worked totally without supervision. The major problem I encountered while working with them began on a bright sunny morning at the halfway drinks hut. This was strategically placed at the ninth hole, where the other crew member would make his way in the car for the changeover. That day it was decided I would walk the first nine holes and by the time I reached the hut, Archie was the worse for wear and the tail car was nowhere to be seen. Rather than bring shame and disgrace on the force by having him stagger over the remaining nine holes, I left him where he was out of sight.

After another few hours, we completed the eighteenth hole and went into the clubhouse. Somehow Archie had managed to drive the car back from the ninth unscathed. The Lord Chief Justice, always fond of a drink himself, turned a blind eye to what had gone on. I, on the other hand, was incensed. I was a police protection officer being dragged down into the gutter by those around me. Other very influential members of the club were by now fully aware of the failings of the Close Protection Unit and I just couldn't believe what was to happen next.

Just when I thought I could get Archie into the car and head home, the Lord Chief Justice commenced another eighteen holes with three other members of the judiciary! As Lord Lowry teed off, I was boiling with silent rage. I really had to work very hard at controlling my temper and rising blood pressure. It was nearly four hours before we returned to the clubhouse once more and I was by now burnt to a crisp by the afternoon sun. Archie was still where I had left him, sleeping in the front seat of the police car in full view of other club members – I was disgusted. Almost apologetically, the Lord Chief Justice woke Archie up as he placed his clubs and bag into the boot of our car. Archie arose as if nothing was out of the ordinary. 'Where the hell have you been? I looked everywhere,' he exclaimed. I felt my right hand make a fist and the only thing that stopped me from belting him there and then was the fact that I considered myself part of a disciplined organisation and didn't really want to stoop to his level. I wasn't going to take part in a slanging match in the car park, so I let my silence be my protest as I changed out of my walking kit.

To all intents and purposes, I was alone that day; I was protecting the Lord Chief Justice on the golf course without even the reassurance of a car to come to my aid. In humiliating fashion, I had to arrange potential cover from the other judiciary teams also out on the course with me. If anything sinister were to happen, then at least I could get him into an armoured car and away to a place of safety.

The ordeal was by no means over, however. By now I was starving and looking forward to dinner in the Magherabuoy House Hotel on the outskirts of the town. Usually we would take it in turns to eat and look after the security of the cars. Even this simple task was too much for Archie to manage but at least the tail car had now shown up again; it seemed they had felt it necessary to head back to Belfast and have a few hours at home!

I had elected to do the first stint of security duty outside in the car park. Half an hour later, a police dog team arrived to check out the grounds of the hotel and, to be perfectly honest, their presence made me feel secure and a bit more relaxed.

Archie and one of the other judges' drivers came out wiping their chins an hour later. He told me that my dinner was just about to be served in an annex room adjacent to where Lord Lowry and the other judges were sitting. It was now dark outside and I grew uncomfortable knowing that the car park was totally unlit. Archie and the other drivers were outside but I couldn't help feeling that the security of the cars left a lot to be desired. My suspicions were confirmed a short time later when I spied them heading back inside towards the bar. I was halfway through my steak, unable to relax and now troubled by the total lack of security outside. Next, I heard a car screech its wheels in the car park and I rose to look out the corner of one of the small windows. It was pitch-black outside; I could see nothing save the reflected moonlight glimmering off the roof of our car parked against the wall. I slammed my knife and fork down in rage and headed to the bar.

'Archie, will you go and see what's going on out there, please?' I asked.

'It's OK, Ed. I've just had a look, it's only some kids having a bit of fun in their car; they're away now.'

As I walked back to the table, I was racked with indecision about whether or not I should finish my meal or head back out to the car. 'Why the hell should I?' I heard a voice inside ask me. 'Surely to God I have the right to a meal after all I have been through today?' I gobbled down my last chips and washed them down into my now well-knotted stomach with my last slug of tea and headed out into the hall. I glanced into the bar only to see them all sitting in a group, hiding from the passing gaze of the general public. Not wanting to stoop to their level, I headed out towards the cars but soon realised I needed the keys. I entered the bar to looks of bemusement at my concern and asked Archie for the keys.

'For fuck sake, Eddie, chill out, will you? Do you want a drink?' Archie asked as he handed me the keys.

'No thanks,' I replied. 'I'll stay outside with the cars.'

As I turned and walked to the door, I could feel the daggers hit my back and could just about detect the snide comments of 'wimp', 'firm's man' and 'moaner' as they chuckled amongst themselves.

I stood at the top of the steps of the hotel, scanning intently for any sign of the police dog van but to no avail. Christ! My heart sank even further. Just when I believed our cars were reasonably secure, I came to the bitter realisation that they were, after all, totally unguarded! I tentatively walked over to them, scanning the scene for anything out of the ordinary, and I had a definite sense that something was wrong. CPU armoured cars have a distinct enough profile, with their flat armoured glass, and ours somehow did not look kosher – something was missing.

'Holy fuck!' I shouted out. Our magnetically attached electronic counter measures (ECM) aerials were missing from the roofs of both cars. Not just missing but the wires which passed through the gap in the closed doors had been cut; I could see the bright copper wire shining in the moonlight.

ECMs, or 'clocks' as we called them, are machines which emit a strong radio-blocking signal, thereby rendering a radio-controlled bomb useless. They were usually to be seen strapped to the back of an army foot soldier as he patrolled the streets of Northern Ireland. Our machines were exactly the same, only mounted into a plastic box placed into the boot of the car with a control wire leading inside the car. The ECM is a very special piece of kit indeed but the world and his wife knew we carried them, as the 'whiplash' aerials were a dead giveaway.

At times like this, the crass stupidity of some members of the RUC took my breath away; I was totally dumbfounded. I had been trying to tell them all bloody night that the cars were not to be left unattended and still they took no heed. Now, because of their stupidity, I too had been dragged into this mire of negligence and madness. But what concerned me more was the condition of the cars. If those so-called kids screeching about in their car had had the time and the courage to remove the aerials, then even the most inept terrorist could easily have planted bombs under both cars. I recoiled immediately as this realisation struck home. Now I was really worried!

I made my way back into the hotel and told Archie of his predicament. He thought I was kidding until he detected the gravity of the situation by the expression on my face. To be perfectly honest, I was by now shaking at the thought of those cars outside being compromised and rigged with Semtex. Archie, on the other hand, was feeling somewhat different. Within minutes, he was outside, had lit a cigarette and was in the car with the engine running. He gave no thought at all to his or anyone else's safety. But still I was not convinced. With a powerful torch I commenced my own very thorough search of the underside of the car.

'What are you going to do now?' I asked Archie.

'Fuck it,' he replied in his usual nonchalant fashion. 'We'll get another two aerials tomorrow and no one will know the difference, will they, Eddie?' he said, looking me straight in the eye.

'No,' I replied. 'You're wrong. *You* will get another two tomorrow, I'm not paying for your fuck up.'

A few minutes later, we got the nod from the clubhouse that the Lord Chief Justice was on his way out. I drove the car over to the steps, not really wanting to apply the brakes too hard just in case someone had indeed planted a mercury tilt-switch device and I had failed to see it. This time we got away with it but it put a whole new perspective on working with this team.

The Lord Chief Justice was pretty well oiled by this stage of the evening, so he was poured into the back seat of the armoured Granada and it was boot to the board out of Portrush. He never objected to being driven very fast, but he wasn't really conscious of it by this stage as he was wedged between the front and rear seats, fast asleep in the rear footwell. But as the journey progressed, predictably enough, he had to have a pee. There was something rather strange about seeing the Lord Chief Justice of Northern Ireland peeing on the hard shoulder of the M2 motorway outside Ballymena. Many cars flashed their lights and sounded their horns in amusement, not really aware that they were watching the cream of Northern Ireland's judiciary in full flow whilst holding onto his police bodyguard. Without further incident, we then delivered him home.

On arrival back at Dundonald, the fizz had somehow worn off the whole episode and I was only too glad to be signing off in celebration at another day's survival in the RUC. Archie, on the other hand, was already covering his tracks by fiddling the books. Each ECM had to be signed out and in each day in perfect working order, and in a clumsy attempt to avoid his responsibilities, he asked me to sign them in.

'No way, José,' I said. 'Do you think I came up the River Lagan in a bubble?'

Archie did indeed start work early the next day and bought two new aerials and replaced them unnoticed. Once again, a member of the CPU had failed in his duty but landed on his feet.

Other special duties with which I was involved included providing protection to special VIP visitors and, over the following years, I had the honour of driving most members of the Royal Family, two Irish presidents and was even on the team looking after President Bill Clinton during two of his trips to the Province.

I had been involved with protecting the Irish President Mary Robinson since her first visit to the Province in 1992 and was on duty on 18 June 1993 when she made one of her most controversial trips. Sergeant C and I were always selected for protection duty with the Irish President; it seemed we had built up a certain rapport with her and, more importantly, her Irish government entourage. Apparently they derived a certain comfort from seeing familiar faces each time they stepped out of the tiny Irish Air Force One.

Just when it was thought by many that she was showing sensitivity to unionist feelings with her recognition of the war dead, her visits to the scene of the IRA bomb explosion in Warrington and to the Queen, Mrs Robinson paid an unofficial visit to a community festival in Belfast that was opposed by the British government and Northern Ireland Office. During this visit, she met with Gerry Adams and shook his hand, causing widespread anger throughout the unionist community, even though the meeting took place out of the public gaze and away from the cameras. They were furious that she seemed to be recognising Sinn Féin as a viable political party at a time when the IRA was still a fully operational terrorist organisation. At this time, however, Mrs Robinson was fully aware of the efforts being made for a republican ceasefire, having read the Hume–Adams document in Londonderry the year before.

In the run-up to the visit, there were indications that it would be difficult for us to be able to guarantee Mary's security on this trip. RUC headquarters and, more importantly, my own office therefore insisted a few days before the visit that they would have to send a large security presence into West Belfast to protect her. But on the morning she was due to arrive, it was made extremely clear by the organiser of the meeting, Inez McCormack, that a large security presence would be seen as a political act, that it would turn a community visit into a confrontational situation and that we would have to take responsibility for that. When the local police commander turned up with over 20 officers, the President's team negotiated a deal – only half a dozen officers would enter the Rupert Stanley Training College in the Whiterock Road to guard stairs and exits.

This was hostile territory for the Close Protection Unit. Our senior officers were apprehensive and nervous – you could see it on their faces. I was armed, guarding the entrance to the main hall, where the local thugs were incensed at our presence and made us most unwelcome. At every opportunity they would deliberately try to instigate a confrontation, only refraining when the Irish officials intervened and warned Sinn Féin to 'call off their dogs' or the visit would be cancelled.

When Mary met Gerry Adams and others, after the cameras had gone, he simply said '*Cead mile failte*' (one hundred thousand welcomes). After this, we headed back out to our cars and found the West Belfast Festival was in full swing. There was Irish music and dancing, and an exhibition of crafts. A local man presented Mary with a bodhran and her husband was given a walking stick. Even though no pictures of this historic meeting were made available, the story was all over the news that evening.

The next day we arrived early at the Culloden Hotel outside Belfast, where she was staying, and prepared to whisk her off to Coalisland for another full day of visits. There was a tense atmosphere and I could see the silent rage on the faces of the Irish officials when it became apparent that the President's pre-arranged hairdresser had failed to turn up at the hotel; they had no doubt it was a protest by those who disagreed with her actions the previous day. She waited and waited but the hairdresser never arrived. It seemed obvious to me that the hairdresser had said 'stuff her' to the woman who had dared to shake the hand of Sinn Féin leader Gerry Adams.

The prospect of Mary Robinson facing a full day of visits to County Tyrone with dishevelled hair brought into play our social skills as we went out of our way to find a suitable replacement. My sergeant and I immediately made numerous calls by phone and radio to our base in an effort to get a hairdresser there before her press conference later that morning, as the press would have had a field day.

Before anyone could be found, however, she had to go ahead and visit Coalisland without having her hair done. Republican activist Bernadette McAliskey (née Devlin) used the occasion to protest against sectarian killings of Catholics and there was a very funny moment at Coalisland Heritage Centre where Devlin was heard to say, 'And she didn't even get her hair done to come and see us!'

When Mary arrived at Balance House, the home of former New Zealand premier John Balance, later that morning, a hairdresser was waiting and the damage was repaired before she faced more of the public and, more importantly, the press. The President was very grateful and she took the time to personally thank us, which was much appreciated.

Mary Robinson did a lot of good work with her trips to the North and she reached out to both unionist and nationalist communities, but overall I would agree with people who said there were too many visits. During the 18 trips she made to Northern Ireland, she attended Catholic and Protestant events, cultural and community gatherings; she attended the funerals of

Senator Gordon Wilson and of his son Peter; but it is always the trip during which she shook hands with Adams that is remembered.

In 1997, when Mary Robinson resigned to take up the position of UN High Commissioner for Human Rights, she was replaced by Mary McAleese, a professor of law at Queen's University in Belfast. While McAleese was a popular appointment among many sections of the community, her election campaign was somewhat tarnished when she had to fight off allegations that she was sympathetic towards Sinn Féin. Certain unionist politicians in Northern Ireland, notably in the DUP, were extremely critical and, after McAleese stated that one of her intentions was to help to 'build bridges' in this divided Province, the DUP accused her instead of 'digging ditches'.

On the day of her inauguration, she departed her home in Rostrevor in County Down in the North as Mrs McAleese and returned across the border a few days later to our waiting cars at Middletown as the Irish President. For security and continuity reasons, the protection team remained the same as it had been with Mary Robinson. I was her driver, with Sergeant C as team leader and two other men in a tail car as back-up.

After her black Garda Mercedes stopped opposite the gates of Middletown RUC station, she made her way over to meet us. You're never sure how people are going to react or what their attitude is going to be towards their protection officers, but I needn't have worried as she was very gracious and seemed somewhat embarrassed by all the security arrangements laid on for her arrival, apologising profusely for keeping us out at this late hour. After the formalities were over and she got into the back of the car, she immediately leant forward to ask my name, and on the short journey to her now heavily guarded home she asked about my family. I assumed that she was just being courteous but she remembered those details for as long as I was her driver and always asked for Agnes by name. The President's husband, Martin, was with her on this occasion and he was also very friendly and down to earth. He was a dentist by profession but had given up his practice in Crossmaglen to support his wife in her political career.

We arrived back at Rostrevor to what appeared to be a street party in her honour. Hundreds of local people and schoolchildren lined the streets, cheering and waving the Irish flag. We didn't stop the car but filtered our way through to her home just off the main square and the steel gates were slammed shut behind us. While under no threat from those within her own community, she would have been considered a prime target for loyalist terrorists.

Once the car stopped outside the door, we were ordered into the house for tea. Somewhat embarrassed at her lack of supplies, she sent her daughter down to the local shop for biscuits and buns. 'I bet the White House would never run out of biscuits,' she said, laughing. This was a marked change from the atmosphere that had existed during her predecessor's period in office. Mary Robinson had always struck me as being slightly mistrustful of the RUC and a strict distance was always maintained. Now there was an open and friendly approach to the RUC in general and I felt that the new President trusted us implicitly.

During Mary McAleese's visits to nationalist areas, it felt at times as though we were somewhat detached from the RUC, as many of the venues she would visit in Northern Ireland would usually have been considered out of bounds to uniformed police, but with a 'wink and a nod' we were ushered through. On more than one occasion, I witnessed phone calls being made from the rear seat of my car to Sinn Féin officials who granted permission for her RUC escort team to enter particular areas. This happened in October 1998, when I drove her into Crossmaglen for a school visit. This was to be the first time in 20 years that a police car would be allowed into the village without any back-up. We were on our own, as local police and army patrols were asked to stay away – two miles away, in fact.

The next day we drove her into the Bogside and Creggan in Londonderry. Again no police or army personnel were allowed in at all; instead, they monitored the situation from the battlements of Derry's walls. On a visit to the Glen Road in Belfast, we were again on our own but were marshalled by Sinn Féin members. They opened the gates of the Christian Brothers Secondary School car park to allow our three armoured cars in, then they closed them and stood guard beside our cars as we sat looking out through the thick bullet-proof glass as the President received a rapturous welcome.

At no time during these visits were we ever attacked – as might have been expected at such venues. Those in control on the republican side knew full well that the Irish President would only be allowed to visit venues in Northern Ireland whilst in our care. If we were attacked, the visits would be stopped – it was as simple as that.

On only one occasion did we lock horns with the republican movement. In June 2000, we had arrived at Strabane Community centre. The President was then escorted inside the building by her Garda bodyguard but, unbelievably, we were refused entry. It was then that I formed the distinct impression that maybe the republican movement had a hand in her protection whilst inside. What upset me more was the implication, though of course I had no evidence to back this hunch up, that this might even have been arranged in advance with the President's private office without informing us on the ground. After much protest, we were told by our authorities to calm down and it was all conveniently brushed under the carpet.

After this visit, I refused to work on this team anymore. I had lost my trust and confidence in the President's Garda escorts, as to my mind we were now being treated with contempt in public. But despite this slightly sour ending to our working relationship, for many years afterwards I received personally signed cards from the President at Easter, St Patrick's Day and Christmas, delivered to our office.

Working so many hours and at this level of stress took its toll. Maintaining that level of alertness for more than a few hours both mentally and physically drained me. My performance would noticeably drop off later in the day – something I always felt to be very dangerous, especially if, due to bad weather, a long road run was to be made instead of using helicopters. While we had the use of the very effective motorcycle escort, we would still have to maintain a very fast pace, moving as part of an overt five-car high-speed convoy.

There is only a certain length of time the human mind can concentrate for and my attention span was getting shorter as the years rolled on. My mind would wander so much I had to keep reminding myself who was on board and where we were heading. Sitting in a silent atmosphere only heightened this detached feeling, as with no one to talk to it was indeed a struggle to remain alert. My mind would gradually focus on domestic problems and I would invariably find myself caught out in traffic by not concentrating on the road ahead. Such a slip-up occurred at Nutt's Corner roundabout one day when I peeled off onto the wrong road with Mary Robinson on board only to face the total embarrassment of forcing three cars to double back. These visits were much rehearsed and trained for, with all possible scenarios being envisaged, except the human factor of tiredness – and by this stage I was getting very, very tired.

Nearly every Ulster policeman suffers stress and tiredness to some degree, even though their macho image bars many from admitting it. We all have different personalities, thank God, and we deal with our demons in our own special ways. Many drink, beat the wife or enjoy chasing a bit of skirt. Many take physical training to excess; some even do drugs. I, on the other hand, had my own special way of coping: I had my motorbikes.

I had been motorcycling since 1973 and have owned 38 machines since then. Unfortunately, most of them have had to be in the over-1000cc category to suit my demand for adrenalin. In 1975, a friend and I owned the first two 1000cc Honda GoldWings in Northern Ireland, setting the local motorcycling scene alight as we fought off onlookers everywhere we parked.

As in days of old, when a man and his horse enjoyed a close working relationship, I trusted my bikes implicitly. Yes, there were many times when I pushed the envelope further than I should have, but by exceeding safe limits I could release the tensions that would otherwise have destroyed me sooner. Fellow bikers would be concerned at times about my wanton disregard for my safety but then, in my darkest days, I didn't give a shit if I crashed or not. In fact, I would have looked upon it as a blessing in disguise. But I eventually started to heed their well-meaning advice and channelled my skills into participating in organised events. I participated in the 1996 World Police Road Race Championships at Donington Park, and competed in the 1999 British Police Trek Championships, winning outright that year and in 2000 as well. As a member of the RUC Motorcycle Club, I held the position of secretary and helped promote skills by becoming a member of the Institute of Advanced Motorists after passing their difficult motorcycle test on my new Triumph Daytona.

My bikes were very important to me then and they did seem to cement my foundations together. There was nothing better than heading off for the weekend with some mates to scratch the roads together. Agnes would often join me on pillion and I particularly remember one fantastic week we enjoyed together in Scotland. On that occasion, I thought it would be best if we went alone, without the temptation of other bikers to chase. Agnes and I headed off on my BMW K100RT and toured most of the Highlands. But what really influenced us both was our visit to the island of Iona.

We had arrived in Oban the night before and, after checking into our hotel, decided it would be fun to take a coach trip to the island rather than sit all day on the bike. In some ways, it would be more relaxing for me as well, seeing that the roads over there were in a very poor state of repair. After crossing to the island of Mull the next morning, we continued on to Fionnphort to catch a small passenger-only ferry over the Sound of Iona and onto the hallowed isle.

For years, I had read of the magical effect this island has on everyone who sets foot upon its soil. I was sceptical but as Agnes had never even heard of it before I felt it would be good to observe her reactions. To say I was stunned would be an understatement; Agnes was immediately overcome with an unexplained feeling of calmness and well-being. I could see it in her face and hear it in her voice. I, too, could not explain my feelings but something magical had definitely taken place within us both. This was no tourist gimmick or a cheap trick; instead, this was undoubtedly the effect this holy ground had upon us. In the year 563, St Columba set up his monastery here after sailing from Ireland after many years of study. It was, in effect, the birthplace of Christianity in Scotland. Over the centuries, millions of pilgrims, and Eddie, have set foot on this holy isle and been touched by its magic.

CHAPTER 17

PRINCESS DIANA WAS
REMARKABLE INDEED

During my 15 years in the Close Protection Unit, I was closely involved in the many visits to Northern Ireland by the members of the Royal Family. There never was a separate Royal Protection Unit within the CPU; instead, there was a ready pool of men, normally attached to other principals, who could also be used for Royal visits. Not every member of the CPU was suitable for this kind of duty, however. Only those men who were blessed with more than a fair share of common sense were ever selected. Our authorities tended only to choose men who could work without close supervision and who portrayed a good image of the police. One particular colleague of mine couldn't understand why he was never selected for duty on Royal visits. He was the friendliest of men with a heart of gold and would usually start a conversation by turning around in his seat and asking the principal, 'What about ye?', as only an Ulsterman can do. Our senior officers felt that he was too forward and that this might not be to the Royals' liking – 'One would not be amused' – and so he was never selected.

Other officers were not considered suitable because they could not do what they were told. Most policemen, by their very nature, are incapable of following even the simplest of orders without asking, 'Why?' Our senior officers only wanted men who could see the logic of doing what they were told and work as part of a team. The following story explains why they were so selective.

On one of his many visits to the Province, I had just driven the Prince of Wales to an army camp in Ballymena for a short visit. He was greeted by army officers resplendent in their best kit and shown into the officers' mess. To my utter horror, the CPU driver of the lead car then decided to get out. Unbelievably, he lit up a cigarette and wandered off into the building behind the entourage, leaving his car unattended! He hadn't realised or just didn't care that we were to move off almost immediately from another door around the rear of the building. Somewhat embarrassed, we drove off without him and the sergeant he was supposed to be carrying. I therefore had to assume leadership of the convoy until they eventually caught up with us 30 miles away: he never performed Royal duty again.

Incredibly, some of the men who were not selected for such duty started a hate campaign targeted at those already established on the teams. There would be allegations of being an 'arse licker' and 'firm's man' thrown at us; some even went to the extent of sabotaging our immaculately prepared cars and I once had the keys deliberately locked inside one of my vehicles.

This selection process did not, however, always ensure that the positions went to the most able of officers. For example, the role of principal protection officer would always go to our desk-bound superintendent who did not carry out close protection duties on a daily basis and was therefore, I felt, the last man in the world who should have been given that position. Thankfully, nothing ever happened while he was on duty, as I have no doubt he would have proved completely ineffectual.

The preparation for each Royal visit was intense. Dry runs (recces) would be carried out weeks before in the lead-up to the visit, and again on the day, to check the route. The cars would be cleaned the day before and checks carried out to make sure they were immaculate. Then, hours before the Royal arrival, we would all form up at base with our eight-bike motorcycle escort. We had all been on a special course to familiarise us with the potential problems associated with using motorcycles on such operations but there was no need to worry on that score, as these riders were fantastic to say the least. They were all very highly trained advanced motorcyclists and had already completed years of traffic duty. Their role was to travel with us at all times, ensuring a safe and trouble-free passage throughout the visit. Some of them would race ahead to close roads before our arrival and then catch up after we passed. It worked like clockwork and, in fact, Prime Minister Tony Blair was so impressed on his first visit to the Province that he asked to speak to them individually on completion of his busy day. The RUC taught that form of motorcycle escort to nearly all UK forces. Before their introduction, it would have taken hundreds of policemen standing at junctions to ensure a safe passage.

In the course of my time in the CPU, I drove most of the Royals at some stage: the Queen and Prince Philip, the Queen Mother, Prince Charles, Princess Diana, the Duke and Duchess of York, Prince Edward, Princess Anne, the Kents, the Gloucesters and other minor members. Some I remember more fondly than others.

The Queen's first visit to the Province was in 1953, an occasion marked by all the pomp and ceremony typical of that period. The young Queen, only one year into her reign, landed at Aldergrove Airport and travelled to her residence at Hillsborough Castle, her base for the three-day tour of the Province, during which she visited Belfast, Londonderry, Lisburn, Ballymena, Ballymoney and Coleraine. In a gesture that would not be acceptable now, she was 'serenaded' by a couple of Lambeg drums at Hillsborough Castle.

She visited again in 1966 and then in 1977, in the company of the Duke of Edinburgh, when she arrived on board the Royal Yacht *Britannia* as part of her Silver Jubilee tour. This trip was more controversial, however, as Sinn Féin organised widespread disruption and protests which eventually erupted into full-scale riots. Undeterred, she carried on with her programme of visits, walkabouts and dinners showcasing the Province's business and sporting achievements and, in doing so, she showed the world a brighter side of life in Northern Ireland.

I was her driver in 1991 as she presented colours to four battalions of the Ulster Defence Regiment at Thiepval army barracks in Lisburn. There was a total lapse in protocol that day when she was left standing in the pouring rain. My authorities panicked as they hunted for a plastic umbrella, which she then struggled to open. From then on it was made standard practice within the CPU to carry the regulation, easy-to-open black umbrellas in the rear of our cars. This was always a standing joke within the unit, as the man detailed to look after them would always be considered on the bottom rung of the Royal protection team ladder.

All senior officers had wanted to be selected for this visit. It wasn't a big event really, apart from Lisburn she was only attending the annual garden party at Hillsborough, but the preparation was intense. I felt that we went over the score sometimes but then there was always an underlying fear among senior uniform officers that something was going to go wrong with the visit while they were in charge. Most of them would come over to the sergeant in charge of the CPU protection team for the visit and ask him discreetly to 'cover their asses'. These senior uniform officers were normally deskbound and therefore had no idea about close protection. They tended to stand well back and only came out of the shadows to claim the credit after a job well done by the hardworking men on the ground.

After the visit to the barracks, the orange helicopter of the Royal flight made its way to Hillsborough where it touched down gently as usual and, after the rotors had stopped, the Queen made her none-too-graceful way out and onto the helipad. After a short greeting from the Lord Lieutenant, her representative in Northern Ireland, she walked towards my car. I sat quietly in the driver's seat as she got in, and her police bodyguard from London then sat beside me in the front. Our inspector showed the Queen's lady-in-waiting to her seat behind me in the rear beside Her Majesty. I was not allowed to leave my seat, no matter what. I had to be in position and ready to drive off at a moment's notice in case anything sinister were to happen.

At this point, it would have been normal to receive some kind of greeting but there was nothing, no acknowledgement at all from the Queen or her bodyguard beside me. He was so arrogant that he just pointed forward with his finger as if to say, 'Go.' There was not even a hello or how are you out of any of them. I drove the short journey to the house in total silence and they got out every bit as quietly as they had got in. The Queen disappeared inside the house for a while then emerged onto the lawn for the garden party. It seemed to me that her smile appeared just at the precise moment it was required and not a moment sooner.

At the end of the pleasantries, she departed later that evening the same way she came and again in total silence. I have found over the years that this aloofness is common to most of the senior Royals. The Queen's son, the Duke of York, was without a doubt the worst, closely followed by Princess Anne.

The Queen returned again in 1995, this time to open the new M3 Lagan Bridge during the first year of the IRA ceasefire. Due to the cessation of hostilities, developers now felt comfortable enough to invest their money in war-torn Belfast and the city was going through a massive building boom that would change the Belfast skyline forever. The Queen was totally amazed at the progress this little Province had made in such a short time.

Another short visit for a garden party in 1997 went off without incident but a hoax bomb alert interrupted preparation for her next visit to Northern Ireland in April 2000, during which she was to present the George Cross to the Royal Ulster Constabulary in recognition of the bravery shown by the force during 30 years of violence in the Province. Army bomb-disposal experts were called in to deal with a suspicious package in Hillsborough where the ceremony was due to take place but they later declared the device a hoax and the ceremony went ahead as planned.

The Queen and the Duke of Edinburgh were greeted by Northern Ireland Secretary Peter Mandelson and the Queen then presented the medal to three officers: Assistant Chief Constable Bill Stewart, representing those with long service; Constable Susan Wright, one of the force's newest recruits; and Constable Paul Slaine, who lost both legs in an IRA bomb attack. Constable Slaine represented the 302 officers who were killed and the thousands injured during the Troubles.

RUC Chief Constable Sir Ronnie Flanagan welcomed the awarding of the George Cross, describing it as 'a momentous day for the force. It is the highest honour that can be conferred upon civilians. It takes precedence over all medals with the exception of the Victoria Cross.' Many within the

RUC, however, including myself, saw the honour as a political stunt aimed at placating the unionist community at a time when the government planned fundamental reforms of the police force to make it more acceptable to Catholics and nationalists. Former Hong Kong governor Chris Patten had submitted his far-reaching report in September of the previous year, recommending sweeping changes to the RUC. The most controversial was the loss of the name. The Patten report dictated that the force's future name should be the 'Police Service of Northern Ireland'. Many RUC officers, and widows of officers, felt the removal of the name was an insult, though in a gracious move, Iona Meyer of the RUC Widows' Association said, 'The award was a tremendous honour for all that had served and given their lives for the force. Even though people are understandably angry and hurt at the proposed change to the name and symbols of the force, we are still proud to see the force receiving this honour, especially from where it is coming.'

Of all our Royal visitors, I found the Duke of Edinburgh the most enjoyable to work with, unless he asked you a question to which you didn't know the answer. He is intolerant of waffle and I considered myself very lucky on one occasion. We returned to the helicopter landing pad at the dockside in Belfast only to find the helicopter was missing! Without telling anyone, it had headed back to RAF Aldergrove to re-fuel and was therefore running late. Somewhat annoyed, the Duke looked over the River Lagan and asked me, 'What are they building over there?' Normally I wouldn't have had a clue what was going on over that part of the river but, as luck would have it, I had just read about the preparations for the new Odyssey Centre a few days before in the *Belfast Telegraph*. I explained it to him in graphic detail, much to the apparent annoyance of his stern-faced English police minder, who sat with his arms folded beside me in the front – it was obvious to me he didn't want someone coming between him and his precious charge. Our conversation continued along that vein for some time until the eventual arrival of his helicopter for his return journey to Aldergrove and home. The Duke then thanked me for my description and paid tribute to my local knowledge.

Without a doubt the most civilised member of the Royal family was

Princess Diana. I always felt she was too good for them and her marriage into that family ultimately led to her severe unhappiness and premature death. She was the most caring and gracious lady I have ever had the privilege of working for. I was on her protection team as a driver on three very memorable occasions.

She would never settle into the rear of the car without first leaning forward and greeting me with a handshake. She always asked had I a family and if they were keeping well. I felt that these were genuine enquiries from a sincere and truly caring person, not just polite small talk. It was an honour to be part of her day and her relaxed presence ensured a great time was had by all. At every venue, she was greeted with bouquets. For practical reasons she could not take them home, so she would always ask me to give them to my wife. The only other Royal who made this gesture was the Duchess of Gloucester; she was in the same mould as Diana and would converse freely with us, much to the annoyance of the stuffed shirts in her entourage.

Diana was really a remarkable person. She had a special gift of being able to calm everyone around her. We would be on edge all day during her very long visits to some of the more unsavoury areas of Belfast and Londonderry. No matter where we went, however, she somehow held the crowd spellbound and could even unite them to a certain degree in common appreciation of her. The mental picture I have of her sitting in full army battle dress in the rear seat of my heavily armoured Ford Granada, while visiting troops at Ballykelly, will live with me forever. She was so self-conscious about her appearance that day that she asked my advice about what would be appropriate, army camouflage jacket or green jumper? At that stage, I was about to commit the cardinal sin of telling her that no matter what she wore, she would still look beautiful – but I didn't. I am sure if I had had the courage to pay her that compliment, she would have shrugged it off with one of the shy little smiles she was so loved for. But her police bodyguard from London would have reported me immediately for being too forward and such a complaint would surely have ended my days on the Royal protection team.

I feel deeply privileged to have known Princess Diana and I will always look back with fondness and affection to those days when she graced us with her presence here in Northern Ireland.

In contrast, my many days driving Prince Andrew, the Duke of York, were tense and uncomfortable. There was a bad atmosphere between us and I feel it stemmed from the first day I spent with him in 1986. This was his first visit to Northern Ireland since his marriage to Sarah Ferguson in July of that year and it was actually my first contact with any member of the Royal Family.

After arriving at RAF Aldergrove, Andrew and Sarah made their way by army helicopter to the RUC sports grounds at Newforge; it was the RUC annual sports day and they were our invited guests. Although I was waiting in the Duke's allotted armoured car in the five-car convoy, we were not required at this stage. We were only there in reserve in case the helicopter was grounded at Newforge due to bad weather. As the conditions were fine, they were able to take off for their next venue in Belfast. Our convoy then leap-frogged to Comber cricket ground to await their arrival a few hours later.

Comber is a quaint little village ten miles from Belfast and famous for its once very important linen mill owned by the Andrews family. Another claim to fame is its connection, through the same family, to Thomas Andrews, the designer of the ill-fated *Titanic*. He lived in the grandeur of Ardara House on the outskirts of the village.

I could sense the keen anticipation among the schoolchildren who had been mustered ever so diplomatically by the Northern Ireland Office. This always seemed the best way to ensure a Royal visitor could be given the flag-waving welcome the NIO wished. Adjacent to the helicopter landing area stood the de rigueur ensemble of dignitaries, including the Lord Lieutenant. As soon as the rotors stopped spinning, the young couple stepped out and, after a short meet-and-greet, they slid somewhat excitedly into the rear seat of my gleaming armoured Granada; their stern-faced police inspector from the Royal Protection Squad in London sat in the front beside me. Sarah had no sooner settled into her seat behind me when she reached over to shake my hand and say hello. To say I was surprised would be an understatement, especially when I detected a look of disdain on Andrew's face as I glanced in the rear-view mirror. I formed the impression very early on that Sarah's genuine show of warmth was not in keeping with Andrew's more aloof nature. His only comment was, 'Oh no, not another redhead', at which I was forced to laugh.

The purpose of their trip was to visit the little town of Killyleagh on the shores of Strangford Lough, of which Andrew had been made Baron by the Queen as a gift after his wedding. All along the road from Comber, people from every hamlet and village were standing on corners hoping to catch a glimpse of the newlyweds. On entering Killyleagh, the streets were again lined with immaculately turned out schoolchildren holding little flags they had made the day before. Sarah and Andrew were joking amongst themselves about who exactly the children were waving at: her or him? Almost sycophantically, the London protection officer assured the Duke that the children were in fact cheering his Royal personage, as he was probably the only one they could recognise!

When not on leave, I was always the driver detailed to serve the Duke of York during his visits; it seemed no one else wanted the task. We never did get on. The days always seemed long and were interspersed with churlish comments on trivial things like the standard of the car or that he was being driven too slow or too fast – it seemed as if nothing I did pleased him. I quickly formed the impression that it was all a bit of a show; I felt he was trying to 'dominate' me but it didn't work – I always looked him straight in the eye and gave as good as I got. I stood my ground where others would have been humbled. After several years, I was replaced – it seemed that all of a sudden they had found someone else. I was delighted!

Prince Edward was so insignificant that I remember very little about the two occasions when I was his driver. He would just sit and make small talk with his entourage. He seemed to lack self-confidence and would never make any attempt to converse with any of us. To be honest, I always had the feeling he would rather be elsewhere and was there as a matter of duty.

His elder sister, Anne, was another different character. Wherever she went in Northern Ireland, I always felt she was tolerated – just. She was never loved to the same degree as Diana or Fergie and I felt she knew it. As hard as she tried, I don't think she ever crossed that barrier and commanded the respect of the people here. She had that noxious trait that Ulster people abhor of appearing to look down her nose at you.

Right from the start, Princess Anne demanded, contrary to all our training drills, to be seated directly behind the driver. This may seem like a minor deviance from the overall plan but let me assure you that, in the event of an attack, it could prove fatal. The very reason for putting a principal behind the bodyguard is that he or she could be extracted immediately in the event of the vehicle being immobilised. The bodyguard therefore does not have to interfere with the driver, who by now should be giving covering fire in the event of us having to leave the vehicle. I have no doubt at all that this was her way of arrogantly stamping her authority on the proceedings. There was no reason given for her charade and, as usual, our command structure had not the backbone to put her right. She was blatantly putting her own life and, more importantly, the lives of all the members of the crew assigned to protect her, at risk; she was not touring through the Cotswolds after all.

Anne should have learnt her lesson after the attempt made to kidnap her in London in March of 1974. Then, an attacker drove his car in front of the Royal limousine and planned to kidnap her and demand a £3 million ransom. As her police bodyguard drew his pistol, the gunman fired and ran into St James's Park, where he was arrested. Both Princess Anne and her husband Captain Mark Phillips were unhurt as a bullet passed between them. A police bodyguard, the chauffeur, a passing taxi driver and a policeman patrolling the Mall were all shot and seriously wounded.

Driving her in Northern Ireland was not a pleasurable experience for me at all. The day seemed long and there was usually total silence from my rear-seat passenger. She would converse with her entourage, by and large ignoring her protection team from the RUC. This trait was common to most of the Royals and also quite prevalent among their travelling staff. They seemed to treat us with utter contempt, which made me feel very uncomfortable at times. At the end of the day, they knew the only way they would be allowed to visit the Province was with our protection but ultimately the Royal protection teams would have preferred to be totally in charge. Thank goodness they were not, however, and a famous incident involving Prince Charles proves my point.

In 1994, Prince Charles was on a visit to Sydney to celebrate Australia Day. The Prince crossed the bay by ferry to Darling Harbour, where, in the company of the governor of New South Wales, the premier and the mayor, he sat on a stage in front of a vast crowd while they sang Australian songs. The Prince was to present two prizes to the schoolchildren of the year and then say a few words, but he stood there feeling rather stupid as nobody seemed to be coming forward to receive their prize. Suddenly, a man leapt out of the crowd to his right and started running towards the stage, firing a pistol as he ran. The Prince first thought that this might be part of the proceedings and that maybe it was one of the prizewinners who was particularly keen to receive his trophy! But then he was barged across the stage by his bodyguard just as the assailant tripped and fell. While the Prince resisted efforts to remove him from the stage, a large number of policemen and officials piled on top of the assailant.

The man with the starting pistol was David Kang, a student from Cambodia who wanted to draw attention to the plight of the Cambodian boat people in Australia. As the television pictures flashed around the globe, viewers were struck by the blasé attitude of the Prince, who did not move until his police bodyguard moved him aside to get between him and his attacker.

This sorry incident just reinforces my conviction that this level of security should not be placed in the hands of more mature senior officers attached to the Royal protection unit in London nor indeed here in Northern Ireland. It is my opinion that his bodyguard took far too long to react to the attack. The men offering this type of protection, in this day and age, need to be young with incredibly sharp reactions.

After watching footage of this incident, it seemed to me that the officer made no attempt to remove the Prince from the scene of danger, preferring instead to embrace him as they both watched the proceedings unfold. No thought seemed to be given to the possibility of an accomplice. I took great pleasure in asking the Prince's bodyguard about the attack when I next had occasion to meet him in Belfast. I was met with a scornful expression and told to mind my own bloody business, such was his obvious embarrassment. I was surprised he was still in the job as, if the gun used in the attack had been real, the Prince would be dead!

CHAPTER 18

'LADIES AND GENTLEMEN, THE PRESIDENT OF THE UNITED STATES'

Undoubtedly, the highlight of my years as a member of the Close Protection Unit would have to be my involvement in the protection of the President of the United States, Bill Clinton. I was an important member of the team on both occasions he set foot on our shores: driving his National Security Advisor Tony Lake behind the presidential limousine on his first visit in November 1995 and as the RUC pilot car leading his limo during his second visit a few years later.

The hype about the presidential visit started weeks in advance within our unit when it became clear that there was every chance he would come to Northern Ireland. There was always some doubt due to the very unstable nature of the peace process at that time. Political infighting behind the scenes ensured that all sorts of obstacles would be thrown in his way.

The RUC had never been involved in such a high-profile visit before and the chance of being involved was very hard for certain RUC men to resist. Normally deskbound senior officers came crawling out of the woodwork of headquarters, training and other branches, trying to get on the team. I was appalled to see fully trained, fit and alert members of the CPU, who had been involved in close protection on a daily basis for years, being replaced by men incapable of carrying out this very crucial role within the protection teams. Thankfully, the inspector assured me of my place on the team, so I didn't have to join in all the jostling.

The CPU now had to come up with a plan of protection for the President that would not only work effectively but, more challenging, would also have to please the American Secret Service. To be perfectly honest, though, at no time during the preparations or the visit itself did I feel the RUC played any meaningful role in the physical protection of Clinton; we were there only to supply cars and drivers for what was, in effect, an American roadshow.

While protecting the President, wherever the American Secret Service goes in this world, they always call the shots. This has, and will again, cause real friction between them and the host police force. When the President is onboard Air Force One on the tarmac or using the limousines, the ground they occupy is treated as US soil and protected as such. These men were at the very pinnacle of their line of work and as such were the most professional protection teams I had ever seen. Nothing, and I mean nothing, was left to chance, as prior to each of his visits everything was thoroughly checked out. Everyone due to meet him was scrutinised and all routes were checked and re-checked. All road manholes along his route were entered, checked then sealed with special non-removable sticky markers that would be destroyed if they were to be tampered with. Secret Service members would be in situ at the various locations of each visit for days in advance and would maintain a sterile area, monitoring anyone who came in and out. They were instantly recognisable due to their apparently standard-issue fawn-coloured long coats, the like of which Belfast had never seen before. These coats started a trend amongst certain of the younger members of the CPU after the visit, much to the amusement of the rest of us.

After long and sometimes heated meetings between the Secret Service and our supervisory officers, the men who would work on the presidential teams were selected and informed of their role. I was selected to drive the

American National Security Advisor Mr Tony Lake and was briefed accordingly. He was never to be out of the sight of the President for reasons I would be made aware of at a later date.

A few days prior to the visit, I was introduced to Tim, the Secret Service team member I would be working with on the big day. We greeted each other as colleagues and headed out to do all the dry runs and to reconnoitre the venues. He was genuinely warm and not condescending at all. I was pleasantly surprised and we formed a good working relationship. But unfortunately my experience wasn't mirrored elsewhere. There was a general feeling of distrust between the two forces and it was obvious that the Secret Service men were control freaks. So deep was the distrust that they placed one of their own agents in Dundonald RUC station to check out the police cars to be used on the visit. One uniform policeman didn't improve relations by remarking to an agent: 'We've had the Queen here many times and she's never been shot. You lot haven't got such a good track record.' Despite such barbs, another agent later said that the RUC was the smoothest-running police force he had ever worked with.

The morning of the visit arrived and we were all to start very early. I made my way to sign on duty, only to be met by a Secret Service agent at the top of the stairs of Dundonald station who had the audacity to question my identity in my own station. I was beginning to get somewhat fed up at this stage and, on seeing my rising temper, Sergeant C duly identified me to him. He had to vouch for each and every one of us as we assembled that morning.

The briefing that followed was all about what the Secret Service wanted and expected from us that day. I looked over to my superintendent and chief inspector, who were sitting somewhat meekly in the corner of the sergeant's room, as if to say, 'Come on, sir, put this clown in his place. This is the RUC, not a police force in some banana republic.' We had been at the cutting edge of the fight against terrorism for nearly 30 years, probably since before this agent was born, and there he was dictating to us in a very condescending manner what his expectations were. I have no doubt this is standard operating procedure for the Secret Service and he was only doing what was asked of him but there will always be scope for conflict when two different cultures and methods of achieving the same objective collide.

In our gleaming cars, we headed up to Aldergrove Airport outside Belfast to the pre-arranged hangar to await the arrival of Air Force One. All seven of our CPU cars had to suffer the indignity of being searched by the Secret Service. Did they really think we would leave the cars unattended and therefore open to tampering? Obviously so. We then waited patiently for some hours as they lined us up in convoy within the mighty hangar just off the main runway. Outside were all shapes and sizes of minibuses, vans and cars they had rented for the White House press corps, baggage, etc., and for these they had employed drivers from some of the more unsavoury areas of the city. Only cursory checks had been done on their backgrounds and I couldn't believe that after all the security they had laid on they had this mighty chink in their armour.

I was in line with the two black limos and just behind the black Jeep with blacked-out windows that they had flown over on a mighty Galaxy transport plane a few days before. This was the command centre of the operation and there were some heavily armed men inside who would act as a quick reaction force. This was all only for the Belfast end of the operation; there was the exact same set-up waiting at Londonderry for the afternoon leg of the visit.

There had been some argument about just how many Secret Service men were to be permitted to carry arms on the streets of Northern Ireland. They all wanted to bring in their guns but the Chief Constable quite rightly put his foot down and restricted them to four firearms certificates. Initially, the Secret Service then wanted us to be disarmed and when we refused they made us wear little metal badges with the letter 'E' painted on to signify who was carrying weapons so they could keep a close watch on us.

With military precision, they stuck large paper signs on our windscreens, some of which had PROTUS printed on them in large black letters and others FLOTUS. Somewhat confused for a minute, I then realised that PROTUS stood for President of the United States and the other was for the First Lady of the United States. This was to indicate two distinct teams that would run together until they arrived in Belfast; they would then split up to carry out their separate programmes of visits in and around the city.

To keep myself occupied as we waited, I walked around the hangar inspecting the mighty Cadillacs which I had seen so many times before on the television. To tell the truth, I wasn't very impressed. They had all the marks and scratches you would expect with cars of their age. The doors were badly fitted, although bearing in mind the thickness and weight of them it was hardly surprising. 'Obviously,' I thought to myself, 'they wouldn't send their best cars to Belfast – would you?'

At the appointed time, we were given the nod and off we headed towards the international arrivals area of the terminal building. To say that this was an amusing sight would be an understatement. There was a snake of approximately 50 cars, trucks, vans and buses stretching all the way back to the hangar and there was not an aircraft in sight. All flights had been put on hold until after the landing of Air Force One. Secret Service agents were running around like crazy, getting each and every vehicle in exactly the right spot, something I have no doubt they have had to do many times in the past, such was the degree of professionalism shown that day. Each man on the team had a certain job to do and carried it out with great gusto. I later learned that they rotate within their unit: some who were parking cars had been protection officers on a recent visit to China.

There was an air of excitement as Air Force One touched down; her gleaming light-blue and grey exterior somehow brightened up an otherwise dreary Aldergrove Airport. 'Now that's something you don't see here too often,' I said to myself as the mighty jumbo taxied up to her resting spot. It's rare enough seeing a jumbo jet here in Northern Ireland, let alone the most famous aircraft in the world! She stopped and we were immediately on the move around the building to our position right at the base of the rear steps that were now in place. The multitude of staff and press corps descended onto Ulster soil and, like a clockwork army, they knew exactly where to go.

After a respectable period of time, the President appeared at the top of the front steps, stopping briefly to wave to the waiting crowd and pose for the international press. His wife Hillary joined him and, hand in hand, they made their way towards the excited throng in a slow and deliberate fashion down the catwalk that was the steps of Air Force One. The rear door of my car opened and a very well-groomed gentleman slid in, saying 'Good morning' as he did so.

'Good morning, sir,' I replied as he reached forward between the seats to shake my hand. I shook his hand with a firm grip intended to indicate my sincere pleasure at his safe arrival. I welcomed him to Northern Ireland, to which he said, 'Thank you,' and introduced himself as Tony Lake. He asked my name and somewhat nervously I replied, 'Constable Gregory, sir.'

'No, no, your first name,' he said.

'Eddie,' I replied, and from then on Ed was my name in every conversation.

By this stage, his own Secret Service agent had already taken up his seat beside me. I looked out of the window just in time to catch a glimpse of the President getting into his limo and then we were off out of the airport and heading towards the waiting city of Belfast.

Northern Ireland had never witnessed anything on this scale before and it left many people mesmerised. Ulster folk, normally very reserved in relation to newcomers, had been swept along en masse as the hype built for the impending visit and they now lined all the routes into the city, hanging from every vantage point to get the best view of that famous black limo. It was clear that there was a real hunger on the part of the people to see the US President come and make a statement about the importance of the peace process, which was well under way at this stage.

The M2 motorway to Belfast had been closed off; every overhead bridge had been manned on the clear instructions of the Secret Service for fear of someone dropping a device as we passed. The snaking convoy of over fifty vehicles now stretched back some two miles, with those carrying the most important passengers towards the front.

As we reached Fortwilliam, the cavalcade became somewhat smaller as the First Lady and her entourage peeled off to carry out her own programme of events at various locations throughout Belfast. An advance party of staff and press had also taken this opportunity to head off to the Mackie engineering factory to set up the most important visit of the day: the President's keynote speech. When we entered Northumberland Street on our way to the Shankill Road on what I thought was the pre-arranged route to the Mackie factory, the Secret Service radio that had been installed in the rear of my car began to ring. Tony Lake lifted it and, from what I could make out, there was to be an impromptu stop just around the corner at the junction of Agnes Street and the Shankill Road.

As a young boy, I had walked these very streets and virtually lived in the Shankill Road Mission only a few doors away. Ten years ago I was patrolling this junction as a member of the DMSU. It was remarkable that this crossroads played such an important part throughout my life. I looked to the corner, my mind racing back to the dreadful nights of rioting I had witnessed. Here I was again, same place, only a different time. When I had stood on that corner as a filthy and hungry urchin, ducking and diving for survival, I could never have predicted that someday I would drag myself out of that mire and find myself in the company of the President of the United States.

This stop was indeed impromptu! There was absolutely no notice given to any of my team. We were totally in the dark and not even aware of exactly where the President wished to go at this location. I tried to warn my sergeant in the lead car by radio but was overruled by the agent beside me. I had to bite my tongue but by this stage it was too late, we had already stopped. It later transpired the Secret Service had taken the decision some days previously that there would be a photo opportunity outside a fruit shop in this Protestant area. This was most important to the Americans as there had to be seen to be some degree of balance between their interest in the two communities, and the main event of the day was to take place at the Mackie factory in a predominantly Catholic area. It was also felt by some that it would be better if he had some contact with the Protestant community before his secretly planned handshake with Gerry Adams due a few hours later.

It might perhaps have meant more to the Protestant community if they had stopped 100 yards further up the Shankill Road at number 273, the scene of the Shankill bombing. This was where nine totally innocent people were blown to pieces by an IRA bomb in October 1993. The bomber, Thomas Begley, was also killed as the bomb he was planting exploded prematurely, causing the whole building to collapse into a pile of rubble. But it was obviously felt that a visit to this site by the President would set the wrong tone for his meeting with Adams.

In a scene of total chaos – as police on the ground were also unaware of this unplanned stop – the President stepped out of his car wearing a long, heavy bullet-proof coat that would cover his shoulders throughout that day when outdoors. The crowds who had gathered to witness his passage along the Shankill were taken totally by surprise as he stopped. The shops emptied as they thronged closer. There were no crowd-control barriers in place due to the total lack of communication with the men on the ground, and the Secret Service members were looking troubled. Everybody on the Shankill greeted him cordially, though, and his visit made a celebrity of the shop owner, Violet Clark. The President bought some fruit and then, as quickly as we had stopped, we were back on the move again, heading on to Mackie's.

We arrived at the 'Protestant' gates of the Mackie factory and swung down towards the side entrance. It was planned to bring the President in by that side door so that he would be closer to the massive stage which had been built on the shop floor. The 'Catholic' gate was around the other side of the building, allowing the Catholic workers to enter from their own area of the town: the workers in this part of Belfast were not yet ready to trust each other.

It had been touch and go whether the President would ever visit the factory at all. For some weeks beforehand, there had been heated discussions with unions and management about the possible visit of Gerry Adams to the factory at the same time and staff had even threatened to lock the President out. The Mackie factory, although in a

Catholic area, is staffed mainly by Protestants and the workforce was not prepared to have Gerry Adams in their factory under any circumstances, even though the workers were slowly but surely overcoming their anti-Catholic bias.

By the time we arrived, the early speakers had started and two schoolchildren, a nine-year-old Catholic girl, Catherine Hamill, and an eleven-year-old Protestant boy, David Sterrett, read out their heart-rending tales of growing up during the Troubles. Their efforts had been selected from hundreds of letters written by schoolchildren from schools close to the factory in the days running up to the visit. After they had finished, the announcement went out over the Tannoy: 'Ladies and gentlemen, the President of the United States.'

I was sitting in my car at the side door, unable to leave the vehicle due to certain equipment that had been placed in the boot that morning – all I was told was that under no circumstances was it to be left unguarded at any time. I wasn't too annoyed, though, as I was able listen to the President's address in full as Radio Ulster was broadcasting it live. It was a great speech and its positive overtones did make me feel that there might be some hope for the future.

The President then left the hall and made his way back to the cars. We managed to get everyone back on board and started to head down the Springfield Road towards the Falls Road junction.

Unbeknown to everyone but the members of the Secret Service, there was to be another deviation from the planned route. Once again, Tony Lake answered a call on the radio. 'The meeting's on,' I heard and the radio handset was put back down as quickly as it was lifted. I wasn't stupid and I reckoned he was referring to the controversial meeting and handshake with Adams, which was no doubt due to take place before we departed Adams' area.

As we approached the junction with the Falls Road, I knew something was about to happen, as the crowd was turning ugly and unruly. The Secret Service agents were out and running on each side of the limo as we passed Springfield Road RUC station, then, without warning, the presidential limo and back-up Jeep turned quickly left into the Falls Road and stopped. As I was right behind the Jeep, I made as if to follow but this time Tony Lake reached forward and held my shoulder, telling me to, 'Stay here and don't follow.' He sat in the car with me as the crowd headed after the limo; no doubt they had been told that there was to be a presidential walkabout. Seeing that there was a need for more manpower on the ground, the agent beside me got out and headed towards the limo to assist. It was chaos as the RUC tried in vain to hold back the crowd, who were jumping the barriers and deliberately ignoring police advice to keep back. I looked in the rear-view mirror only to see Tony Lake with a look of contentment on his face as he gazed out at the unfolding scene. Here for the first time, there was going to be a televised acceptance of Sinn Féin as a respectable player in the peace process by the US government, something that would infuriate the unionist community.

Gerry Adams had been waiting where he had been told by the Secret Service – in the doorway of McErlean's bakery – and as the President's car came to a halt, he was called over as the door opened. Clinton stepped out wearing his bullet-proof coat and smiled as he shook hands with Adams who said, 'Cead mile failte.' This was it. This was the day the republican movement had been dreaming of for so long. Here on the Falls Road was the President of the United States of America paying homage to the president of Sinn Féin, the political wing of the IRA, a fully armed and operational terrorist movement with the blood of over 1,500 men, women and children on their hands. Politics is a dirty business.

Adams and Clinton then headed into the bakery. Outside, the crowds were now getting out of hand. My car was now well and truly in the thick of it and once it was recognised as a police car it received its fair share of kicks and bangs from the thuggish element now starting to amass. Tony Lake was clearly getting a bit concerned as he was on the radio telling the agents to 'wrap it up'. Clinton came out and was jostled and cheered by the crowd, who had closed right in to that sterile zone which the Secret Service should have been keeping clear. One woman even managed to grab the President, throwing her arms around him as she kissed him. A drunken man thrust a pint of Guinness at him, which was quickly removed and poured onto the street by an agent, no doubt worried it may have been spiked with poison. His agents managed to push him into his car and we were off again down the Grosvenor Road and into the city centre.

It was important that the President should now be seen to visit the Protestant area of East Belfast. After his open and very friendly courtship of the republican element, he had no choice: he had to meet the 'Prods'.

CHAPTER 19

ARE YOU AN RUC MAN
OR A POLICEMAN?

With the convoy now re-formed, we headed through the city on our way to the next venue at the East Belfast Enterprise Park. We were all now in a much more relaxed mood after the obvious tensions of the morning but this was not to last. As we were driving up towards the Albert Bridge, the President had spotted hundreds of schoolchildren furiously waving flags and singing at the tops of their voices. The call came over the radio that he wanted to stop. I could see the colour drain from Tony Lake's face, as this was obviously a stop they hadn't planned and therefore they had no control over the situation. We, the RUC, were also very apprehensive about it as we were right on the edge of the notorious Markets area of Belfast, scene of some of the most brutal killings in the city. No security sweep had been done nor were there enough police personnel on the ground should they be needed for crowd control: this had all the potential of turning into a very ugly scene.

When the presidential limousine came to a halt, all the Secret Service agents jumped out looking very nervous. The President hadn't even time to don his heavy bullet-proof overcoat, so his agents provided very close body cover instead. The entire local school of 300 pupils was now out on the street with their little paper American flags that they had meticulously painted just for this special day. I could see the preceding sleepless night of excitement on their tiny faces, just knowing that they would be seeing the President drive by. Never in their wildest dreams would they have expected him to stop. The press corps were totally furious as they were in a van some distance behind. They could be seen running forward carrying all their equipment as we drove off again after this very brief stop.

Back in the cars, we breathed a sigh of relief as we headed over the Albert Bridge towards our next appointment at the Enterprise Park just off the Albert Bridge Road. It was very noticeable that public support here in Protestant East Belfast was nowhere near as enthusiastic as it had been across the city on the Falls Road but, then again, the President wasn't here to curry favour with this side of the community. We were travelling adjacent to the Newtownards Road, a hotbed of militant Protestantism, and the crowds were sparse. True, there were some of the more inquisitive lining the route but the hard core of the working classes, no doubt, had more important things to do with their time.

The motorcycle escort headed away from us, as only five of our cars were to enter the small parking area of this new collection of compact business units. The advance party of Secret Service agents who had been here over the previous days welcomed us in as they closed the large steel gates behind my car. The agents had carried out their duties well at this venue and had even gone to the trouble of having sheets of metal attached to the top of the gates, thereby blocking out the view from some overlooking buildings. Unfortunately, this turned out not to be such a great idea, as the wind was blowing a gale and just prior to our arrival all the sheets had come crashing down into the yard.

The President stepped out of his car while removing his heavy coat. It was felt, considering the high security in the area, he could dispense with it. He started to walk the line and shake the hands of all the gathered dignitaries, including the MP for the area, Mr Peter Robinson.

Peter Robinson was the deputy leader of Ian Paisley's DUP party. He was hardly thrilled about this visit but realised that there was no way he could be seen to snub the President of the United States. As a Member of Parliament, he was also very interested in portraying a good impression of the area with reference to any future American investment. The Americans always felt that, of all the DUP politicians, Robinson was the one they could do business with.

As they all headed off into the main building for discussions, Tony Lake and I settled down in the car to feast on a packed lunch provided by the agents who had taken up residence here. This period of relative calm gave us time to converse 'off the record' and some thorny issues were raised by Mr Lake. I had to be very tactful, as the last thing I wanted at that stage was to be quoted over what I perceived to be force policy.

One question he did ask which had me thinking long after this visit was: 'Do you consider yourself a policeman or an RUC man?'

I answered him truthfully, saying that when I joined the RUC in 1980 I wanted to be a policeman and serve the whole community but due to events beyond my control I found myself being moulded into an RUC man. There is a subtle difference depending upon an individual's thinking and the term RUC man is usually meant to depict an officer who sees his role as serving the unionist cause. It was damn near impossible to carry out the prescriptive role of a policeman here in Northern Ireland due to the ongoing security situation. He praised my answer, saying that he too had always detected there was a difference depending on a man's viewpoint.

With lunch now over, the entourage was starting to assemble in the car park and within minutes we were off again on the relatively short journey to the Belfast City Airport adjacent to the harbour complex, where the President's US Marine Corps helicopter was waiting to take him to Londonderry. I drove around the rear of his very large, green Marine One helicopter, emblazoned with the presidential crest and the words United States of America, and stopped at one of his support helicopters, where Tony Lake said goodbye. I wasn't being used on the Londonderry side of the visit but I would see him later that evening upon his return to Belfast. With a salute from two white-capped Marines, the President boarded Marine One and took off to Londonderry. That was the end of the first Belfast portion of the visit, so it was back to base at Dundonald and some well-earned R&R.

Later that evening, Marine One landed back on the taxiway of Belfast City Airport. After another very smart salute, the President and the First Lady descended the few steps back onto Belfast soil. A crowd of 80,000 had been building all day to witness the President switching on the Christmas lights and, in fact, some had taken up their positions outside the City Hall at 10 a.m. that morning. So many high buildings surrounded the platform that the Secret Service had dictated that all office lights be left on so they could see into every office. Five large panes of bullet-proof glass had been set up on the stage to give some protection to Clinton, as the agents were very concerned at the possibility of an attack by some hot-head in the crowd.

Curtis Stigers and Van Morrison were entertaining the very excited crowd as we arrived at the rear gate of City Hall. So many vehicles were now involved that all roads in the vicinity had been closed off. I parked behind the presidential limo as the President headed into City Hall with his entourage. Tony Lake made a few calls on his radio then made his own way into the building. The music reverberating around the high buildings only heightened the atmosphere of this great event, the likes of which Belfast had never witnessed before. Seeing that all our vehicles were now parked in a secure and monitored area, it was felt that more manpower was required at the front of the crowd. The Secret Service had decided, after consultation with my chief inspector, that they would guard the cars if we – the RUC bodyguards – could be sent in to mingle with the crowds. Our local knowledge would obviously have been of some use in identifying any potential troublemakers.

With 'Van the Man' singing out the unofficial anthem to the peace process, 'Days Like This', I took up a position to the left of stage beside the main railings of the front gate and scoured the crowd. A noisy group, who I later found out to be students from nearby Queen's University, were generally making a nuisance of themselves by shouting out abuse about the American influence in the Middle East. I was not prepared to allow them to argue their case in the middle of this great event and so I called for assistance and had them removed immediately. There was no way I was going to tolerate behaviour like that. Uniform police unceremoniously dumped them outside the secure cordon in Great Victoria Street.

While the John Anderson big band was playing the Glenn Miller hit 'Don't Sit Under The Apple Tree', they were interrupted by the huge crowd screaming for the President: 'We want Bill. We want Bill.' Following Mayor Smyth, the President climbed the few steps and walked out onto the stage. The pent-up anticipation of the crowd erupted into rapturous applause and shouting, while thousands of flash bulbs went off taking the pictures that would fill the world's newspapers the next day.

The Mayor greeted the Clintons and immediately turned his message into a sermon quoting Matthew 1:22, 23. He received some abuse from the crowd for this unexpected lesson from the pulpit and I cringed in disbelief, wondering what the world would think. Thankfully, it didn't go on too long and Mayor Smyth then called on the President to switch on the Christmas tree lights. Clinton pulled the dummy lever as the crowd called out the countdown from ten down to one, while a workman threw the real switch under the stage and the lights flickered to life.

After saying thank you to their hosts, the President and First Lady got back into their limo for another very short journey to Queen's University. The route was lined with hundreds of uniformed RUC men and women, all an equal distance apart and facing away from the cavalcade as they scanned the crowd. They were obviously under strict orders, as not one of them turned around as could have been expected on such a momentous day.

Clinton was scheduled to have face-to-face meetings with all the political leaders in Northern Ireland. It was good to see Peter Robinson and other members of the DUP breaking their traditional stance and mixing in the same surroundings as the leaders of Sinn Féin – they were now breathing the same air, which must have been a sign of political progress! Having said that, Peter Robinson instructed his members to keep their hands in their pockets and shake hands with no one unless they knew who that person was. The group never moved from their spot at the opposite end of the hall from Sinn Féin.

When all the talking was over, the President and First Lady made their way to the cars and their well-earned overnight stay at the Europa Hotel. We headed back down Great Victoria Street from the university, swung into Glengall Street and entered the covered parking bays that had been secured for our use. The doors slammed behind us.

The President, while visibly tired, took time to say goodnight to each of us in turn, issuing us with the regulation trinkets of pens and cufflinks in thanks for our services. With a firm handshake, he wished me goodnight and then entered the service lift to his tenth-floor suite to freshen up before a meeting with Ulster Unionist leader David Trimble. Tony Lake removed his papers and kit from my car and thanked me warmly for my company that day, presenting me with a small memento as he did so. The Secret Service agent removed all their secret kit from the boot of my car and I was free to head back to base.

Agnes and my kids were so proud when I told them of my involvement that day. I showed them the pen and cufflinks presented to me by the President – while they could be considered tacky, they were, after all, gifts from the President of the United States in recognition of a job well done.

The next day was a bit of an anti-climax, as we had a very quiet and uneventful run to Aldergrove Airport and Air Force One, that mighty jumbo jet waiting to fly him to his next leg in Dublin. President Clinton later said of his trip:

> Our day in Northern Ireland was indeed one of the most remarkable of our lives and a highlight of my presidency. I am still deeply moved by the warmth of the reception we were given and the palpable desire of the people we saw to come together in peace and reconciliation.

I was and still am very proud to have been a part of this first visit and the memories of that great day will live with me forever. True to his word, he did return to our shores and in 1998 he visited Armagh as well as Belfast and Omagh. Again, I was fully involved in assisting with the security from the RUC end and this time drove the lead car just in front of the same mighty black Cadillac limousine. Sergeant C joined me on this occasion, along with a Secret Service agent with whom we had spent the previous week doing all the dry runs to perfection.

It was truly humbling to lead the President's limo up the stunning Prince of Wales Avenue from the front gates of Stormont to the massive white Portland stone steps. Inside, he met all 108 elected members of the new Northern Ireland Assembly, again addressing them about his hopes for the ongoing peace process. True to form, Ian Paisley accused him of 'ongoing interference in Northern Ireland affairs'.

Clinton's next engagement was in Belfast, where he made a visit to the City's Waterfront Hall. This had been the venue for a women's conference called 'Vital Voices', at which the First Lady was guest speaker. It was also planned for them to travel on to Omagh, to attend a wreath-laying ceremony and to meet some of those who suffered as a result of the Real IRA bombing on 15 August 1998, which killed 28 innocent men, women and children. The President met local people, along with the emergency personnel who worked at the scene on that dreadful day.

On the day of the bombing in Omagh, Agnes and I were driving down to our favourite bolthole in Norfolk for a long weekend with our great friends Nick and Lesley when we heard the news broadcast over the radio. We were so shocked that I had to pull the car over to the side of the A1 just outside Grantham. I felt really saddened and sick to the pit of my stomach.

We normally headed down to Norfolk in an effort to place the horrors of Northern Ireland behind us for a few days; this time we were taking them with us. Nick and Lesley were totally gutted by the time we arrived, no doubt having already seen it all unfold on the television. I detected the earnest confusion on their faces as they tried to come to terms with the scene of utter horror and how people in Ireland could be so cruel towards each other.

Bill Clinton returned for an unprecedented third visit just before his presidency finished in 2000. He had always promised the people of Northern Ireland that he would return before he finished his term and he gained a lot of respect from the hardliners for keeping to his word. The fizz had now gone out of his presidency and he didn't draw as much attention this time, possibly due to the sordid Lewinsky affair. It was felt by some that this trip was an attempt at repairing his tarnished image. I was not directly involved in his visit to Belfast this time but I feel that all he had to say was extremely important.

Then, after stepping down as President, Bill Clinton again made another visit to Belfast in May 2001, this time to receive an honorary degree from Queen's University for services to peace in Northern Ireland. He travelled again to the Guildhall for his only public speech and then on to Enniskillen to open the William Jefferson Clinton International Peace Centre on the banks of the beautiful River Erne. His involvement in the politics of Northern Ireland was at an end but I have absolutely no doubt at all that the three visits he made in his capacity as President of the United States did galvanise the peace process. They made Ulster people stop and think deeply about the future, particularly the future of our children.

CHAPTER 20

A CANARY IN A CATTERY

Along with providing protection for these VIP visitors, I had continued to look after the same judge throughout much of this period. It was a fairly easy task, as all I had to do was take him to court in the morning and stay with him until it was time to go home. As he neared the end of his career, he was promoted to the position of Belfast Recorder, which, amongst other things, meant he was sitting permanently at the old Town Hall in Belfast. This gave me the opportunity to look around the law courts in Chichester Street, just across the road, where I was introduced to the infamous 'table of knowledge'.

This was a somewhat misleading description applied to a certain old piece of furniture that filled a dark and dingy private room in the bowels of the Belfast law courts building in Chichester Street. This imposing building of gleaming Portland stone bears the scars of a bomb that nearly destroyed it some years before. It is the centre of High Court law in Northern Ireland and the cream of Northern Ireland's judiciary, from the Lord Chief Justice down to the lowly Masters dealing with probate, can be found here. Inside its beautifully restored marbled reception hall and through double brass doors is the main hall, with grand entrances to the courts along one side and the Bar Library on the other.

A CANARY IN A CATTERY

Just off the main hall and around a darkened corner beside a tearoom is the door to that inner sanctum where the table of knowledge could be found. This was the room occupied by the 'barrack-room lawyers' of the CPU (so called because these men sat around all day dissecting rules and regulations in an attempt to trip up our authorities) and during my years of service it was symbolic of all that was wrong within the Close Protection Unit.

It was not a very large room and certainly not in keeping with the grandeur of the rest of the building. There was no wood panelling or marble here; instead, there were nicotine-stained walls and broken chairs. The object that immediately commanded your attention when you entered was a massive, old, dark wooden table, sitting square in the middle of the room. In its centre lay a collection of dog-eared Argos catalogues and tabloid newspapers. It was a table totally devoid of any decoration but its strength was evidenced by its very survival after many years of coarse use by the world's best furniture-tester – the policeman. Around the table was a collection of well-worn chairs and in the far corner of the room were a number of rickety cupboards and a filthy tea-stained sink. A plastic bin complete with week-old contents only added to the already pungent atmosphere. There had been attempts to impose a no-smoking policy but this was ignored by some of the older officers.

Confined to one corner were members of the uniform police guard squad, which was responsible for the day-to-day security within the court building. They occupied a tiny table and had one cardboard box to use for storage. The dominant presence was the many men who were involved in the personal security of the Lord Chief Justice and his High Court judges. There was no tenure of employment in force within the CPU and therefore many of these men had been entrenched in their positions for well over 15 years. They viewed the room as their turf and behaved very arrogantly towards new officers. There was always a lethargic atmosphere in that room and I felt that many good men were tainted by time spent wearing out their elbows around that infamous table.

There was something fundamentally wrong with allowing so many well-paid men to sit around all day doing nothing for up to ten hours. The situation bred laziness and apathy, and some officers became very lackadaisical with regard to the security arrangements for their principals. The CPU authorities must have realised things were getting out of hand, as at one point a supervisory sergeant was placed in the room on a permanent basis. He detailed the CPU men to carry out some very basic security checks on their judges and armoured cars, as it was obvious that without this supervision they could not motivate themselves to carry out these very simple tasks.

The room itself was affectionately called 'the bunker' by some men and I was relieved that I wasn't attached to a judge who would normally frequent this building on a daily basis. When I had to be in the building due to judges' meetings, I preferred to stand in the hall watching life go by. I was not part of the clique in the bunker so was never made to feel very welcome; instead, I carried on looking after my judge in the old Town Hall for his last few years until he announced his retirement in 1996.

I then had a choice to make about what I was going to do next. Would I stay with him and spend endless days on the golf course or, worse still, shopping, or would I ask for a move to another crew?

As I pondered my decision, another new chief inspector had arrived on the scene in the CPU. He was a bit of a whizz-kid and had apparently been transferred with orders to stamp out the corrupt practices that were earning the unit a bad name. He soon recognised the guilty parties and set about gathering the necessary evidence to have them brought to book. He set up covert observations at various venues and used security cameras aimed at the gates of Dundonald RUC station to check on men who left the base just after signing on in the morning and then returned surreptitiously to sign off duty later that day, thereby fooling our authorities into thinking they were in fact working. He seized the videotapes of the relevant days and had them enhanced to expose the culprits.

Other scams included fiddling overtime and making bogus meal claims. Two men were caught red-handed claiming overtime while their principal was sitting at home. Another two were caught claiming for non-existent duty on a rest-day at the law courts in Belfast. In all, six men were transferred out to uniform duty, taking with them the stigma of their unceremonious removal from the CPU. At Christmas, one of the barrack-room lawyers thought it would be a great idea to get up a collection for these disgraced officers to make up for their lost overtime. I refused to fund their lifestyles, but many men were psychologically bullied into handing over their hard-earned cash. In a ham-fisted attempt at shaming me into paying, he asked me again for a donation, this time in the packed canteen of Dundonald station. I told him there was no way was I paying money to that load of scoundrels, why should I? In response, he threw a childish tantrum, cursing at me in front of everyone.

As a result of this petty incident, I was ostracised by many of the other members of the unit, which really hurt. If the tongue were a bone, I would have been battered to death! The atmosphere at work became very strained, which took its toll on my mental health, and again I found myself falling into a state of total despair. My self-esteem hit an all-time low and I really felt that I hated the job and everything to do with it. For me, there was little pride to be found in being a member of the CPU, nor indeed in being a policeman.

I had no choice but to carry on, however, and I decided to ask for a move. In fact, I asked to be placed on the crew looking after one of the most high-profile men in Northern Ireland, Mr Peter Robinson MP, deputy leader of the Democratic Unionist Party led by firebrand loyalist the Rev. Ian Paisley.

'Are you right in the head?'

That was the general response from the men within the CPU when my request became common knowledge. 'The man is a workaholic' and 'He never goes home' were some of the milder observations from men who had previously worked with Peter.

In 1979, after a few years serving on Castlereagh council, Peter Robinson won the election for the parliamentary seat of East Belfast, defeating William Craig of the UUP by 64 votes. He won at the first count and has been Member of Parliament for East Belfast ever since. In 1988, both he and his wife Iris served short prison sentences for failure to pay fines imposed for public-order offences and though this didn't impress me much I still felt he was one of the best politicians around in Northern Ireland at that time.

I was already well aware of Peter's hectic schedule, as I had worked with him on a number of occasions while covering for men on his team who were going on holiday or required a night off. There was never any regularity to his working day, which I have to say appealed to me quite a lot after all the time I had spent sitting on my backside for hours looking after a judge in a courtroom. I would be back out on the street as bodyguard to an instantly recognisable public figure and this would be a challenging task considering he had many enemies. Peter was a high-profile target and under very real threat of attack. He had recently been targeted by the IRA in London and had had a parcel bomb delivered to his home.

The only grey cloud on the horizon arose from the fact I was to be inserted into Peter's crew as the officer in charge of his security. This decision, taken by my authorities, caused some consternation amongst the already established members on the crew – I was being transferred in to replace a man who had asked for a move after serving some years with Peter, and the other three members of the crew weren't happy at all. They saw my transfer in above them as a slight on their ability but it was pointed out that none of them had the necessary operational experience on the street to take control of his security.

I settled in very well after making a few of my own changes, resulting in a more efficient working relationship between my crew and Peter. Prior to my arrival, it was common knowledge that certain members of this crew had attained the dubious reputation of being some of the highest overtime earners in the CPU. I was called into the chief's office two months into my tenure to be shown figures demonstrating a 35 per cent drop in overtime since I took over. He praised me for my efficient management and asked me for some form of explanation as to the high level before my arrival, probably hoping I would finger some members involved in claiming overtime for work not done – of which I was aware. I told him, with all due respect, that this was not my problem and he should question the men who had worked in the crew before me, and after that I heard no more about it.

I was, however, concerned about a certain degree of complacency amongst the other crew members. They didn't vary their routes on a daily basis and would commit the cardinal sin of setting routines in relation to daily movements to and from his home. I had to ask them to alter the pick-up times and routes both inward and outward, something I shouldn't have had to do, bearing in mind these men were supposed to be trained to the same standard as myself.

Right from the start, I adopted a hardline approach to Peter's security in that I would not tolerate slackness or downright dangerous practice. After all, it was not only his life I was concerned with but also, more importantly, my own: I would be no bloody good to him dead! This stance did cause some conflict with the other members of the crew and I was horrified by the behaviour of one of the men in particular. This officer had very little service under his belt and I felt that, as a result, he hadn't developed that instinct for survival that becomes second nature to a long-serving RUC man. He was never switched on in relation to possible attacks, seeing the whole branch as some sort of glorified taxi service. More times than I care to remember, I would catch him asleep in the armoured car outside an office while I was inside with the principal. On one occasion, Peter had to knock very loudly on the windscreen to gain entry to the locked car – an unbelievable situation. He was even caught by staff at Peter's office sleeping upstairs stretched out on some chairs while he was supposed to be guarding the main door. In the end, and after numerous warnings, he had to go. After much complaining, he was replaced by a better man and the crew worked together in relative harmony.

This duty was very different to protecting a judge. Judges had a certain degree of anonymity, as no one outside the court circle really knew what they looked like without their gowns and wigs. They were, by and large, free to walk about on their own in relative safety and quite a few of them did so. It was always considered they were under greater threat during the more predictable times of their week and so full cover was always supplied for the journey to court in the morning and home again that evening. Security was somewhat more lax at weekends, even to the degree of using a non-armoured and therefore more comfortable car for shopping trips or golfing excursions. Peter was a different kettle of fish altogether. He was constantly at high risk and, without exception, he always travelled in an armoured car. If there were times when I wasn't actually involved in his personal security, I would be subconsciously going over numerous attack scenarios in an attempt to work out the best plan of action and escape. At the end of a long day I would be very tired, both physically and mentally.

The fact that he was Paisley's deputy, as well as being somewhat outspoken, would have made Peter a 'prize kill' for some of the smaller republican terrorist groups. I believed it would have been counter-productive for the IRA to take him out: the political backlash would have been devastating to Sinn Féin and they were also only too aware that such an attack would lead to all-out war with Protestant militants. The smaller republican organisations had less to lose. I also had to be fully aware of the possibility of an attack from within the loyalist community, as some elements there were to be trusted even less than the IRA.

As I got to know him, I formed the impression that Peter enjoyed the fact that he had a car and two policemen at his beck and call. He was, after all, from a humble background and I felt we were massaging his ego. Being tied to such a busy schedule, it would have been very inconvenient to drive himself to and from literally dozens of meetings per week. He already had previous experience of this hardship as on 7 August 1986, the Chief Constable, Sir John Hermon, unceremoniously removed Peter's two police bodyguards and their car from his use after he led a large group of Protestant protesters into the small town of Clontibret, across the border in County Monaghan. The protesters caused widespread damage and seriously assaulted two Irish policemen. Local residents were verbally abused, intimidated and terrified as the rabble ran riot in their little town. When Garda reinforcements arrived, only one man was arrested – Peter Robinson – even though he was not directly involved in any of the vandalism or violence.

Peter was in serious trouble in custody across the border and, with the prospect of being held on remand in Mountjoy Prison, where no doubt the IRA would be waiting, frantic efforts were made to raise the bail money. With a sigh of relief, he was released on bail to appear at a later date (whereupon he was found guilty of unlawful arrest and fined 15,000 Irish punts). But when he returned home, he arrived in time to witness the removal of all his security equipment. I was there myself, having been held on duty after dropping off another principal at his home and, with the assistance of one of our sergeants, we called to remove the police radio equipment from his home. We were greeted at the gates of Peter's home by loyalist thugs wielding baseball bats, as they were now in overall charge of his security. In what very nearly developed into a mini-riot, we gained access and removed our equipment. A few days later, Peter Robinson was to be seen being driven around Belfast in an old second-hand armoured Mercedes hurriedly bought from a car dealer in England.

As Peter was a Member of Parliament at Westminster, Sir John Hermon came under extreme pressure to restore his protection. He had the guts to refuse and when asked what the Secretary of State would do if Robinson were murdered, he replied sharply, 'He would blame me!' Peter's protection was not restored until several years later, just before Sir John Hermon was due to retire. In some ways, I think that was a wake-up call for Peter. I had noticed by the time I was protecting him in 1996 that he was making a conscious effort to distance himself from situations which might develop into such violence.

There were still occasions, however, when I questioned some of his actions and one of these was his visit to Billy 'King Rat' Wright in Maghaberry Prison in March 1997. Wright was a hardened loyalist murderer who was generally thought to have carried out his first murder at the age of 21 and was eventually charged with the drive-by shooting of a Catholic man, Peadar Fagan, in 1981. It came out in the court case that he had carried out the shooting in retaliation for the IRA murder of the Rev. Robert Bradford, Member of Parliament for South Belfast, as he was holding his political surgery in a community hall in the Finaghy area of Belfast. Wright was later acquitted when the case collapsed.

After a period of freedom, Wright was jailed for eight years in March of 1997 for threatening to kill a woman. She and her son had to leave Northern Ireland and live under police protection at a secret address in England. This time, Wright was incarcerated in the isolation unit of Maghaberry Prison and he was crying out for help. Word was out that republicans were out to kill him.

I was standing in Peter's Belmont Avenue office when the phone call came in. Billy wanted Peter to visit him in prison – and soon. The phone call caused reverberations in the office that day and I was dumbstruck by the way Peter responded to this request. Billy Wright wasn't even a constituent of his and yet here he was running to the aid of a murderer in prison.

A few days later, on 18 March 1997, we arrived at the gates of the prison. Peter had no papers or files with him that day, which was very unusual, as he was always to be seen with something under his arm. Obviously, on this occasion, he was here on an advice-only basis. We checked in to the legal visits area, made our way through the prison and were shown to the room where the visit was to take place. At the appointed time of 2.30 p.m., Wright arrived in the room flanked by two burly guards. They walked him around the small table and sat him down on a plastic chair that had been chained to the floor, then left to observe through the toughened glass. Wright looked at me and caught me sizing him up. He hadn't changed at all since the last time I had seen him, when he had been orchestrating a riot in Portadown some years earlier. His close-cropped hair and sharp features only accentuated his dark and sinister psychopathic eyes. I felt a shiver run down my spine as I realised that I was peering into the black heart of a man who would kill without emotion or remorse. He didn't display any animosity to me but, then again, as Peter's bodyguard he would have viewed me as 'kosher'.

This was a bizarre situation indeed: here I was in the presence of a mass murderer who, in any other part of the UK, would be classed as a serial killer and, as such, kept under constant supervision at all times, but the guards in Maghaberry had now cleared off for a cup of tea! I was satisfied as to Peter's security, though, so I also left the room in order to let them speak confidentially and stood by the closed door.

After the relatively short meeting was over, Peter rapped the door and I entered the, by now, very stuffy room. Billy looked drawn, as if all hope was lost. Whatever Peter had told him, I don't think it was to his liking. The normal hard-man image that he portrayed was fading as I again made eye contact and, instantly, I detected the fear in his very soul. Peter wished him well and we departed the way we had come.

As I wasn't privy to the conversation that day, I don't know what went on between Peter Robinson and Billy Wright, though I was convinced that it had something to do with Wright wanting to move from Maghaberry to the Maze Prison. Nothing was said in the car on the way back and I don't believe Peter could have influenced such a decision, though in April Wright's transfer did go ahead. On 27 December that year, it was reported in the news that the 37-year-old Wright had been shot dead in the yard of the Maze Prison by a fellow prisoner who was a member of the hardline republican Irish National Liberation Army.

I had been surprised by how willing Robinson seemed to be to meet with Wright, as he had been furious about the televised appearance of DUP Assembly Member the Rev. William McCrea sharing a stage with Wright at a rally in Portadown just the previous year. A massive attempt at damage limitation had been launched after this incident but it didn't last long and I felt the DUP continued to show empathy towards convicted loyalists.

Another source of controversy was the visits made to the home of Neil Latimer in Armagh. Latimer was one of the Ulster Defence Regiment's infamous UDR4, four local soldiers who had been convicted of the murder of a 24-year-old Catholic in 1984. Three of them were cleared in the Appeal Court in 1992 but Latimer's appeal failed and he remained in prison.

Peter Robinson, the Rev. Ian Paisley and his son, Ian Paisley jnr, visited Latimer's parents' home on 30 December 1996 for what appeared to be a very cosy reunion. Ian Paisley jnr was the DUP security spokesman and a leading campaigner for the UDR4. I was quite surprised to be welcomed into the house, but maybe it was because his parents looked upon me as a member of 'their' police force. I felt uncomfortable throughout this visit and still questioned whether politicians should be seen paying lip service to what was, to all intents and purposes, the family of a convicted murderer. They weren't their local politicians but leader and deputy leader of the Democratic Unionist Party.

Latimer was released after serving 14 years. Three Appeal Court judges sitting in Belfast on 9 February 2004 turned down an unprecedented third appeal against Latimer's conviction and he is still fighting to clear his name.

On one occasion, the slogan 'DUP = LVF' was daubed on the walls of Peter's constituency office in Belmont Avenue in bold white paint. As soon as the office staff reported for work that morning, they realised that what made this particular incident even more worrying for Peter was the fact that in a few hours' time there was to be a televised press conference from this very office. We arrived soon afterwards with a visibly very angry Peter Robinson. No sooner had his feet hit the street than he had his staff out scrubbing the door and walls in panic before the arrival of the press. A front-page picture of this slogan in the *Belfast Telegraph* could have destroyed years of sterling work in keeping the DUP's nose clean in the eyes of the political world. I am sure his agitation was enhanced by the fact that all the other residents of the street were by now standing on their doorsteps. I invoked further bile by refusing to help remove the paint from the door – that wasn't my job and he knew it. As hard as they tried, they could not remove the white stain left by the paint on the brickwork and when the press arrived they asked the staff some pretty direct questions 'off air' regarding the possibility of there being any truth in the slogan.

Peter Robinson is a razor-sharp politician with an incisive understanding of the political scene. In some ways, I would now see Paisley as Peter's deputy, as he slowly takes control of an evolving DUP. I have always felt that Peter has real political ambition and I believe he will not rest until he becomes Lord Gransha or Lord Castlereagh. Peter loves politics, he lives it and his very existence revolves around the debating chamber – but I can't help feeling his biggest political blunder was walking away with his party from the discussions leading up to the Good Friday Agreement or Belfast Agreement, depending on which side of the fence you sit. They should have stayed in there, as the unionist people of Northern Ireland would have extracted a much better deal, and I felt Peter knew it. He was following the party line but I could see real hunger in his eyes. I felt he yearned to be in Castle Buildings with all the participants in those historic talks, which would ultimately lead to the political reshaping of this Province.

I was gutted as we drove out of those gates in July 1997 in that characteristic DUP 'No, never' huff; I think Peter also knew it was wrong. I could sense the internal conflict he was experiencing as he headed home on the quietest journey of my four years with him. I was excited as the talks were reaching a crucial stage and it would not be a lie if I said that everyone in that building could feel real progress at last being made on this island.

You could feel it in the air and in the packed corridors of Castle Buildings.

Even though Peter was now taking no part in the proceedings, I volunteered after my shift to return to Stormont to relieve members of other crews looking for time off. Just prior to the signing of that historic agreement, I must have been at Castle Buildings every day. Even when off duty, I would observe the proceedings from the press gallery. I wanted to be part of history – and I was. I have my own personal copy of the agreement signed by all involved in those talks, including the Prime Minister, Tony Blair, the Taoiseach, Bertie Ahern, and the 108 members elected to the new Assembly at Stormont.

I continued protecting Peter as he prepared for the elections in June 1998. This, I was assured by the other crew members, would be the real test of my resolve, as we would rack up long hours and high mileage while Peter canvassed all over Northern Ireland helping to raise the profile of other less well-known party candidates fighting for, or hoping to retain, their seats.

As I have probably said before, politics has never been one of my greatest interests. I have a mind of my own and don't toe any party line. I always formed the impression that there was never any love lost between the DUP and the RUC. They would use us when it suited them for poster campaigns seeking votes but cast us aside as soon as we had served our purpose. According to the DUP, we were the best police force in the world until we faced up to the loyalist thuggery at Drumcree from 1996 onwards, then overnight the RUC became the villains!

While attending an election rally in Kilkeel, I observed a side to DUP loyalism that sickened me beyond belief. I was protecting the life of Peter Robinson while at the same time the crowd was baying for my blood as an RUC man. We had arrived in our armoured car into Kilkeel in the dark of evening and made our way through the hostile crowd who had assumed we were a normal unmarked police patrol car until they sighted our passenger. On arrival at the lorry trailer made into a platform bedecked in red, white and blue bunting, Peter mounted the stage to the rapturous applause of the hundreds of supporters who had turned out in the cold drizzle to hear him speak. But all through the proceedings, the chants and taunts came raining in from the rear of the crowd: 'SS RUC, SS RUC' and 'Burn, burn, burn the bastards'. To say I was getting a bit concerned would be an understatement: we were, after all, totally alone without uniform police back-up, as the local police patrols had been advised by the organisers to stay out in order to avoid trouble.

I had already witnessed on previous occasions what a hostile crowd like this was capable of and I gave very serious consideration to extracting Peter from the venue. Then Peter rose to address the crowd and I half expected some support from him, maybe a warning to the crowd to behave. No chance! He commenced by castigating the RUC's actions at Drumcree and telling the crowd that as the RUC were refusing to let Orangemen walk down Garvaghy Road they would have to face the consequences. I was incensed and the crowd was now growing uglier by the second. I sent my driver off with the armoured car and machine gun to the police station for his own protection and gave serious consideration to departing myself. This course of action would have been well within my standing orders and my actions would have been fully supported by my authorities. The meeting ended without further incident, however, and Peter was conveyed home in total silence. He must have known I was disgusted at his lack of support. At times like this I felt very conflicted about what I was doing protecting such a man.

At the height of the Drumcree stand-off in 1998, Peter made me aware of his intention to attend the loyalist protest at Drumcree church one evening. There was no way I was going to risk my life and the life of one of my crew members so he could attend this hate-filled venue and I seriously questioned why a Member of Parliament wanted to go there anyway.

For some weeks before, Orange Order protesters had relentlessly pasted the police lines, attempting to break through and triumphantly parade down the Catholic Garvaghy Road. I had no doubt at all that the very sight of our unmarked police cars at Drumcree church would have placed us in great danger. It had come to my notice that the Rev. Ian Paisley also wished to attend, so I liaised with his crew to find out what measures they were planning. On that night, his two regular constables were off duty and the protection of Paisley was entrusted to a full-time Reserve constable who wasn't even aware of the standing orders in relation to police visiting

Drumcree church. As an act of bravado, he was prepared to take Paisley to the church, compromising his own safety and that of his crew. I had to put a stop to this, so I contacted our inspector and explained the situation. The problem, as I saw it, was that if Paisley had gone to Drumcree in his police protection car then Peter would have travelled with him, leaving the CPU and myself with egg on our faces in relation to future visits.

No CPU policeman entered Drumcree that night. Instead, against all advice, Paisley and Robinson were dropped off at the Birches roundabout on the M1 motorway and made their own way to the church in cars belonging to other DUP party members. We then waited in Lurgan police station for their safe return to us in the early hours of the morning.

By now I was getting really fed up with Peter Robinson's antics and being the butt of jokes about protecting such a man. There was no pride to be derived from my work but it didn't alter the fact that Peter was still under very serious threat of assassination. On an everyday basis, we found ourselves under the constant threat of an attack; we didn't know where or when, we couldn't drop our guard at all. I was usually exhausted by the end of the day, not only by the physical aspect of duty but, more importantly, drained psychologically by maintaining that high level of alertness for so long year after year.

The dark evenings were undoubtedly the worst for me, as I felt this was the easiest time for terrorists to attack. It wouldn't have been difficult for anyone to find out Peter's planned movements, as his attendance at meetings or rallies, particularly in more rural areas, would be treated as a great event. It was always uncertain what time he would leave home and sometimes he would be forced to change his plans at the last minute, but it was always certain that after his departure from a venue he would be heading home to Dundonald. If an attack was on, I felt it would most likely occur in the dead of night when we were tired and had let our guard down after assuming we had survived another day.

Bearing all this in mind, I was always very cautious about our chosen route back to Peter's house. Much to the annoyance of my tired crewmate, and indeed Peter, I would often dictate a last-minute change of route, sometimes heading streets away and coming in from a totally different direction. But try as hard as we could to fend off any possibility of an attack, we still had to travel the Gransha Road to his house and this was where the hair would stand up on the back of my neck. With full beams and spotlights burning the road ahead, I would scan the area for something out of the ordinary. Why is that wheelie bin there? Is it refuse collection day? Which house does that car belong to? Why is that street lamp out? Approaching the gates, I would ensure that no traffic was in front of us and our car was in first gear ready for a speedy exit or a hand-brake turn. With monotonous regularity, I would put brand-new batteries in the remote control that opened the gate. So many variables existed that sometimes, I'm not ashamed to say, we just held our breath and hoped for the best.

Once inside, the gates were immediately closed behind us and we could relax to a certain degree – but not totally. Peter's gardens are huge, to say the least. His rear fence was so far away that it would be in total darkness. I never felt fully secure until I had him in through the bullet-proof door and it was locked for the night.

After a while, I did begin to wonder whether I might be taking the job too seriously. Men before me seemed to have been so blasé concerning Peter's security that my pedantic nature was now causing serious friction within the crew. At this time, I was also subject to the most massive mood swings imaginable. Some days I would be fine and then it would be all change the next morning. I had learned to manage my depression to some extent but I couldn't hide my troubled state completely and colleagues at work, including my crewmates, were beginning to question my sanity.

During a very low spell, I invented an excuse to leave Agnes and did indeed leave the family home one night for a while. I had begun to think that if I was out of the way then maybe it would make life easier for her, but after many hours walking in the cold night air I came to my senses. 'What the hell am I doing?' I remember shouting out. By the time I got back to the house, Agnes had raced off in the car in a dreadful state, as can be imagined. She drove around for ages, tears streaming down her cheeks and not knowing where to go. In all honesty, I didn't expect that response; my self-esteem was now so low that I thought she would have been glad to be rid of me.

Robert and Cassandra were now fully aware of what was going on between their parents. They were also badly affected by what I had instigated that night and it must have come as a complete shock to them to see the state I was in. In the past, while I would have been stressed out at times, I would normally have been in total control.

My massive mood swing had by now gone completely the other way and I was doing all in my power to heal the hurt I had inflicted. Through a tearful night, Agnes and I patched things up and over the following weeks I slowly regained my balance; it appeared my outburst on that night had somehow released some pressure within. I felt much better and our relationship improved beyond all recognition now that some of my demons were out in the open. Robert and Cassandra were aware their father was at breaking point and they both went out of their way to ensure that nothing stressful was placed in his way. With the benefit of hindsight, I now believe that the pressure of maintaining the high level of alertness required by the CPU had become too much over a protracted period of time. Rather than leaving my work-related problems in Dundonald RUC station, I was bringing them home in my head.

It was Agnes, as head of the household, I felt great pity for. She was always working away behind the scenes ensuring I ate properly, was clothed well and that our home ran without a hitch. I invariably took her for granted, never noticing the little things that made our house a home or appreciating the strain that I put her under. It was thanks to her support that I was able to continue as long as I did.

No sooner had the new Assembly been established at Stormont than the DUP came crawling back to the table. I felt they had been left out in the cold for too long and realised they were losing credibility as things were really starting to move on the political front. On the DUP's first day back, Monday, 20 July 1998, and under massive scrutiny from the world press, I escorted Peter through the west door and into the palatial grandeur of the Parliament Buildings at Stormont. He settled into his office as if he had always been there. I detected startled looks on the faces of some of his more militant supporters, no doubt under the impression that the DUP were there to wreck the place. Quite the contrary, in fact; they were filling the teapot, opening the biscuits and getting their feet well and truly under the table. Their appointed offices were on the second floor on the south corner – just up the hall on the other corner was their arch enemy, Sinn Féin.

In the new Assembly at Stormont, Peter accepted the role of Minister for Regional Development and, as such, he had responsibility for roads and transport. In his new position, Peter had decided that a proposed multi-million-pound bypass in the staunchly nationalist area of Toomebridge was to be given the green light. This action seemed to cause some raised eyebrows within the DUP as another equally valid request had already been placed with his department for a similar bypass in the mainly Protestant County Down village of Comber. I couldn't help feeling that Peter's decision was an attempt to appease the stunned locals and he knew that it would undoubtedly show him in a good light at government level.

Toomebridge is a very small village halfway between Belfast and Londonderry. It is 100 per cent Catholic and has always been considered a hotbed of republican terrorism. The Toomebridge police station, with its two massive armoured sangars, has the look of a veritable fortress as it nestles at the end of the main street. Its light-brown brickwork and hideous green-painted high steel fence and mesh wire would not look out of place on a mountain pass in Afghanistan. Directly across the road and in full view of the police observers cocooned within its sangars is a massive marble cross, a republican memorial to Rody McCorley, who was hanged on this spot for his part in the rising of 1798; a reminder, if one were needed, of the continuing struggle for Irish freedom and the willingness of its activists to die for their cause.

The official launch of the project was to be held in the rear function room of the O'Neill Arms Hotel in the centre of Toomebridge village. This venue caused me a lot of anxiety, as there were many people in the area who would have had a grievance with Peter Robinson and everything that the DUP represented. We were tasked to deliver him right into the midst of this potentially very hostile crowd.

After a conference with my authorities, it was decided that every effort would be made to have him at this venue without uniform back-up and regardless of local public opinion. I was aware that certain assurances with reference to a 'safe passage' had already been gained from the local councillor and MLA at Stormont, Mr John Kelly of Sinn Féin. Not that this completely put my mind at rest.

We arrived at the venue and made our way to the rear of the building where the function room entrance was marked out by beautiful shrubs in ugly plastic tubs. I entered the crowded room, keeping close to Peter's side. The hubbub stopped immediately as everyone was made aware that the minister had arrived. The subordinate Regional Development staff and officials obediently made their way over to welcome him. I scanned the room and noticed that a large number of well-known active IRA men were present. Bearing in mind the political connotations of this visit and the republican hunger for that elusive picture of a handshake between Sinn Féin/IRA and the DUP, Kelly made every attempt to thrust unknown Sinn Féin party members into Peter's path. Kelly was hoping Peter would be duped into a handshake, which would be captured on film by their stalking photographers. It wasn't for me to stop this petty stunt but then again I also had to be fully alert to the possibility of an attack by the IRA. One of the thugs was standing beside the bar openly 'trigger fingering' his head, no doubt in an attempt to cause a confrontation with me that would leave Peter vulnerable. The scene was starting to turn really ugly and I had to physically manhandle Kelly out of the way a number of times. I had now made Peter aware of Sinn Féin's obvious intentions and the 'meet and greet' aspect of the visit was cut short as he took to the podium to commence his speech concerning the building of the bypass.

At this point, the men I had recognised as IRA members left the meeting. I was worried about where they had gone and what they might have planned for our departure, so I called the driver of my armoured car on my radio and asked him to contact the local RUC station and request that they provide cover when we left in 30 minutes. This request wasn't met, however, and I reflected bitterly on the fact that in so many cases the local police rarely helped out the CPU unless they were in receipt of an operational order from headquarters. Somewhat gingerly, we left the building, thinking Peter was now departing Toomebridge, only to have him commence a walkabout in the village, no doubt as an act of defiance aimed directly at Sinn Féin.

I could see the anger in the faces of the local people as he gave a televised interview in the middle of their main street and he was literally drowned out by verbal abuse and the sounding of car and lorry horns. This disturbance eventually drew the local police to the scene and they were livid at this blatantly provocative act, which would no doubt result in an overspill of anger that they would ultimately have to deal with later on that evening.

At last, I managed to get Peter into our car, which I had instructed to follow us. We then left the village without further incident on a totally different route than would normally have been expected. In order to cause confusion amongst any waiting IRA units, we headed off in the other direction towards Londonderry before doubling back cross-country towards Belfast.

This was only one of many times Peter would openly come into conflict with his political enemy, Sinn Féin, and I always asked myself whether he would be so brave if it wasn't for his two police bodyguards and their armoured car that shadowed his every move. I think not. Would a canary in a cattery sing so loud if it didn't have a cage?

It was around this time I noticed there was renewed interest within the CPU in relation to possible duty within my crew protecting Peter. Young and very keen members who had just joined the unit were constantly asking me to 'put a good word in for them' within the CPU hierarchy. I was somewhat puzzled until I realised that there were some men who, like me, wanted to get their sleeves rolled up and do the job they were actually getting paid for.

Escorting the Secretary of State or the other government ministers was generally felt to be totally detached from the real CPU protection world. These ministerial protection crews had everything done for them and they didn't have to think for themselves, as everywhere they went there was an army of uniform police waiting to ensure their safety. Government ministers rarely walked the streets of Northern Ireland and shied away from trouble spots. In effect, the job of their CPU minders was to act as a taxi service, delivering them to their next venue and into the protection of the local police. There also appeared to be too much of that old 'Yes, Minister' ethos prevalent in their everyday duties: the Secretary of State Mo Mowlam apparently even used her two policemen to collect her shopping! Working for a high-threat politician such as Peter was seen as much more of a challenge.

Bearing in mind that Peter Robinson and his DUP party were well known to be staunchly Protestant, any new CPU member would always, inevitably, find himself working in that environment. I was somewhat surprised, therefore, when I was called into the chief inspector's office to be informed he had a certain Catholic member of the unit that he was going to transfer onto my team. I told him I had absolutely no problem with that and indeed I was very surprised he had brought it to my attention. But he then informed me that this officer had made allegations that he was being discriminated against as a Catholic because he never got to work with any of the high-ranking political principals. At the same time, he also alleged he never got to perform duty on Royal (Category) visits, and again stated that this was because of his religion.

Unwritten practice within the CPU had been to avoid placing Catholics with overtly Protestant politicians such as Ian Paisley, Martin Smyth, David Trimble and Peter Robinson. This practice had nothing at all to do with discrimination but was more to do with avoiding serious embarrassment to the policeman, bearing in mind the very contentious locations he would find himself in on a daily basis. Protestant rallies, band parades and meetings in Orange halls were the normal events you found yourself caught up in when attached to these high-profile politicians. Although I felt some unease at the position in which I was being placed, I informed the chief that, as far as I was concerned, I had no problems and would welcome him into my crew.

The man in question went on to prove himself a very worthwhile member of my team. He was very conscientious and alert. He brought with him many new ideas, worked really well with the other men and as such only strengthened us as a unit. On his first day, he opened up his heart to tell me of the reasons he found himself on my team. He told me that, while he had wanted to change team and felt he had been overlooked in the past,

Peter Robinson certainly wouldn't have been his first choice of principal and he felt that the chief had put him there out of spite after he had complained. I sympathised with him to a certain degree but also felt he could have gone about addressing his situation in a more diplomatic way. I felt he could only see the problem from his side, oblivious to the operational problems that could ensue from a wrong placement. He didn't spend very long on our team and after coming to some arrangement with our authorities he was voluntarily transferred out of the CPU and into an office job somewhere in headquarters.

Whether intentional or not, he had left behind a legacy of blame and counter-blame, as accusations were flung around our unit, resulting in a witch-hunt among our more senior members, some of whom retired early as a result of the stress created. The CPU would never be the same again. Our authorities were now constantly going out of their way to appease the minorities within our branch. A new set of guidelines and regulations were drawn up and strictly adhered to from then on. The chief inspector drew up this new Equal Opportunities Statement, issuing each member with his own copy and getting us to sign to prove we had received it:

CLOSE PROTECTION UNIT
EQUAL OPPORTUNITIES STATEMENT

Allocation of officers to principals will primarily take into account the skills and experience of the officer, their developmental needs and the nature of the principals' duties.

All officers will be provided with the opportunity to perform protection duties on Category visits. Any decision on allocation will be based upon the skills and experience of that officer, his/her developmental needs, the principal and nature of the visit.

Operational necessity, coupled with the health and safety of officers, will be the overriding factor in determining allocation to principals or deployment on Category visits.

No officer will receive less favourable treatment on the grounds of gender, marital status, religion, political opinion, race, or sexual orientation.

> None of these guidelines preclude any officer from drawing to
> the attention of a supervisory rank any concerns he/she may have
> in relation to his/her duty with a particular principal or
> deployment on Category visits.

This really seemed like a bit of overkill when I thought about it, considering we only had approximately eight Catholics out of a total complement of one hundred and thirty.

As the peace process progressed into the new millennium, I became more and more dissatisfied working for Peter Robinson and felt myself suffocating in the negative atmosphere of DUP politics. For the first time in history, politicians in Northern Ireland were making real progress on the very big issues that had caused conflict here for generations but the DUP remained entrenched in their negativity, refusing to make any concessions in order to facilitate the process. At every turn, I witnessed them disrupt progress in the formation of better community relations by their childish tantrums in and out of the Assembly chamber at Stormont. To be perfectly honest, I sometimes felt that Robinson was being strangled politically by his close association with Paisley and would better serve Ulster politics by starting up his own less bigoted and more tolerant party.

Negativity rubs off on you; it's like cigarette smoke as it sticks to your clothes and skin, and you can feel its effects for days. Over a period of time, you become accustomed to it and no longer find reason to despise it. Eventually you build up a subconscious barrier to anything positive and view everything in life with a defeatist attitude. I was becoming more and more concerned for myself working in this contagious environment and I realised it was time to move on before I too fell victim to the dreaded 'No, never' view of life.

CHAPTER 21

I HAD SUFFERED ENOUGH

Ever since the last bout of deep internal conflict, I had been attempting to stay on an even keel. With Agnes's help, I had managed to keep going. On many occasions, I found myself on the verge of re-establishing contact with the RUC Occupational Health Unit when I felt myself sliding into deep despair. Nothing specific would cause this worsening of my stress disorder; rather it would be a culmination of factors that would build until one day I found I could take no more.

The political climate in the run-up to the publication of the Patten report didn't help my frame of mind. I couldn't believe the news that was filtering out about the future plans for the force. I would be the first to agree that the RUC did require radical change but I could not believe it when I heard that the force of which I had been part for 21 years, putting my life at risk to serve my community, was to be replaced by the new Police Service of Northern Ireland. I felt as if we were somehow being blamed for the events of the last 30 years and the politicians were trying to erase us from history.

This feeling was reinforced by the increasingly prominent role of the Police Ombudsman. On 4 November 2000, I read a story in the *Belfast Telegraph* concerning the opening of the new Police Ombudsman's office in Belfast. The title of the story summed it up very well: 'Police watchdog shows new teeth'. It was clear to me after reading this story that Nuala O'Loan could not wait to get her teeth into the RUC. She even boasted that her 'civilian investigators' would have the same powers as police officers, as they could obtain search warrants, secure evidence and even make arrests. It felt as though a witch-hunt was being conducted and it really scared me to think what they would do when they eventually got their hands on our files or even our service records from the personnel department. There have already been many stories of policemen being suspended on the totally unsatisfactory evidence of criminals.

I looked around me with disgust at the many so-called 'reformed' terrorists who now held positions of power in our government and at the mass murderers now free to walk the streets of Northern Ireland. More shocking still was the realisation that there were over 1,800 unsolved murders still on the books in Northern Ireland. I would not, could not, be part of their 'new police service'; it would be to deny everything I had gone through.

I have no doubt at all that it was this enforced process of change that was causing me great trauma around this time and was fundamental in bringing my past problems to a head. The hinges on that bulging chest of memories had now burst open; the contents were spilling out all over the floor.

On Monday, 6 November 2000, I had to go off sick from work. I knew this was to be my last working day as a policeman. I finally made the decision I had been thinking about for many years; in the interests of my sanity, I had no choice.

I finished compiling a 28-page report containing the specific details of my ugly past and presented this to the Occupational Health Unit. While handing it over, I told them in no uncertain terms that I felt my career had come to an end. It is very difficult for a stranger sitting in an office to grasp exactly what a policeman goes through and how he copes with turmoil, so I felt it would be of great benefit to them if I created a written portrait of a troubled man and presented it to them. I had been keeping accurate records for years in journals and official police notebooks of all incidents I had been involved in and the effect the trauma had on my overall well-being. The act of recording it somehow felt as if I was unloading it onto someone else. After a lengthy assessment, the Force Medical Officer decided that I had suffered enough and it was time for me to leave the organisation for good. He said he had no hesitation in recommending my medical retirement, as he was in no doubt that I had been psychologically injured on duty. I was told that I would not be returning to the ranks and would eventually be retired, but I now had to go through the long process of securing that retirement on medical grounds.

It was early evening before I arrived home that day from the Occupational Health Unit and explained to Agnes all that had happened and my future plans with regard to my career. She was understandably quite concerned and wanted to know what was going on. I told her that maybe it would be a good idea if we headed off somewhere first, away from the house, maybe to the pool for a swim. I had to get out into the fresh air for a while. We headed off and had a good soak and steam, talking on the way; it felt good to get some of this off my chest.

The next day, I had to tell her all that had happened in the years gone by. I knew this was going to really hurt her but I thought it was time she was told of my past. During 26 years of married life, I had refused to share with her the details of what I was involved in at work and I was now about to drop the biggest bombshell she would ever have to deal with. I gave her a copy of the report I had handed to my authorities and then went outside to do some gardening and await her reaction.

About one hour later, I came back in to find her crying her eyes out; I had never seen Agnes in so much pain and it frightened me. She was pale, shocked and devastated to learn of some of the things that I had been through. We embraced and I found it near impossible to retain my composure. 'Thank God,' I thought to myself, 'now it's all out in the open.' I felt great relief, as if some enormous burden had been lifted from my shoulders. Now I had a number of people in my corner who could help me to fight my demons. There is no doubt that the solution in a situation like this is to get everything out. This is what I was trying to do and it seemed to be working.

The next few days at home were spent in quiet contemplation of what might lie ahead and what direction I would move in. To be quite honest, I was excited and looking forward to the future and what path I might take. One thing I was certain about was the fact that never again could I hold down a stressful job or even one which entailed a high degree of responsibility, such was the damage that had been done to my confidence over the years.

As the days passed, I became aware that in order to make as full a recovery as possible I would have to remove myself completely from any association with the police. I was offered assistance from the Police Retraining and Rehabilitation Trust (PRRT) but as that meant I would still have to work with other policemen within a structured environment I turned down the offer. I just had to get away from them all. I was also concerned about the large number of civilians on the PRRT staff to whom I would have to divulge my personal details. My concerns proved well founded when a serious security breach took place at the neighbouring offices of the Police Fund at Maryfield outside Holywood in November 2003. The names and details of hundreds of serving and retired officers went missing and two members of staff were arrested.

I decided that it would be a good idea if Agnes and I headed off on a short holiday to the west coast of Ireland. I don't really have any hang-ups about crossing the border; in fact, quite the opposite – I can really relax as I blend in with the tourists. While crossing over, I often feel as though I am moving into a different time zone and one in which there are few reminders of the troubles of my previous occupation. We had a fantastic weekend in County Mayo, relaxing as best we could in our idyllic surroundings and enjoying each other's company to the full. It was good to get away from it all.

By way of distraction, my friend Tommy arrived from Australia a few months later. We chewed the fat together and spent a lot of time discussing the way ahead over the coming months. He really is a tower of strength and someone whose advice I will always value. During his stay, however, world events were to overtake us and shatter the fragile sense of peace I had been starting to construct.

Tommy, Agnes and I had just arrived at Quincy's Restaurant in Bangor for a meal on 11 September 2001, when I heard the report about the attacks on the World Trade Center on the car radio. I sat frozen, taking in all the sketchy details as they unfolded, scarcely believing them to be true. I could hardly bear to think about what the poor people in those towers were going through. I had not been so upset for a very long time as I struggled to come to terms with the scale of this attack and the thought of the human carnage. I toiled through our meal that evening in a trance, unable to keep a straight head, oblivious to all around me.

On arrival home later that evening, we were bombarded with all the gory televised details and I'm not afraid to say that at times I felt sick and had to leave the room. I believe I kept this emotion secret from Agnes and Tommy but at times I felt my eyes welling up and had to think of something else to take my mind off those terrible events. I kept thinking in graphic detail about exactly what those poor souls were going through as they burned to death, and some, unable to bear the torturous heat in their offices, jumped out of the windows to a certain death below. That night the demons of the past visited me in my bed. I could smell the death and destruction as I buried my head deeper into my pillow. Flashbacks from the past lit up my darkened room as I struggled for some composure. Surrendering to those demons, I eventually wandered downstairs for a large vodka, then another, until I collapsed exhausted in a heap on the settee.

Suffering like that I will never be able to comprehend. It is on a scale of hurt that makes my own problems seem so very trivial. But I could well imagine the psychological trauma those brave rescue workers lucky enough to be alive were going through. Images they saw as they clawed their way through the rubble in a vain attempt to find survivors will live in their minds forever. Some, like me, will never get over it. The fallout from this catastrophe was a tidal wave of emotion and retribution. After the smoke settled, some people were saying that, at last, America had been bombed into the real world after she had sat back, watched and even condoned global terrorism for many years. It took an atrocity like this on their own soil to kick the Americans into action on the question of terrorism. We in Northern Ireland, meanwhile, had been witness to its bloody results for over 30 years. Events were staged worldwide to raise money for the victims of this sad day and yet I had to ask myself just how many American dollars found their way to the families of over 300 dead policemen here in Northern

Ireland (in contrast to the vast sums of money that were raised for the coffers of the IRA through groups like NORAID). While not belittling the suffering of those affected by this terrible tragedy, I also felt incensed that it was only now that people began to take the threat of terrorism seriously. Nobody seemed to care about the many good RUC men and women who had lost their lives to this scourge.

A few days later, I received a phone call from my supervisory sergeant, the one and only call I would receive from him throughout the whole retirement process. He told me that he was just ringing up to see how I was, as it formed part of his welfare duties. We had a general chat and he asked me if there was anything he could do for me. I told him I was OK and added that, if he wanted, he could come down some day on a visit. He seemed keen on this idea and said he would be in touch, but I never heard from him again. This sergeant was a good man-manager and I liked him a lot, but the chemistry between us was never really there. We worked well as part of a team but he would never have called me one of his buddies. Unbelievably, I didn't receive support from any of my former colleagues after leaving the force.

With all this time away from work, I felt it was vitally important to believe I could still make a positive contribution to society, that I still had something to offer. When you're not working, it can be hard to feel positive if you vegetate at home in front of the television. One way in which many survivors of trauma have reconnected with their communities is through volunteering with youth programmes, medical services, literacy programmes, and so on. I decided to immerse myself in one of my biggest interests – helping to maintain the maritime history of Belfast. I now had renewed interest in life and as I had decided to embark on a humanities degree I also had a specific goal. I became expert at administering my own psychological self-care. I made time for self-reflection and read literature that was totally unrelated to work. I opened myself up and listened to my thoughts. I successfully challenged my judgements, beliefs, attitudes and feelings, and revelled in completing tasks totally new to me. I developed a new self-awareness and moved away from the normal 'know it all' attitude endemic amongst policemen. In effect, I decreased the stress in my life by engaging myself mentally in totally new areas. I also made a lot of new friends completely outwith police circles.

This would be the advice that I would offer to fellow sufferers. You have to take control of your own lives and set your own agenda; don't accept being labelled as a basket case. It has been difficult to accept at times but I have come to realise that without my past years of neglect and hurt I would not be who I am today. I have now turned the dark days of my childhood and the RUC into a colourful appreciation of life today.

On 1 October 2001, I received the greatest news I could ever have wished for: on 19 November I would be officially retired. This was such a relief to me as it had taken a whole stress-filled year to sort out my retirement and pension. I had been hurting inside for so long that the relief at being given my leaving date released all my pent-up emotions. At long last, Agnes and I could start to make plans for our new life together.

All that was left to do now was to call into Dundonald station and clear out my locker, and I decided to do this on a Sunday night when I knew it would be quiet. I had no desire to run into any of my former colleagues, who had now ostracised me over my early retirement.

There was no wave goodbye, no handshake nor pat on the back; there was nothing, not even a card. I was one of the longest-serving police bodyguards in Northern Ireland but, after I had emptied my locker, it was as if I had never been there at all. It was somewhat sad to realise that this would be the final time I would stand in that locker room as a policeman, but then again, bearing in mind all I had been through, a voice inside me was also cheering out loud. Over the last year, there had been many petty incidents that only reinforced my desire to sever all links to the force. I was denied my Police Long Service and Good Conduct Medal. I had to arrange delivery of my uniform to stores myself and had to deliver my own warrant card to the personnel branch. My framed RUC certificate of service went missing in Dundonald RUC station and after one year I had to ask for a duplicate: all in all, a very sad state of affairs. As I closed my locker door, I reflected that I had never been given the choice of being a policeman on the beat; I served all my 21 years in specialised units. All I had collected in those years had now been stuffed into black bin bags, sorted into what would be dumped, retained and handed back to stores. I did keep my proud green RUC cap and whistle as reminders, if any were needed, of the good old days that – for me – mostly turned out bad.

Another milestone was reached on 3 November 2001 – the last operational day in the life of the Royal Ulster Constabulary. From midnight the force would be renamed the 'Police Service of Northern Ireland'. All I had worked for would be consigned to history and I felt very sympathetic towards those members of the RUC who would from then on be trapped within a service they had not chosen to join.

Outside police circles, it appeared to me that no one really cared and the story didn't even make the news headlines. I drove past the main gates of Police Headquarters at Knock only to see a bright shiny new sign bearing the words 'Police Service of Northern Ireland Headquarters' on its nondescript façade. I felt as if the struggles we had gone through were being erased from collective memory and the only thing that lifted my spirits was the fact that some kind person had placed a small bunch of fresh flowers at the base of the sign as a memorial to our sacrifice and pain.

At midnight on 19 November 2001, I finally felt that the saga was coming to a close. I was no longer a serving police officer but an ordinary member of society again. The second sorry chapter in my life was over and I felt I could now start living again.

I can only hope that it is third time lucky.

GLOSSARY

ATO	Army Technical Officer – bomb disposal
B SPECIALS	Ulster Special Constabulary – part-time reserve Protestant RUC officers, disbanded 1969
DMSU	Divisional Mobile Support Units – RUC riot squads
DUP	Democratic Unionist Party – founded in 1971 by the Rev. Ian Paisley and Desmond Boal
ECM	electronic counter measures
FENIAN	slang term used to describe a Roman Catholic
FRG	federal riot gun
GARDA SIOCHANA	Irish Republic's police force
INLA	Irish National Liberation Army – founded in 1974 after breaking away from the IRA
IRA	Irish Republican Army – used to indicate Provisional IRA for the purposes of this book
IVCP	illegal VCP set up by terror groups
LVF	Loyalist Volunteer Force – breakaway group from the UVF in 1996
MI5	Military Intelligence – Britain's domestic military agency

OHU	Occupational Health Unit of the RUC
OOB	out of bounds
OTU	Operational Training Unit
PROD	slang term to describe a Protestant
PRRT	Police Retraining and Rehabilitation Trust
PTSD	Post-Traumatic Stress Disorder
PUP	Progressive Unionist Party – formed in 1979, political wing of the outlawed UVF
PSNI	Police Service of Northern Ireland – formerly the RUC
QC	Queen's Counsel (also denotes a cheap fortified wine mentioned in this book)
RECCE	to reconnoitre a route or location
RIR	Royal Irish Regiment – formerly the UDR
RIRA	Real IRA – dissident IRA splinter group
RUC	Royal Ulster Constabulary – disbanded in November 2001
RUCR	Royal Ulster Constabulary Reserve
SANGAR	sentry box
SINN FÉIN	political wing of the Provisional IRA
SLR	self-loading rifle
SMG	Sterling sub-machine gun
SPG	RUC Special Patrol Group – forerunner of the DMSU
TARA	a secret Loyalist organisation (now inactive) formed in the mid-1960s by William McGrath
TOUT	informer
UDA	Ulster Defence Association – loyalist paramilitary group formed in 1971
UDR	Ulster Defence Regiment – British Army regiment now the RIR
UVF in	Ulster Volunteer Force – loyalist terror group formed 1966
VCP	vehicle check point – RUC or British Army
WPC	Woman Police Constable

BIBLIOGRAPHY

Anderson, Chris, *The Billy Boy*, Mainstream Publishing, Edinburgh, 2002

Brewer, John D. and Magee, Kathleen, *Inside the RUC*, Clarendon Press, Oxford, 1991

Birney, Trevor and O'Neill, Julian, *When the President Calls*, Guildhall Press, Londonderry, 1997

Dickens, Charles, *Great Expectations*, Oxford University Press, Oxford, 1993

Dillon, Martin, *The Shankill Butchers*, Arrow Books, London, 1990

Dimbleby, Jonathan, *The Prince of Wales*, Warner Books, London, 1998

Elliott, Sydney and Flackes, W.D., *Northern Ireland Political Directory*, Blackstaff Press, Belfast, 1999

Gilmour, Raymond, *Dead Ground*, Warner Books, London, 1999

Hermon, Sir John, *Holding the Line*, Gill and Macmillan Ltd, Dublin, 1997

Ingram, Martin and Harkin, Greg, *Stakeknife*, O'Brien Press Ltd, Dublin, 2004

McDowell, Jim, *Godfathers*, Gill & Macmillan Ltd, Dublin, 2001

McKittrick, David, Kelters, Seamus, Feeney, Brian and Thornton, Chris, *Lost Lives*, Mainstream Publishing, Edinburgh, 1999

Needham, Richard, *Battling for Peace*, Blackstaff Press, Belfast, 1998

O'Leary, Olivia and Burke, Helen, *Mary Robinson: Authorised Biography*, Hodder & Stoughton, London, 1998

Ryder, Chris, *The RUC: A Force Under Fire*, Arrow Books, London, 2000

The Report of the Independent Commission on Policing for Northern Ireland (Patten Report), Crown Copyright Unit, St Clements House, Norwich, 1999